Kirk, John M.

José Martí, mentor of the Cuban nation

José Martí

A UNIVERSITY OF SOUTH FLORIDA BOOK
UNIVERSITY PRESSES OF FLORIDA
TAMPA

José

JOHN M. KIRK

Martí

MENTOR OF THE CUBAN NATION

Library of Congress Cataloging in Publication Data

Kirk, John M.
José Martí, mentor of the Cuban nation.

"A University of South Florida book."
Bibliography: p.
Includes index.
1. Martí, José, 1853–1895—Political and social views. I. Title.
F1783.M38K57 1982 972.91'05'0924 82–15920
ISBN 0–8130–0736–4

PRINTED IN U.S.A. ON ACID-FREE PAPER

The substance of the material in chapter 1 has previously appeared as an essay in *Latin American Research Review,* Chapel Hill, and in *Norte/Sur,* Montreal, and is reprinted by their permission.

University Presses of Florida is the central agency for scholarly publishing of the State of Florida's university system. Its offices are located at 15 NW 15th Street, Gainesville, FL 32603. Works published by University Presses of Florida are evaluated and selected for publication by a faculty editorial committee of any one of Florida's nine public universities: Florida A&M University (Tallahassee), Florida Atlantic University (Boca Raton), Florida International University (Miami), Florida State University (Tallahassee), University of Central Florida (Orlando), University of Florida (Gainesville), University of North Florida (Jacksonville), University of South Florida (Tampa), University of West Florida (Pensacola).

Contents

Acknowledgments

Though I accept full responsibility for the views expressed in this study (and also for the translation into English of quotations from Martí's work, undertaken to facilitate a wider understanding of José Martí), I have been aided by a variety of colleagues, friends, and institutions. The Inter-Library Loan Office at the University of British Columbia helped to obtain much of the bibliographical material I consulted, while financial support was kindly provided under the auspices of a MacMillan grant, and by an award from the Canada Council. The manuscript was typed by Elizabeth Howarth and Wanda Hebb.

I am particularly grateful to Roderick and Jean Barman, both of whom constantly offered advice and encouragement during the gestation of this work. Others who have contributed with their insight are José Agustín, Peter Beardsell, Gordon Brotherston, Enrique Caraciolo-Trejo, Derek Carr, Nicholas Collins, Keith Ellis, Juan Esteve, Casiano Fernández, Roberto Fernández Retamar, Maurice Halperin, Joan and Edward Kirk, Harold Livermore, Harriet Moshowitz, Emilio Mozo-Adán, Frank Pierce, Isaac Rubio-Delgado, Antonio Ruiz Salvador, Don Schmidt, and John Walker. All my former students at the University of British Columbia, Simon Fraser University, the University of Denver, and Dalhousie University (most of whom have suffered the excesses of the author's "Martí-mania") must be thanked for their patience and forebearance.

Finally, and most important, my sincere gratitude to my wife,

Margo, truly a perfect companion during the long hours spent on this study.

To all of the people responsible for the appearance of this work, my heartfelt gratitude.

Preface

To explain the importance that José Martí possesses for the Cuban people is no easy task. In attempting to illustrate his impressive contribution both to the formation and to the development of Cuba as a nation, Martí can of course be compared with other figures who played similar roles in their own countries, such as Mahatma Gandhi in India, Abraham Lincoln in the United States, Simón Bolívar in Venezuela and, most recently, Mao Tse-Tung in China. Such comparisons, however, are only partially successful, since all fall short of depicting the true importance of Martí's nation-building role.

Within the last three decades José Martí may be said to have penetrated the consciousness of the Cuban people as a whole; and, as one critic has correctly noted, in effect Martí represents the keystone of what can be termed the Cuban national identity.[1] This intensely loyal devotion to Martí by Cubans of all political leanings has led to the rather confusing present-day situation in which Martí is still revered as devoutly as ever by Cuban exiles, while in revolutionary Cuba he is presented as the underlying inspiration, the *autor intelectual* to use Fidel Castro's term, of the revolution.

Because of the many widely differing interpretations of Martí's political ideology, the need for a reasonable, clear, and objective overview of his sociopolitical thought has been at all times the fundamental goal of my study. Fortunately removed from the political pressure of both common interpretations (outlined in chapter 1), I have deliberately refrained from employing either official presentation as a departure point because such a technique would only serve to antagonize the protectors of the rival philosophy.

Consequently, instead of following the more traditional method of analyzing Martí's political thought from a strictly theoretical viewpoint, this work attempts to pursue a different approach. After a detailed examination of his *Obras completas (Complete Works)*,[2] it appeared that a more satisfactory and representative technique was possible, for Martí did indeed possess clear and fairly substantial goals for the liberated Cuban *patria* (motherland). In essence, therefore, this study allows Martí's thought to speak for itself, presenting a well-documented synthesis of his aspirations concerning the type of political, social, and economic structures that undoubtedly Martí would have striven to introduce into an independent Cuba. The intended result of such a study, in reality the blueprint of Martí's sociopolitical designs, is to clarify earlier theories concerning the *Apóstol*'s (Apostle's) ideological beliefs (for many camps have claimed Martí as a partisan supporter of their particular aims) and also to illustrate the extremely pragmatic—and consistently underrated—nature of his specific goals for the *patria*.

To conclude these introductory remarks, a general observation. Because of the unfortunate (though understandable considering Martí's importance for all Cubans) polarization of views on José Martí, any study of his sociopolitical thought is bound to invite criticism from *martianos* (Martí specialists) of differing political opinions. This present work is expected to arouse controversy, perhaps even more so because it purports to offer an essentially "neutral" overview of Martí's sociopolitical thought and, therefore, is open to criticism from all sides. Despite these potential obstacles, this study may contribute to the necessary reappraisal of Martí, particularly warranted here in North America where his political thought has been grossly misrepresented, while at the same time encouraging *martianos* of all political backgrounds to search for the complete sociopolitical goals of José Martí:

> We must study the man in all his tumultuous and intense reality. Let us not fear these major examinations. There is such personal and historical grandeur in José Martí that one can—and should—fearlessly

approach the most intimate aspects of his work, and the apparent contradictions. This searching through the thick forest of material has to be undertaken, however, with a noble objective in mind: no place should be avoided . . . no accident should distract us from a transcendental overview of Martí's work.[3]

To
Margo, Lisa, and Michael

I. HISTORICAL ANALYSIS OF MARTÍ STUDIES

1. From *Místico* to Revolutionary

Travelers in Cuba are almost forcibly made aware of the overpowering presence of Martí throughout the Republic. In Havana, for example, they arrive at the national airport outside Havana known as the Aeropuerto José Martí; they may visit the imposing National Library, the Biblioteca Nacional José Martí, and the central square of Havana known as the Plaza José Martí. Even the most obscure villages of Cuba are equipped with their own monuments to Martí, whose portrait is invariably encountered in the island's schools and can be observed of course on a variety of Cuban banknotes and postage stamps. It is therefore no exaggeration to claim that "to a certain degree Cuba is a country which revolves around one man—Martí."[1]

However, this deeply rooted Martí cult was late in blossoming, in effect manifesting itself thirty years after Martí's untimely death in 1895. Not until the 1930s did the Cuban populace begin to take an active interest in Martí, a process which culminated—from the point of view of quantity rather than quality—in the 1953 festivities held to celebrate the centennial of Martí's birth. Martí had "arrived" as a national hero, with a standard, albeit debatable, "profile" being widely presented of him.

In order to appreciate the most definite need for an objective study of Martí's nation-building role in Cuba, it is important to be aware of the incredible degree to which Martí has been traditionally exploited as a political symbol, especially in his homeland. From the discussion in this first chapter of the two main, and fundamentally opposing, trends in the formulation of Martí's image, readers will be equipped with a basic awareness of these different ideological interpretations. Hopefully, they can look beyond such claims and be prepared to delve into the work of Martí with the intent of deriving an honest, more representative understanding of the true *esencia martiana* (essence of Martí's thought).

To date, remarkably few attemps have been made to provide a systematic classification and analysis of the plethora of studies on Martí as a political (as opposed to literary) figure. The most notable analysis in recent years was that of Andrés Valdespino, who categorically divides the studies on Martí. "The treatment of the figure of Martí in Cuban literature has passed through three distinctive phases: the beatification of Martí (presenting him as a mythical figure); the humanizing of Martí (showing him as a human being); and the falsification of Martí (Martí as a poster of political propaganda)."[2] However, political considerations play an undue part in Valdespino's analysis, and a more balanced examination of the bulk of material written on Martí since his death suggests that there have been only two—and quite noticeably different—periods in the general presentation of Martí to the Cuban people. The watershed between these two periods was, predictably enough, the successful revolution led by Fidel Castro in 1959. This study delineates the prerevolutionary interpretation of Martí and its present-day continuation in the writings of the Miami-based Cuban exiles as the traditional, and the new, post-1959 interpretation as the revolutionary.

One of the most characteristic features of the traditional approach to Martí was the constant reference to him in idealized, reverential, and semimystical terms. Salvador Agüero, writing in 1936, described Martí as a person "whose mind possessed the radiance of a genius, and whose breast contained the saintliness of an apostle."[3] Of the many studies written in 1942 (the fiftieth anniversary of the Partido Revolucionario Cubano [Revolutionary Cuban Party], founded by Martí), Miguel L. de Landaluce's "Vía crucis de Martí" is in fact nothing less than a quasi-religious oration, complete with a series of meditations accompanying each "station of the cross,"[4] and Federico de Córdova's plastically lyrical tribute to Martí deserves quotation.

> On January 28, 1853, the residents of Havana who looked at the sky, believed that they had discovered a new star. And they were not mis-

taken because on that day José Martí was born. . . . Like the inspired leader of Nazareth he was coming to unite men to liberate them from their captivity, to inspire in them faith and trust in good works.[5]

Among the multitude of texts inspired by the Martí centennial of 1953 were several portrayals of Martí as a saintly, Christ-like figure. José Manuel Cortina referred to Martí as "a mystic and a saint,"[6] while Rufino Blanco Fombona was more adventurous, calling him "that second Jesus, that preacher."[7] Finally Félix Matos Bernier, writing in 1952, informed his readers: "Do not look for the moral influence of Martí in the present period. His brother lives in the times of the oldest legends; his brother is Jesus Christ."[8] Even the two most accomplished biographies of Martí from the traditional period suffer from this same reverential awe, as their titles indicate: Félix Lizaso's *Martí, místico del deber (Martí, Mystic of Duty)* and Jorge Mañach's *Martí el Apóstol (Martí the Apostle).* The tendency to sanctify Martí, a standard feature of traditional studies, has understandably vanished from the studies of Martí written in Cuba since 1959.

However, what is perhaps the most prominent characteristic of the traditional studies of Martí was a conscious and sincere desire of many *martianos* to achieve a proper and objective understanding of both the life and personality of Martí. Since Rubén Darío first wrote on Martí's character in 1905, praising his superlative moral qualities and advocating that all Cubans emulate the man he personally called *maestro,* numerous studies have been written in an attempt to shed fresh light on the details of his extraordinary life. With the exception of a few, noticeably mediocre attempts to provide a novelized, overly romantic view of Martí's life, most of the biographies in the traditional period were interesting, well-written, and reasonably accurate accounts of Martí's life and personality. These works were written not only by Cubans but also by authors of the other Spanish-speaking nations. Some of the studies, notable for the quality of their portrayal and their pioneering nature, deserve specific mention, particularly those of Andrés Iduarte, Félix Lizaso, Néstor Carbonell, Jorge Mañach, Raimundo Lazo, and Manuel Isidro Méndez.[9]

With the single exception of Iduarte's excellent work, the outcome of his doctoral dissertation at Columbia University in 1945, even these good studies of Martí share one common defect. They concentrate on the life and not the ideas of Martí, and they particularly neglect his political and social writings, his vocation as a revolutionary, and his plans for a liberated Cuba. Of their absorption with the fascinating life of Martí to the exclusion of all else, the Argentine scholar Ezequiel Martínez Estrada has commented in no uncertain terms:

> Biographies and bibliographies suffered the same fate. The objective was to suppress those aspects of Martí seen by the self-satisfied republican leader as products of his temperament, a "badly adjusted" nonconformist, a rebel and conspirator. They went to the extreme of encouraging among his contemporaries and devoted successors the basic anecdotes and data of his travels, appointments as consul for various Latin American countries, work as a journalist, personal relations and the like—all of which was equally applicable to any citizen of the Cuban bourgeoisie.[10]

The vast majority of studies written in the traditional period agreed in presenting an apolitical, uncontroversial, and neutral image of the *Apóstol,* who was frequently portrayed as "a sort of celestial star, chemically pure, as far removed as possible from our miserable human condition."[11] Relatively little attention was paid to the political thought of Martí. Among the small number of studies that did consider the subject, two very different approaches were present. On the one side and a very distinct minority were those writers who championed a radical and even revolutionary interpretation of Martí's political thought. On the other side were the more numerous authors who supported, though without much investigation of the evidence, the concept of Martí as a moderate in politics.

The leading proponents of the radical interpretation—a school which, it must be repeated, was never more than a tiny minority among the abundant studies of traditionalist *martianos*—were Antonio Martínez Bello, Emilio Roig de Leuchsenring, and Juan Marinello. However, whatever impact the revolutionary interpretation might have had was further dissipated by disagreements among these writers as to the precise nature of Martí's radicalism. For instance, in a letter published at the end of Martínez Bello's important study of Martí's political thought, Juan Marinello took issue with Bello's claim that Martí subscribed to the ideas of Marx:

> The illustrious patrician [Marx] coincided exactly with the thought of our own Apostle. Martí was aware of the need for an alliance with those socialist parties, not only because of the convenience that assured the maintenance of peace and social equilibrium . . . but also because he recognized in these parties the legitimacy of their ambitions to impose social justice. That is, Martí would have recognized those radical parties, because MARTÍ, who identified with the urgent necessity to bring about social justice and the economic liberation of the proletariat, was a SOCIALIST.[12]

To spend much time considering the quarrels between the proponents of a radical Martí would be misleading, because, of the few authors who did consider Martí's political thought, the clear majority supported the concept of Martí as a moderate. The leading proponents of this viewpoint were Guillermo de Blanck, Federico de Córdova, Ramón Infiesta, Raimundo Lazo, Jorge Mañach, and Emeterio S. Santovenia. Their common attitude toward Martí's political aspirations for Cuba is perhaps best conveyed by Santovenia's simplistic and indeed naïve interpretation of the "Constitutional Bases" of Martí's political program:

> 2. The Republic is to be organized according to the concept of "a united, caring, astute motherland."
> 3. All the rights essential to human freedom are to be specified.
> 4. There is to be an equitable sharing of the products of association. Men who work have to live with self-respect and respite from their labors.
> 5. All those elements particular to our motherland are to be subordinated to the human objective of well-being and respect. This is to be achieved by methods that are in keeping with the country, and which can function without any confrontations.
> 6. The injurious past is to be wiped away, and the present is to be prepared for a future that, although confusing at first, will afterwards be secure—as a result of the totally just administration of a learned, industrious freedom. . . .
> 12. These means which will lead to the solution of political and social conflicts (that are already present) will be adopted.[13]

To present Martí as a moderate, it was necessary for these writers to ignore or minimize the more militant of Martí's observations, to downplay drastically the role of Martí in the struggle for liberation of Cuba, and to pay little if any attention to his plans for the future Republic. The general trend of these studies was to present Martí "more as an impassioned, poetic master of ceremonies than as a judicious planner of a carefully thought-out program."[14]

The best evidence of this "neutered" view of Martí's political thought is to be found in the traditionalists' handling of Martí's views on the United States. Without going so far as Aquiles Nazoa, who claimed that anthologies of Martí's writings on the United States were deliberately shorn of their offending critical references to North America, it can be stated that the anthologies did present a biased and essentially unrepresentative selection of Martí's views on the United States. With the important exception of Manuel Pedro González's excellent work, *José Martí, Epic Chronicler of the United States in the Eighties*, the same criticism can be made of the general studies of Martí and North America.

Indicative of the attitude of these works is a passage of Lizaso in which he describes Martí's famous "Escenas norteamericanas" ("North American Scenes") as "a masterly painting of movement and color in one of the fundamental decades for the creative process of the great North American people who were striving to bring about grandiose structures and projects."[15] Also typical of this approach was the constant comparison by the traditionalists of Martí to famous American presidents: to Lincoln, Franklin D. Roosevelt, even to Woodrow Wilson and Theodore Roosevelt—who was remembered with such gratitude by the Cuban people, in the words of one critic, "because he came, leading his valiant roughriders, to struggle for the freedom of Cuba."[16] In sum, Martí was widely presented as having been totally enamored of the United States, very impressed by the many basic freedoms to be found there, an ardent admirer of the country's noble institutions, indeed desirous of transferring many of these established institutions to his own country, and an enthusiastic defender of Pan-Americanism.

Writing in 1928, for example, José A. Giralt claimed in the face of abundant evidence to the contrary: "Pan-Americanism—that desire to secure, by means of spiritual solidarity and the political cooperation of all the nations of the New World, a future of glory and prosperity for the Americas—had in Martí an eminent defender."[17] Some twenty-five years later at the Congress of Martí Specialists (held in Havana to celebrate the Martí centennial), two American writers displayed an extraordinary ignorance of the work of Martí. In their presentations, they attempted to substantiate that Martí "with his profound understanding of that country [United States] . . . could appreciate well the Pan-American ideals of Henry Clay and James G. Blaine."[18] Such a blatant disregard for Martí's express rejection of Pan-Americanism in favor of Pan-Hispanism, "Nuestra América" ("Our [Hispanic] America"), was not unique. The very words quoted were proudly repeated in the preface of Richard Butler Gray's work, *José Martí: Cuban Patriot,* as late as 1962. In the face of such misuse of the evidence, it is only possible to repeat the words of Manuel Pedro González: "Just as so many infamous acts have been carried out in the name of Christ, so too that of Martí is frequently invoked to cover up and disguise fraudulent and unspeakable acts of cunning."[19]

Although in the traditional interpretation considerably less attention was paid to the social, political, and economic thought of Martí than to such topics as the details of his life, his character, his psychological traits, and his religious and philosophical affiliations, nonetheless a standard if debatable interpretation of Martí's political thought did exist before 1959. The subject was thus not entirely neglected. The cumulative effect of the traditionalist studies of Martí was to portray the *Apóstol* as a great and selfless Cuban, determined to give his life for the *patria,* a noble—but somehow alienated—patriot: in short a Cuban version of Don Quixote.

As was mentioned earlier, the climax of this portrayal by the traditionalist school occurred during the Martí centennial of 1953. A truly astounding quantity of remarkably obscure works was produced. "The 'Martí and . . .' writings were voluminous before the centennial, and they now threaten to become a flood," as Duvon C. Corbitt shrewdly remarked at the time.[20] The dominant theme of this period was one of harmony, with a conscious effort being made to demonstrate that Martí's fears about foreign incursions into Cuba had not been fulfilled and that, in fact, his desires for the *patria* had been generously accomplished.

If any one item can be said to summarize all these characteristics of the traditional interpretation of Martí, it was an advertisement inserted by Simmons International Ltd.—purveyors of

Beautyrest, Deep-sleep, and Hide-a-bed products—in *The Havana Post* of January 28, 1953. The advertisement displays a large drawing of Martí in a serious pose with a quill behind him and a book in front. The advertisement also contains an interesting quotation from Martí, which not only typifies the "low profile" image of Martí presented in Cuba before the revolution but which is almost certainly bogus as well: "What is important is not that our cause should triumph, but rather that our motherland should be happy."[21]

It was one of history's ironies that in the very year this traditional representation of the *Apóstol* reached its peak with the centennial celebrations, a young revolutionary named Fidel Castro should have presented, in most dramatic fashion, a radically new interpretation of Martí and his thought. In the speech, later published as *La historia me absolverá (History Will Absolve Me),* given by Fidel Castro after his arrest following the Moncada uprising, he made many references to Martí as the *autor intelectual* of both the revolt and its political goals. In this way a very different portrayal of Martí originated, one diametrically opposed to the existing standard interpretation. As a fresh generation of *martianos* sprang up in Cuba, they presented a revitalized view of the man, no longer as an *Apóstol* but instead as a "revolucionario radical de su tiempo" ("radical revolutionary of his time").[22]

While the new revolutionary interpretation of Martí has understandably triumphed in Cuba since 1959, the traditional viewpoint has not disappeared but persists among the writers of the Cuban exile community in Florida. These writers have quite deliberately continued to maintain in their studies of Martí the same thematic concerns that predominated before 1959, with Martí still regarded as a type of quasi-divinity to be revered as a sacred object. In Hernando D'Aquino's recent work, *Sinfonía martiana (Vida y pasión),* the nine cantos revolve specifically around the "parallel between the Redeemer of Nazareth and the most human Apostle of Cuban independence."[23] Typical of the work is the description of the birth of this "Cuban Christ," complete with the presence of "three peasant Wise Men" who had come "to offer the Child / tobacco and sugarcane / and the nectarine coffee / fresh from the coffee pot."[24] There is even a sketch of the event included in the work.

This small group of Cuban exiles has also continued to proclaim defiantly Martí's admiration for the United States, displaying as little balance and as little concern for the evidence as their predecessors. There is the same blind insistence on highlighting Martí's praise for that country, while avoiding quite deliberately the many criticisms by Martí of the "monstruo" (monster) as Martí referred to the United States in his last, famous letter (IV, 168). In one of the few moderate and balanced discussions of Martí's views on the U.S.A., Carlos Alberto Montaner has also consciously minimized Martí's criticisms. "Martí, with all his integrity, grew hoarse warning the peoples of America, Cubans, and all North Americans of the imperialist maneuvers which some delirious and ambitious financial interests wanted to bring about."[25]

Behind this insistence on Martí's admiration for the United States there clearly lies an element that was absent from studies produced before 1959. A handful of delirious and ambitious Cuban exile writers employ Martí's praise for the United States as a means of discrediting and attacking Fidel Castro, whose outspoken denunciations of U.S. foreign policy are well known. Typical of this technique is the pamphlet *Martí y los norteamericanos en su propia palabra (Martí and the North Americans in His Own Words)* published by the Directorio Magisterial Cubano (Exilio). The quotations are, as always, carefully selected to provide a favorable impression of the United States. Martí's report of President Garfield's death is followed by a very revealing comment:

> Only a man devoted to this country and its legitimate values can write with so much emotion on President Garfield.
>
> Martí depicts the grandeur of the American soul.
>
> Martí depicts the nobility of the American spirit. . . .
>
> What can the communists say—the ones who only use Martí's name to profane it—when faced with his authentic words showing his intimate ties with North America? . . . In free Cuba, republican Cuba from 1902 to 1958, we never heard Martí named as an enemy of the United States of America. . . . But since the first of January of 1959, when the communist treason destroyed Cuba's freedom, trampled over her total sovereignty and darkened the horizon of her genuine independence, José Martí has been an instrument of this exploitation by the Marxist-Leninists.[26]

When Martí is not presented as a supporter of the United States and advocate of Cuban-American friendship, he is often employed as no more than a stalking horse for attacks on Fidel Castro and his regime, even by exiled *martianos* such as Rafael Esténger and Carlos Márquez Sterling who earlier enjoyed respectable reputations as Martí scholars in Cuba. Esténger has gone so far as to claim that Fidel Castro pays only "fingida reverencia" ("simulated respect") to Martí, for fear that the Cuban people might turn against him if he did not:

> That is why, before the unfortunate masses in the Civic Plaza, the almighty Fidel Castro was able to announce the abolition of the liberal and democratic Republic. But never would he have dared to destroy the gigantic image of José Martí, whom he frequently uses in his demagogic harangues. Even though he profanes the image with his deeds, Castro continues paying him a simulated respect. Castro has not yet been sufficiently crazy enough to loathe publicly the revered memory of Martí. He knows well that Martí is a leader who cannot be jailed or killed.[27]

Quite unfortunately, Martí, his life, and his thought have become for many of the Cuban exiles no more than vehicles for expressing their frustration and sources of ammunition to hurl against the hated Communist regime. In this respect Martí has indeed become what Valdespino termed a "cartel de propaganda" ("poster of propaganda"), although Valdespino undoubtedly had no intention of applying that term to his own political *confrères*.

The works of the Cuban exiles on Martí can therefore be summarized as presenting Martí in a manner similar to that in which he had been portrayed in prerevolutionary Cuba. As a person he is regarded with reverential awe, with remarkably little attention being paid to his political and social aspirations for Cuba. In short, the exiles' interpretation—or, it could be argued, misinterpretation—is intended to be a continuation of the earlier traditional approach with the addition of an unfortunate attempt to use Martí as a means of mobilizing opposition to the present Cuban regime.

In revolutionary Cuba, meanwhile, a very different development in the area of *estudios martianos* has occurred. Initially, particularly in the first three or four years after 1959, a determined effort was made to demonstrate the direct relevance of Martí's teaching to the contemporary scene. The titles of the articles written in this period reveal an obvious desire to associate José Martí with this revolutionary process: "Trajectory and Actuality of Martí's Thought,"

"El mentor directo de Nuestra Revolución" ("The Direct Mentor of Our Revolution"), "Martí y la Revolución Cubana" ("Martí and the Cuban Revolution"), "El pensamiento de Martí y nuestra Revolución Socialista" ("The Thought of Martí and Our Socialist Revolution"), and "Raíces martianas de Nuestra Revolución" ("The Influence of Martí in Our Revolution"). This new approach to Martí has been well described by Manuel Pedro González, who made an apt comment on the linking of Martí and the revolution. "In this decisive moment, it is both logical and natural that the Cubans should invoke and emulate the ever-fresh example of their heros of yesteryear, and especially their principal founder and guide."[28]

Another major characteristic of Martí studies in Cuba during the early years of the revolution was clearly influenced by the national anger at external pressures on Cuba such as the Bay of Pigs invasion, the economic sanctions against Cuba imposed first by the United States and subsequently by the OAS, the Missile Crisis, and covert CIA activities. Heavy emphasis was then placed by many *martianos* on the numerous critical references made by Martí to the United States. Little attention was paid in the early years of this revolutionary process to the praise expressed by Martí for the North American republic, as the Cuban critics—relishing the opportunity to present what may be termed the other side of the coin previously ignored by traditionalist writers—concentrated on publishing the Martí thoughts that could be construed as anti-American. Typical of this mood was a comment of Juan Marinello in January 1962:

> In fact our liberator could note from within "the entrails of the monster" not only its limitless greed but also the elements which nourished its corruption.
>
> A third of Martí's work, and perhaps the best part, is intended to offer us a precise, surprising panorama of the "discontented and brutal North which despises us."[29]

Gradually, as the years passed and national confidence grew both in the Castro government and in the ability of Cuba to survive, as the economy became comparatively stable, and as sweeping social changes took place in Cuba, a considerable shift occurred in the revolutionary interpretation of Martí. The successful literacy program in 1961, christened the "Year of Education," in which

Martí's works were employed extensively as texts, introduced José Martí to the generality of the Cuban people, who now began to read his work in some detail. The publication by the Editorial Nacional de Cuba of a new and extremely thorough edition of the *Obras completas* between 1963 and 1966 introduced a new phase of interest in Martí's writings.

With the single exception of Raúl Roa's article, "José Martí. El autor intelectual" published in 1973, there has been a complete abandonment of what were often labored and overbearing comparisons between the general aspirations of Martí and the aims of the *fidelista* government. Instead, the new generation of *martianos* concentrated on indicating and explaining what they now saw as the fundamental, if long ignored, substance of Martí's work—his political and social thought. Particular attention was given, virtually for the first time since Martí's death, to the role and the organization of what Martí clearly intended to be the microcosm of the liberated Republic, the Partido Revolucionario Cubano.

As this mood of national confidence grew, there was a very distinct change in the emotional approach of the critics. The early, highly critical references to the United States were generally replaced by a more reasonable, objective interpretation of Martí's views on the United States. However, to the Cuban exile writers, even this modified interpretation is still a misreading of Martí. "The antiyankee feelings attributed to Martí have nothing to do with that senseless and racist hate which is preached today," as Carlos Montaner has noted.[30] What is perhaps the most reasonable and most balanced summary of Martí's attitude toward the United States is to be found (despite Valdespino's criticism that this particular writer is among the most conveniently partisan of *martianos* in contemporary Cuba) in a recent study by Roberto Fernández Retamar.

> It is not a case of [Martí] rejecting the United States mechanically, en masse; rather it is a case of underlining the negative aspects borne in that country's breast ("Perhaps it is inevitable that worms make their nests among the roots of all great trees"), as well as the tremendous danger that they represent for Latin America. Besides, in the United States as in Europe there are many useful aspects for our countries. Among the most important is their knowledge: science, technical advances, and the vast wealth of art and literature which Martí shared copiously among his Latin American readers.[31]

Since the middle of the 1960s the main thrust of the revolutionary interpretation has been a determined, if at times overdone, attempt to analyze the steady progression of Martí's thought from a standard liberal viewpoint toward a stance of opposition to colonialism and, more importantly, to imperialism. The result has been a series of studies that have returned to a similar interpretation of Martí presented by Roig de Leuchsenring many years earlier as Cuban critics portray Martí's struggle for the independence of Cuba as a firmly committed and anti-imperialist action. The quality of the vast majority of these studies is excellent, exemplified by the thorough studies of Isabel Monal, Juan Marinello, and Angel Augier; but a few articles, for instance that of Ariel Hidalgo, are replete with revolutionary clichés and not much else.

As a result of this new school of Martí studies, the general interpretation of Martí has not simply been altered or revamped—it has been utterly changed. No longer is Martí presented as a mystical, apostlelike figure. He is now seen as a man deeply committed to the revolutionary struggle, both in his own country and in the other countries of "Nuestra América." Studies concerned with purely biographical details, so numerous before the revolution, are now rarely if ever encountered. Far more common is a thorough examination of Martí's ideas, with particular emphasis being given to the fact that Martí was not simply fighting to overthrow the Spanish and win political independence for Cuba but was also fighting as an international revolutionary to secure the liberation of his continent, and indeed of the world.

Gone too are the studies dealing with Martí's philosophical and religious leanings, as are the psychological analyses of his character. The order of the day is to present Martí as a convinced anti-imperialist, a man also with a profound interest in the situation of the working class, and of course a dedicated revolutionary. No longer is Martí compared with American statesmen such as Abraham Lincoln or Franklin D. Roosevelt. Instead his contribution to the *patria* is frequently likened to that of other revolutionaries such as Petofi, Lenin, Fanon, Ho Chi Minh, Fidel Castro, and Che Guevara. As might be expected, the quality of these studies varies enormously, from the excellent studies by Maldonado Denis on Martí and Fanon and by Fernández Retamar on Ho Chi Minh and Martí, to less successful attempts such as the articles by Jesús Sabourín and Eduardo López Morales.

Within the mainstream of this revolutionary interpretation of Martí a fairly clear trend is identifiable, one which closely parallels the growing maturity or institutionalization of the revolution. The original and somewhat heavy-handed tendency to sell the work and thought of Martí for their relevance to the revolutionary situation in Cuba has been steadily replaced by a more profound and fairly balanced view of Martí's work. Indicative of this new and essentially well-reasoned interpretation of Martí is a recent observation by Carlos Rafael Rodríguez, deputy Prime Minister of Cuba, a comment that reveals the maturity of the current revolutionary approach:

> And so we have now a Martí equipped with all the ingredients for today's battle. We do not have, however, (and it is good to repeat it) a socialist Martí. On some occasions, in a desire to take Martí farther than he himself could reach, mention has been made of the socialist nature in Martí. But really what we find is Martí's respect for socialism. . . . All of that seems part of the admirable nature of Karl Marx, but he does not reach the same conclusions in regard to the class struggle or the revolutionary forces in that class struggle. . . . The society that Martí wanted to construct was one in which he thought that the balance of classes and social reconciliation were still possible.[32]

The general tone of works published in Cuba most recently is well balanced and informative. The best indication of this mature approach is the valuable *Anuario del Centro de Estudios Martianos (Annual Report of the Center for Martí Studies).* In a recent (1980) issue, for example, a series of well-reasoned papers were gathered around the central theme of Martí as a "democratic revolutionary." Minister of Culture Armando Hart set the tone for the collection, noting that Martí possessed "an extremely advanced revolutionary thought, but one which could not be termed that of a scientific socialist."[33] The existence of the Centro's solid work, in addition to other studies published in recent years, indicates a scholarly objectivity survives in the works by revolutionary Martí specialists.[34] All agree with Fernández Retamar's definition of Martí as "a democratic revolutionary who was becoming increasingly radical."[35]

The movement toward an objective interpretation of Martí's thought by the Cuban scholars concludes a brief but comprehensive outline of the ways in which José Martí has been presented to the people of Cuba and of the world. The crucial element in this evolving presentation has certainly been the different profiles with which he has been endowed. If the Beautyrest advertisement in *The Havana Post* of 1953 can be taken as a fair summary of the profile of Martí contained in the traditionalist interpretation, then the profile presented in the revolutionary interpretation is well illustrated by a collage composed by the Cuban writer and artist Fayad Jamís and included in a special edition of Castro's *La historia me absolverá* prepared by the Casa de las Américas.[36] The collage contains a bold portrait of Martí in the center of the page over which a photograph of Fidel Castro, taken in 1953 after his arrest, is superimposed. On the forehead of Martí is a star with the words *autor intelectual,* the implicit message being reinforced by the appearance on the facing page of a quotation from Fidel Castro's speech referring to Martí as the intellectual inspiration for the outbreak of revolution on July 26. Thus, from being regarded as an innocuous, well-intentioned, and somehow mystical figure, José Martí evolved into a convinced, hardened, and devoted revolutionary.

That such different and flatly contradictory interpretations of Martí's work as the traditional and the revolutionary can exist suggests two possible explanations. Either, as Richard Butler Gray has claimed, his ideas were so inherently "disorganized and contradictory" that "the prolixity of Martí's writings has resulted in his becoming 'all things to all men',"[37] or else Martí's ideas, in reality quite coherent, have since his death been tempered or overemphasized, taken out of context or selectively ignored. What is now needed in the study of Martí and his thought has been most succinctly expressed by Manuel Pedro González:

> It is necessary to call a halt to this frivolous competition, in which every ignoramus has ordained for himself the right to participate. These "experts" have not read Martí, have not meditated on his teachings, and have not the slightest intention of emulating him.[38]

The need thus exists for a fresh, constructive, and essentially "neutral" study, not merely of carefully selected passages but rather of the totality of Martí's works; only in this way will Martí's thought be properly deciphered and the true *esencia martiana* be gleaned. An important step in this direction has been taken in revolutionary Cuba, although for historians and critics both in North America and in the countries of "Nuestra América" to use Martí's term, there still remains much soul-searching and methodological investigation to be done before a thorough and objective overview of Martí's thought can emerge. The study of the twenty-eight-volume *Obras completas* is indeed an arduous task but one which is necessary if we are to truly understand and appreciate the work of José Martí, "el hombre más puro de la raza" ("the purest man of the Latin race"),[39] and one of the most advanced social thinkers of his time. The following chapters prospectively constitute an important step in this necessary reassessment.

II. THE MOLDING OF A VISIONARY

2. Origins of a Political Career

José Julián Martí y Pérez was born in Havana on January 28, 1853, the son of two *peninsulares* (literally, born in the peninsula of Spain) of humble birth, Mariano Martí and Leonor Pérez. During his short but extremely full life, José Martí managed to accomplish far more than most men, fighting for many years to instill a sense of patriotic dignity in his corevolutionaries, while steadfastly encouraging them to liberate (in the fullest sense of the term) their *patria*. When Martí's life was cut tragically short in 1895, much still remained to be done in Cuba, but at least the path along which the process would follow had been blazed. As this study will reveal, the basic plans for the program of liberation had been carefuly outlined by Martí, a liberation of which he himself was certain, as he noted the very month in which he was killed in a skirmish with a party of Spanish troops:

> I know how to disappear. But I know too that my ideas will not disappear, and that I will not grow bitter with this temporary neglect. As soon as our ideas have taken shape, action will be taken—whether it be my destiny, or someone else's. (XX, 163)

Ironically Martí's father had come to Cuba as a sergeant in the Spanish army and for the majority of his life served with various official peacekeeping bodies on the island. Obviously don Mariano's official position, as well as his firm allegiance to the Spanish crown, were both unacceptable to the young Martí. In fact, in order to understand properly the original motivation for his extraordinary revolutionary career, his notable obsession to liberate Cuba, and indeed his whole approach to life, an examination in some detail of Martí's childhood and adolescence is absolutely essential. Therefore, based on a close study of Martí's early work (and of course including his personal correspondence, notebooks, etc.), much of his thought can be explained not by means of any supposed intellectual influences but rather through an examination of the extremely unusual chain of personal experiences Martí endured during this period. A thorough study of this time in Martí's life greatly assists our understanding of the intensely moral and idealistic foundation for this thought, one of the key elements in his planned liberation campaign.

Of exceptional importance in the formation of José Martí's character was the influence of his parents on him (or rather Martí's negative reaction to that influence in the case of don Mariano). Martí's relationship with his mother was very deep, as illustrated by his poem, "A mi madre" ("To My Mother"), written in 1869 and generally considered to be the first verse he ever wrote. During his traumatic prison experiences in 1869 and 1870, Martí did not write to his father, indicative of the strain in their relationship, but wrote consistently to his mother, even sending her a photograph of himself in prison garb accompanied by a poem (XVII, 29), and related to her on numerous occasions the harsh conditions in prison.

There was evidently a very profound love between the young Martí and his mother. Through his letters, doña Leonor is revealed as an extremely tender and loving woman who, despite her lack of sympathy with or even proper understanding of the lofty goals for which her son was fighting, nevertheless, suffered immensely during his unfortunate experiences in San Lázaro. In a letter to his Mexican friend Manuel A. Mercado in March of 1878, Martí summarized this aspect of his mother's character:

> My mother has her many strong points, and I respect her for them, and as you know, I love her deeply. Unfortunately she will not forgive me for my wild independence, my brusque, unyielding nature, or my opinions concerning Cuba. (XX, 45)

However, despite the obvious love that Martí felt for his mother, the key psychological relationship in his childhood was quite clearly that between himself and his father; and in fact it is plausible to claim that during his adolescence Martí's character evolved largely as the result from his clear rejection of his father. By nature don Mariano appears to have been a strict and rather harsh individual, scrupulously honest and totally unyielding when he considered himself in the right, who on several occasions was disciplined by superiors because of this lack of flexibility. He was a man whose gruff manner and reticent character gradually alienated his young, sensitive (and equally single-minded) son.

Mariano Martí's military background, compounded by a lack of formal education, obviously conditioned his outlook on life; in essence he knew no other life than that of the barracks. Pedro N. González Veranes' sketch of Martí's father provides a fair representation. "His character was strong, extremely coarse and despotic—in both moral and material affairs, an exact likeness of the Roman *pater familia* [*sic*]. He met all his domestic obligations zealously, and at all times insisted on exercising his supreme authority over his family."[1] Certainly Martí's own comments on his father support the commonly held view that during his adolescence they shared a rather strained relationship. Significantly, on the few occasions later in his life when Martí does write about his father, it is frequently accompanied by an allusion to this early "difficult" period when they did not understand, much less respect, each other fully. Typical of this late appreciation of don Mariano was Martí's letter to his sister Amelia in 1880.

> My dear Amelia, you don't know just how much tender respect and veneration our father warrants. While at first he may appear full of grumpiness and silly notions, in fact he's a man with extraordinary virtue. Now that I'm an adult, I can appreciate the value of his energy, as well as the rare, sublime merit of his pure, forthright nature. (XX, 287–88)

Similar sentiments are expressed several times by Martí, for instance, in a letter to Jorge García (XX, 319) and another to Fermín Valdés Domínguez in which he again refers to his tardy understanding of his father: "You can't imagine how I came to love him after I really got to know him" (XX, 321). Evidently Martí did not initially respect or appreciate his father until the late 1870s, when he discovered what he later termed "a pride that grew every time I thought of him, because no one lived in such a miserable period. Yet no one, despite his apparent simplicity, emerged from this time purer in spirit and deed" (XX, 319).

Understandably, the young Martí—so obviously different in temperament from don Mariano—evaded the normal childhood stage of introjection,[2] clearly refusing to imitate or identify with the attributes of his father's character. The somewhat rude and uncompromising attitude of his father must have been totally unacceptable to Martí who, noting the military position of don Mariano as well as his unquestioning acceptance of the many injustices committed in Cuba in the name of the crown, may well have identified his father's uncompromising and rigidly authoritarian approach with that of the official Spanish policy. Quite possibly Martí, unconsciously comparing his father's attitude with the repression practiced in the name of the crown and increasingly dissociating himself from don Mariano, became a potential revolutionary earlier than is generally thought.

When Martí was only nine years old his father, recently appointed to a minor official post in the town of Hanábana (in the province of Oriente), took José with him. Scarcely competent to handle all the paperwork involved with the position, and also desirous to provide the young José with some valuable work experience, don Mariano employed his son as a general clerk–secretary. It was during his stay in Hanábana that an experience usually depicted as having roused Martí's social conscience took place; he became alarmed at the cruel treatment he saw meted out to the Negro slaves on the surrounding plantations. And although it may seem rather extreme to claim that "at this point Martí resolved to fight Spanish oppression against Cubans, regardless of race, color, or creed,"[3] nevertheless this time spent in Hanábana did represent an important formative experience in Martí's growing awareness of the many ills and injustices of colonial Cuba, reflected in an observation found in his later *Fragmentos.*

> And the blacks? Who has ever seen a friend physically whipped and does not consider himself forever in that man's debt? I saw it, I saw it when I was a child, and I can still feel the shame burning on my cheeks. (XXII, 189)

On another important level, Martí's stay in Hanábana also increased the rift between him and his father since don Mariano, despite his influence in the district, refused to intervene to stop such cruelties, a passivity which his son could never accept.

Meanwhile doña Leonor, convinced that exposure of José to the harsh conditions of life away from the capital would be detrimental to her son, finally persuaded her husband to let José return to Havana. Soon after he returned to the capital, Martí's mother entered him in the school of San Anacleto, where he was a remarkably successful student. Ironically his success in school only served to increase the tension between Martí and his father, who insisted that Martí leave his academic studies and concentrate on finding a job. The further education that Martí longed for was regarded by don Mariano as both unnecessary and wasteful, especially since the young Martí had already proved himself an exceptional accountant and general clerk and would therefore have few difficulties in finding a well-paid commercial position. Fortunately Martí's mother was able to dissuade her husband from this course of action; in March of 1865, Martí entered the Escuela Superior Municipal de Varones (Municipal Senior Boys' School), the director of which was Rafael María de Mendive, a poet of some fame on the island and a man viewed by the Spanish as harboring dangerous and seditious ideas. A new and important part of Martí's life was now to begin.

When José Martí began to attend the school of Rafael Mendive, the *maestro* had already gained an impressive reputation in Cuba, having edited two journals in the late 1840s and founded the prestigious *Revista de La Habana (The Havana Review)* in 1853. Moreover he had published several volumes of poetry and was generally regarded as one of the leading Cuban men of letters at that time. Mendive was also a firm believer in the necessity of Cuba gaining her political independence from an increasingly demanding *madre patria* (mother country, Spain), and he was a fervent admirer of the man generally regarded as being the first revolutionary intellectual of Cuba, Father Félix Varela, whom he met in New York in 1848.

After returning to Cuba in 1852, Mendive busied himself with his literary concerns, eventually turning to teaching; he opened two institutes, a private college called San Pablo, and the famous Escuela Superior de Varones that Martí attended. At this point he was not particularly active politically in Havana nor did he have, it can be argued, any particularly revolutionary plans for Cuban society after independence had been won. Indeed, despite his great respect for the leading proponents of independence in nineteenth-century Cuba—Félix Varela, José Antonio Saco, and José de la Luz y Caballero—it is quite likely that had it not been for the refusal of the Spanish *Junta de Información* in 1865 to allow badly needed tax relief and some minor reforms for the colony Mendive probably would not have greatly concerned himself with the movement for independence. However, with the failure of the Spanish government to alleviate the tax burden on the Cubans and instead to actually increase direct taxation on the citizens of Cuba during 1866 and 1867, many middle-class islanders became deeply antagonistic to Spain, seeking a more radical solution to their problems—political independence—than that afforded by this mild attempt at reform.[4]

The confused state of young Martí's mind as he entered Mendive's school is not difficult to imagine. There were several obvious clashes between his own lofty patriotic ideals and the lackluster reality afforded by his home life, between his own intense desire for knowledge and his parents' lack of education. Furthermore, the rebellious, inquisitive nature of his temperament clashed quite noticeably with the stern, unflinching loyalty of his parents (in particular that of his father) to the established set of values typified by the crown.

It was thus José Martí's extremely good fortune to enter Mendive's school at this time of crisis. Faced with a lack of understanding on the part of his family and convinced that he was essentially very different from them, Martí much needed and gratefully accepted Mendive's understanding, for he saw in the *maestro* a spirit very similar to his own. Moreover, with the possibility for a normal process of identification with his father having been relinquished, Martí willingly turned to Mendive as a father-substitute for guidance and affection. However, not only did he internalize Mendive's attributes, but also he became intrigued by Mendive's interest in political independence for Cuba, later developing the ideas of the *maestro* to a degree never even considered by don Rafael.

Based on a study of Martí's references to Mendive, it is clear that he recognized in Mendive a truly kindred spirit, a genuine *maestro* in the fullest sense of the Spanish word, who would gradually shape Martí's literary and political potential into a strongly humanistic "cosmovision." Mendive's role as a substitute father to the young Martí is perhaps best shown in Martí's own words. In 1868, for example, he concluded a letter to Mendive in this way: "Until tomorrow, Sr. Mendive. Feel free to order your follower who loves you with filial respect, José Martí" (XX, 244). Even more illustrative of this obvious devotion to Mendive was Martí's reply to a critical note from his adviser. "I don't think that a generous father should have to remind his adoring son of his duties. That is why I was so amazed at your note, when at every moment I would give my life for you—a life which belongs solely to you—and a thousand others if I had them" (XX, 245).

Martí could not have helped comparing the harsh, somewhat resentful attitude of his father with the gentle, affectionate nature of Mendive. Unlike Martí's father, Mendive stimulated and encouraged his young charge, heaping lavish praise upon him, gradually building up both his self-confidence and his moral conscience. To understand Martí's undying devotion to Mendive and at the same time his displeasure at his own father, an observation of this time made by Martí in a letter to his teacher is enlightening. Apparently don Mariano, still intent on making his son abandon his studies altogether in order to contribute in a more tangible fashion to the Martí household, had driven the young José to the point of desperation. "I work now from six in the morning to eight at night, and I earn 4½ ounces which I hand over to my father. Every day he makes me suffer more and has hurt me so much that—I confess to you with all the candidness you know in me—only the hope of seeing you again has stopped me from killing myself" (XX, 246). As a result of his father's actions, Rafael María de Mendive became José Martí's true *padre espiritual* (spiritual father), paying for his education when Martí's own father refused to, personally teaching his young protégé, and continually encouraging him to appreciate his *cubanidad* (pride in being Cuban).

What is particularly interesting in the Mendive-Martí relationship is that the *maestro*'s influence on Martí was not restricted to time spent in school; Martí was a frequent visitor to Mendive's home, where he was accepted almost as one of the family. Especially important in the formation of Martí's fervently patriotic outlook were the many famed *tertulias* (social gatherings) that he eagerly attended at Mendive's house. Mendive's outspoken defense of the need to liberate Cuba from Spain was well known, and at these evening meetings there were not only discussions about literature and art but also the idea of an independent Cuba was seriously studied. At these *tertulias* Martí cultivated veritable passions for justice and beauty; and, faced with the rather dry background of unquestioning *españolismo* (love of things Spanish) at his father's house, he willingly immersed himself in the heady atmosphere of revolutionary *cubanismo* (love of things Cuban).

In 1868 the first important Cuban revolt against Spain occurred, led by Manuel Céspedes.[5] This rebellion, commonly known as the "Grito de Yara" ("Cry of Yara") after the small town where the uprising broke out, impelled the evening discussions in Mendive's home to take on an increasingly political nature. By this time Martí had been "adopted" by the *maestro* and participated actively in these sessions, remembering many years later how he feverishly joined the discussions on the Céspedes uprising while he "followed with his elbows resting on the piano the march of Céspedes through the swampy scrubland" (V, 251). He also recalled how on another occasion all the *tertulianos* (people at the social gathering) conspired to hide a Cuban rebel, recounting that "José de Armas y Céspedes, who was being pursued by the police, was hidden in Rafael Mendive's room" (V, 251).

Meanwhile in Mendive's school the students composed and recited poetry that was critical of the Spanish governor of Cuba, Francisco Lersundi. "On the patio, beneath the banana trees, we would recite Señor Mendive's sonnets to Lersundi" (V, 251), Martí later wrote. Indeed, for the first time in Cuban history there was a general feeling of rebellion and of national awareness in the air, as Julio Le Riverend has indicated.[6] As a result of this widespread desire for a liberated Cuba and of the strongly nationalist and separatist views of Mendive, as well as the extremely close ties between Mendive and his young charge, it seems impossible for Martí not to have been imbued with this newfound revolutionary zeal.

But while the struggle against Spain had become a holy crusade for Mendive, for whom the conduct of the *madre patria* was totally unacceptable, Mariano Martí steadfastly continued to support the Spanish point of view. Mendive interpreted the ruthless suppression of progressive ideas (which for him included the notion of political independence) in Cuba as a dastardly crime, a vicious attempt to protect Spain's brutal exploitation of the island, while Martí's father continued to pledge his seemingly unquestioning allegiance to the crown. It was at this point that the young Martí clearly decided to spurn the way of life typified by his father's conduct, preferring instead to follow the path shown him by Mendive.

Consequently, Mendive's influence on José Martí should not be underestimated. For after a signally unhappy home life—Martí refers in fact to the "bitter memories of my house" (XX, 32) and in contrast to Mendive's home as "a house that belonged entirely to the angels" (V, 251)—Martí willingly allowed himself to be taken under the wing of his *padre espiritual.* With Mendive as mentor, Martí's vague feelings of discontent aroused by seeing the slaves whipped at Hanábana, his dislike of the blind acceptance by his father of the many injustices committed in the name of Spain, and finally his growing indignation at the prevailing atmosphere of oppression, all coalesced and ultimately found their form in a fervent desire for independence that he shared with Rafael Mendive. At this particular stage in Martí's somewhat vague political aspirations, the dominant influence upon him had been the conviction of Mendive that the *patria* had to be liberated before there could be any manner of national dignity. Under the *maestro*'s tutelage, José Martí thus became a convinced believer in political independence for Cuba. The relationship between the two men was admirably described by Pánfilo D. Camacho. "From a spiritual influence such as Mendive, nothing else could really result: a poet and a revolutionary."[7]

Under the guidance of Rafael María de Mendive, Martí basically learned three valuable lessons: to compose beautiful and yet simple poetry; to inspire his fellow Cubans to believe in the necessity of political independence from Spain; and finally, perhaps most important of all, to preach without respite the details of the selfless and humanitarian society that had to be instituted in Cuba after political independence had been won. Moreover, Martí was never to forget the importance of these lessons taught to him by his *padre espiritual,* even after the application of Mendive's teachings led to the arrest, imprisonment, and eventual deportation of the young boy. Grateful to Mendive for both his instruction and love and fully aware of the enormous influence that Mendive had exercised upon him, Martí wrote to the *maestro* shortly before being deported from Cuba in January of 1871.

> In two hours I will be deported to Spain. I have suffered much but feel that I have suffered well. If I have been strong enough to meet this and if I am able to be a true man, this is all due to you. Indeed, all the warmth and kindness I have is due solely to you. . . . My best regards to Mario, and to you, the soul of your son and disciple, Martí. (XX, 247)

The year 1869 constituted an extremely important stage in Martí's embrace of the separatist cause. On January 4 a new and more liberal captain-general, Domingo Dulce, arrived in Havana to replace the rather harsh administration of General Lersundi. He had arrived with the express intention of introducing a program of moderate reform in Cuba, including token representation in the *Cortes* (the Spanish parliament), freedom of assembly, and freedom of the press. As a result of these new-found liberties, within eighteen days (from January 10–28) no less than seventy-seven periodicals and newspapers sprang up, the vast majority of which appear to have been critical of the Spanish control of the island. Two of these journals were the direct work of José Martí.

On January 19, Martí published the journal *El Diablo Cojuelo (The Limping Devil)* which he directed with Fermín Valdés Domínguez, another student of Mendive. Four days later Martí's second work, *La Patria Libre (The Free Motherland)* appeared, the costs of both paid by Mendive. Meanwhile Martí's relations with his father had continued to deteriorate and don Mariano, realizing the dangers to which his son was exposing himself by adopting this defiantly anti-Spanish attitude, tried hard to dissuade him from such a course of action. All was in vain, however, since Martí had eagerly embraced the revolutionary cause. Don Mariano could then only watch helplessly as his son, increasingly convinced of the inherent need for an independent Cuba, plunged headlong toward the inevitable confrontation with the Spanish forces.

Both of these initial publications of José Martí are important for they reveal the degree of commitment he felt at the time toward the idea of an independent Cuba. Moreover, both understandably revolved around the young Cuban's fervent patriotism, which is probably best expressed in his drama *Abdala*, published in *La Patria Libre*, by the young protagonist.

> We children of the motherland, born in Nubia, will know how to die for Nubia. Dying for her, the last breath from my lips will be for Nubia—since our strength and valor were created for our native land. (XVIII, 14)

In both *El Diablo Cojuelo* and *La Patria Libre* there are two fundamental levels on which Martí based his opposition to the Spanish domination of Cuba. There is his objective appreciation of the "Cuban situation," in which Martí praised the establishment by General Dulce of many basic liberties previously unknown in Cuba. "Thank God that in these sweet times [tiempos *dulces*] there is a fair distance from one's house to the Morro Castle. During the time of don Paco [Lersundi] it was a different situation" (I, 31). Also clearly evident are Martí's subjective feelings in regard to the historical era in which he was living, as well as his own family situation. Consistently criticized by his parents for his strong interest in the cause of Cuban independence, yet attracted by a deeply patriotic longing to help his country, Martí's personal anguish is portrayed by a remarkably similar set of circumstances in *Abdala*. In the drama the protagonist is torn between his mother's pleas that he concentrate instead on his family obligations and his profound desire to fight for the independence of his country, Nubia, and to defend the *patria* with his life if necessary. Abdala eventually decides on the latter course of action and in fact dies fighting for Nubia—in much the same way as Martí would be killed while struggling for his nation's independence in 1895.

However, although the message of patriotism is mercilessly underlined throughout the drama, it is easy to detect that Abdala's noble love for his country also stems largely from the expectations of personal glory that he will receive in the aftermath of battle. Typical of this attitude is his immediate reaction on hearing that he had been selected to lead the army against the foreign invaders.

> At last my brow will be crowned with glory.
> I'll be the one to free my distressed country,
> And to wrest the oppressor from my people
> Who are now being destroyed in its claws! (XVIII, 15)

Indeed, in this early period of Martí's work, if patriotism is viewed as an obviously desirable quality, it is not considered totally selfless since one of the prime reasons for such dedication to the *patria* is the thirst for *gloria* and personal renown. At this stage, then, the juvenile Martí possessed rather romantic and vague ideas about such patriotic emotions; following his traumatic experiences in political prison, his attitude would change dramatically.

Although the tone of these early publications is cautious, yet firm, Martí was fully aware of the definite need for a radical solution to Cuba's problems. In *El Diablo Cojuelo* he categorically stated: "If I were an orator . . . I would not base my policies on what the French would call an outrageous *hésitation*. Either Yara or Madrid" (I, 32). Yet despite this apparent conviction of Martí, the reader of these early works receives the impression, when comparing them to all of the work written after his imprisonment, that Martí was in fact speaking from a somewhat distant and inexperienced position. It was as if he were accepting the teachings of Mendive principally because of his great devotion to the *maestro* without understanding precisely what had to be changed in Cuba. Consequently, Martí at this point can be classed as a theoretical revolutionary, searching both for a definitive explanation of his patriotic leanings and for a platform of reforms with which to support his willing acceptance of the cause.

Shortly after the publication of *El Diablo Cojuelo,* an incident occurred that changed the lives of both Mendive and Martí. Despite the attempts at moderate reform by Governor Dulce, the paramilitary *voluntarios* remained the dominant political body on the island, outnumbering the members of the regular Spanish Army 33,500 to 7,000.[8] They attacked Dulce because of what they interpreted as the lack of a firm approach toward the Cubans and harassed him into suspending all the newly acquired liberties—less than a month after his arrival. The Cubans, after the welcome taste of these moderate reforms, were understandably bitter.

Then on the night of January 22, 1869, during an evening performance at the Villanueva Theater, one of the actors broke forth in a patriotic outburst, which summoned a band of Spanish soldiers who stormed the theater, arresting and killing many of the spectators. Neither Martí nor Mendive were present at the performance, but the teacher's political feelings were well known, and an example was needed at this point to show the more militant Cubans that such conduct would not be tolerated. Accordingly, Rafael Mendive was arrested and subsequently deported. José Martí's respect and devotion to Mendive entered a new phase, for at great personal risk he applied for a special pass to visit the *maestro* during his five-month stay in prison. Martí also helped to take care of Mendive's family and assisted actively in the running of his school. However, when Mendive was deported to Spain, Martí became inconsolable.

It was at this time that he and his former schoolmate Fermín Valdés Domínguez discovered that another student from Mendive's school had joined the hated Spanish *voluntarios.* They composed a sharply worded note criticizing his thoughtless and selfish disregard for the memory of Mendive but decided against sending the letter.[9] Soon afterward the two young Cubans experienced personally the excesses of Spanish "justice"; and, as in the case of Mendive, the slightest evidence was used to prove their seditious intent. A party of *voluntarios,* suspecting themselves to be the object of laughter they heard coming from the Domínguez house, burst into the room and discovered the letter. Martí and Valdés Domínguez were arrested.

Taken into custody on October 21, 1869, Martí was accused of treason, a charge based exclusively on the offending letter, and on March 7 of the following year he was convicted. Because Martí accepted full responsibility for the letter and also because of his defiantly Cuban attitude toward the court, he was sentenced to no less than six years of hard labor in San Lázaro political prison; Fermín Valdés Domínguez received only a six-month sentence. A new and vitally important period of Martí's life began.

Martí's imprisonment, particularly the time spent in the *presidio político* of San Lázaro, was of exceptional importance from the point of view of his revolutionary "apprenticeship"; it represented the watershed between his early identification with the theories of national independence and his subsequent decision to fight actively for the liberation of Cuba. His imprisonment, correctly judged the "supreme formative experience of his personality" by Ezequiel Martínez Estrada,[10] proved to Martí the need for a radical liberating process in the *patria* and convinced him that he personally should take the responsibility of bringing about this liberation. Consequently when Martí left San Lázaro, as Andrés Iduarte has noted, he was a changed man; although physically debilitated from his rigorous prison experiences there, he had acquired a noticeable determination to lead his country to independence.

> Martí spent six months of his seventeen years splitting rocks beneath the tropical sun, his feet chained. It was a savage punishment that marked him both physically and morally forever; he emerged with medical problems that would continue to plague him, two scars on his ankles—and a series of political convictions.[11]

It was while in prison that Martí obtained the necessary overall view of the many problems of Cuba. Indeed, the reader of Martí's works of this period, in particular *El presidio político en Cuba (The Political Prison in Cuba)* and *La República Española ante la Revolución Cubana (The Spanish Republic Faced by the Cuban Revolution)*, realizes that Martí now saw the island as one huge political prison; the cruelties and manifest injustices that he had witnessed in captivity represented to him only a microcosm of the severe injustices and lack of essential liberties suffered by the country as a whole. Moreover, his experiences in San Lázaro dramatically complemented the earlier lessons of Mendive. From a discontented and patriotic young Cuban, Martí had emerged a committed revolutionary, fully prepared to give his life selflessly for the liberation of his *patria*. He had come to realize not only that this political independence constituted the first necessary step for Cuba but also that the entire sociopolitical structure of the island would have to be replaced. More important, he now firmly believed that it was his obligation to contribute to the liberation by directing the interest and the endeavors of his compatriots. This change in Martí is well illustrated by the dramatic development in his literary work: the uncertainty of *La Patria Libre* was replaced by the conviction of the following work, *El presidio político en Cuba*, published in January, 1871.

Martí was aware that the struggle to attain the first of these goals, political independence from Spain, would be both long and severe, for the crown had too much to lose in Cuba and would obviously punish—in brutal and exemplary fashion—any threat to its continued exploitation of the island; the extremely severe sentences given to himself and Mendive were ample evidence of this.

But, undaunted, Martí did not waver from his firm desire, having made a conscious resolution to offer himself as a victim on what he interpreted to be the "altar" of the *patria.* And, as if to remind himself always of this all-important vocation, he afterward carried with him a ring fashioned from a link of the chain that he had worn in San Lázaro as No. 113 inside of which he had engraved the word CUBA.

Consequently, if as Martí's own testimony shows, the young boy's profoundly emotional interest in his homeland originated from his personal devotion to Rafael Mendive, then a close study of his literary works written shortly after his captivity reveals the extent to which Martí's thought had subsequently evolved. He had been imprisoned for a little more than twelve months, of which the last six months, spent in the *presidio político* of San Lázaro, constituted part of his original six-year sentence. Afterward, weak and infirm, his sentence was commuted to one of exile; on January 15, 1871, the youth—for Martí had not yet reached his eighteenth birthday—was deported to Spain.

A comparison of Martí's literary production before and shortly after his prison experience discloses several important developments. Although there is the same general desire for sweeping reforms in Cuba and basic liberties for the people—concisely, for long-term solutions to Cuba's many problems—the tone of Martí's work intensified. The pamphlet *El presidio político en Cuba,* which he is reputed to have started on the voyage from Havana and which he published shortly after arriving in Spain, offers an emotional, highly personal interpretation of life and conditions in a political prison. A life so brutal, Martí claimed: "If a provident God existed and were to see all that, with one hand He would cover His face, and with the other would hurl that negation of all He stood for into hell" (I, 45).

The measured, somewhat artificially rebellious tone of *Abdala* had been replaced by one of righteous indignation. On one level Martí preached to the Spanish people on the stifling oppression imposed upon Cuba by the *madre patria,* which continued to exploit the island to the limit of its endurance. Taking full advantage of his position in the heart of what could be called the enemy camp, Martí presented to his Spanish readers a disturbing picture of prison life, challenging them to explain their continued selfish interests in the island, which he saw as the fundamental reason for the existence of such miserable institutions.

> Why do you sign with your assent the extermination of the race that has suffered most at your hands, that has been most humiliated, that had the most faith in you, that has been most submissive—until desperation or mistrust of your promises caused her to shake her head? Why are you all unjust and so cruel? (I, 50)

On a more personal level Martí criticized the blatantly unjust Cuban legal system, which was fully prepared to take whatever measures that were deemed necessary to suppress any form of dissent. Martí's personal imprisonment had obviously moved him greatly; despite this, he spent little time discussing his "case history," preferring to relate the atrocities committed on other inmates. Although for Martí much worse than the deplorable conditions and the lack of compassion shown the prisoners by their guards was the fact that most of the inmates, including Martí, apparently had been incarcerated for manifestly unjust reasons. Their suffering was all the more damnable because they had committed no crime to warrant such brutal treatment. The young Martí, indignant and angry, thus learned from his own experiences the extent to which the Spanish government was prepared to go to suppress even the suspicion of dissent. "That prison," Martí wrote, "was the prison of Cuba, the institution of the government" (I, 61), obviously a government that had to be drastically changed.

Another measure of the change in Martí's thought after his harsh imprisonment was his presentation of the noble practice of patriotism. In his earlier work *Abdala,* Martí had placed great emphasis on the value of patriotism, which at that time for him was based on a romantic and somewhat melodramatic appreciation of his native land and a strongly adolescent concern with the idea of *gloria.* Moreover, before experiencing at first hand the rigors of San Lázaro, Martí had loyally supported Mendive's interpretation of the need to overthrow Spanish oppression without really understanding the fundamental problems facing Cuba. In other words, Martí's interpretation of the concept of the *patria* before he was imprisoned (as seen in his earliest works) was almost a flirtation with patriotism: the official "wedding" resulted from his experiences in San Lázaro. Thereafter he would no longer associate this patriotism with the concepts of *fama* (fame) and *gloria*, preferring to employ a new vocabulary composed of such terms as *deber* (duty), *sacrificio* (sacrifice), and *martirio* (martyrdom).

This new, evangelizing intent of Martí, never seen in his earlier publications, appeared very noticeably in his first two works after he left San Lázaro. In his two short-lived journals, Martí revealed the basic immorality and injustice of the Spanish domination of the island; in his later works he was not content, as he had been in *El diablo cojuelo*, simply to present a record of these ills. Instead he chastised the Spanish people for their previous lack of interest in the "unchristian" way in which their colony was governed. Moreover, faced with counterclaims on the part of the Spanish government that Spain was only protecting its "integridad nacional" by this conduct in Cuba, Martí offered in reply a moving description of prison life, concluding: "There you have your national integrity; there you have the government that you have approved, that you have endorsed, and unanimously applauded" (I, 63). In both of his post-*presidio* works written in 1873, *El presidio político en Cuba* and *La República Española ante la Revolución*, Martí actually confronted the Spanish people, hurling out a challenge to them: how in the name of justice could Spain claim to be a freedom-loving country and yet sanction such opprobrious conduct?

> Now approve the conduct of the Government of Cuba.
>
> Now, you State Elders, tell us that in the name of the *patria* you sanction this most wicked violation of morality, this complete disregard for every feeling of justice.
>
> Say it, sanction it, endorse it—if you can. (I, 74)

Consequently following his imprisonment, José Martí clearly accepted the image of the *patria* as the central axis of his existence around which the rest of his life would revolve. With an astonishing degree of selflessness, Martí thereafter dedicated himself totally to what he interpreted as the immediate necessity of his country, the political independence of Cuba, and all else had to be subordinated to this goal, including his most personal desires. His message had become one of exemplary Christianity—to help both his fellow Cubans and the *patria*, which is summarized by an entry made later in a private notebook. "There's no responsibility and no evil like those of feeling able to bring about happiness to others (at one's own expense) and because of self-centered peace deciding not to help one's brother" (XXI, 166). Martí's dedication to achieving this goal was complete, as Manuel Pedro González has rightly noted. "From then on Martí dedicated his activity and his genius to the ideal of liberating his nation. This yearning became an obsession for him and on its altar he sacrificed everything: fortune, well-being, family, literary glory, and, finally, his life."[12] "Martí revolucionario" had been born.

The influence of these early formative experiences on Martí's thought is quite clear, but also Martí was known to have read widely. There have been many interesting hypotheses advanced to show the influence on Martí by a variety of literary, philosophical, and political schools of thought; Martí has been linked to a multitude of possible influences, from Plato to Krause, from Marx to Whitman; and, most recently, José L. Mas has attempted to show the influence on Martí of social romanticism. Though Martí was a well-read man and despite traces of—or at least similarities with—stoicism, Platonism, Spanish mysticism, transcendentalism, Krauseanism, and a basic spiritualism, among others, Martí was touched less by these reputed influences than by the experiences of his early years, a claim supported by almost all reputable studies made on Martí's thought including the works of Medardo Vitier, Manuel Isidro Méndez, Raoul Alpizar Poyo, Antonio Martínez Bello, and Andrés Iduarte.[13] Typical of the reaction of these critics is Martínez Bello's summary of such influences.

> Idealism, Krauseanism, Emersonianism or transcendentalism, Senecanism, stoicism, Spencerianism, theosophism, and many other philosophical "isms" can all be located easily if only partially in his multi-spirited work. He went to all these philosophical doctrines, as he himself said, precisely in order to avoid belonging specifically to any one. He embraced them all, lovingly and knowledgeably, taking from them the particular essence that complemented his own philosophical ideals.[14]

All critics who have studied this question of philosophical or intellectual affiliation have commented on Martí's voracious reading habits; and, indeed, he read everything from modern scientific and agricultural techniques to Hindustani mythology, from the Spanish classics to the poetry of Emerson, from Darwin to Oscar Wilde. Therefore, it seems unlikely that any particular intellectual influence gained preeminence, which is affirmed by Martí's statement:

> I adore simplicity, *but not that simplicity which comes from limiting my ideas to this or that circle or school.* Rather I prefer the type of simplicity to say what I see, feel, or think with the least number of words possible—using words that are powerful, graphic, energetic, and harmonious." (XXII, 101) [my italics]

Thus Martí is best understood as a true philosophical eclectic, reading widely and extracting from all the works that he studied anything that he considered of value, yet never limiting himself to "este o aquel círculo" ("this or that circle"), as he put it. The view of the Mexican critic Andrés Iduarte perhaps best reflects the generally accepted interpretation concerning the dominant influences on Martí: "Everything else—what Martí acquires in Spain, Mexico, and the United States and through his numerous readings—is an addition, enrichment, ratification, improvement. However, the marrow of his thought will remain until his death what he learned in Mendive's College."[15]

It is useful to compare both the tone and content of Martí's early works, examined in this chapter, with those he would write toward the end of his life, for there are outstanding similarities. A close examination, for instance, of *El presidio político en Cuba* and his last, famous letter to Manuel Mercado, written a few days before Martí's death, reveals the same moral base and the same selfless dedication to the *patria*. Consequently, despite a difference of some twenty-four years, the Martí of *El presidio político en Cuba* is indeed the definitive Martí who would later compose the numerous collections of poetry, the revolutionary exhortations found in his journal *Patria,* the famous declaration of pride in *Nuestra América,* and the magazine for children, *La Edad de Oro (The Golden Age).* Commenting on the similarity of all Martí's post-*presidio* work and echoing the opinion of his colleague Manuel Isidro Méndez, Julio Le Riverend accurately noted, "the Maestro appears thoroughly formed in 1870."[16]

Martí's revolutionary energy, and actually his entire approach to life, can thus be explained largely as a result of the extraordinary events that befell him before 1870, in particular by the circumstances surrounding his relationship with Mendive and by his subsequent imprisonment. Faced with a lack of understanding at home, the young Martí turned instead to Rafael María de Mendive, his *padre espiritual,* whose teachings on the sad plight of Cuba and on the human condition in general deeply impressed the young Martí. These lessons were later illustrated more fully for Martí by his own traumatic experiences in prison, after he had been arrested on clearly unfounded charges. Through these two experiences Martí assimilated a series of moral values that would remain basically unaltered for the remainder of his life—hence the similarity evident in all of his works.

Writing with his characteristic clarity to his future corevolutionary Máximo Gómez, the young Martí explained to the general the major formative experiences in his brief career. All was extremely straightforward, he claimed: "Perhaps no one will agree with it, but Rafael Mendive was my father; from his school I went to jail and then to political prison; then I was deported, and later was deported again" (XX, 263). Thereafter Martí devoted himself totally to the application of his high ideals to the struggle for the full and meaningful liberation of his *patria.* His revolutionary apprenticeship had been completed.

3. Evolution of Sociopolitical Thought

It has been ascertained that following a series of disturbing experiences—and in particular his harrowing incarceration in San Lázaro—José Martí's political awareness developed quickly during his adolescence. Indeed, a strong case can be made to support the claim that almost by force of circumstances Martí acquired a mature, radical, and articulate political consciousness unusual in one so young. And it was noted that if a comparison is made between the central political ideas of Martí at this time with those found in his final works, remarkable similarities are discovered in tone, purpose and, most noticeably, in moral content. Thus, as Julio Le Riverend has accurately noted, "at the age of fifteen—in 1869—the young Martí appears to have the fundamental elements of his thoughts and plans properly formed."[1]

A study of Martí's works reveals that there was no single incident especially responsible for the development of his thought after he left San Lázaro,[2] and equally obvious that it is neither possible nor representative of Martí to separate the development of his thought into clearly divided periods.[3] However, the interpretation of Julio Le Riverend correctly outlines the two fundamental conditioning factors on José Martí—the effect on him of his personal experiences in Cuba before his deportation, and that of his travels abroad, particularly his fifteen-year stay in the United States.

> There were two clearly defined stages in the formation of Martí: a first, fundamental stage in which his thoughts and plans acquire

> some of their permanent characteristics, paralleling both his own experiences and those of Cuba; and a second period in which those elements were strengthened by aspects resulting from Martí's study of the world at that time. It should be emphasized that his knowledge of Latin America, his experiences in Europe, and his profound analysis of the shattered innards of North American society, at a period when an aggressive, voracious capitalism was emerging, were all exceptionally important for the universal application of Martí's thought.[4]

Based on this approximation of Martí's development and with the intention of preparing the reader for the salient details of Martí's aspirations for the *patria* to be studied later, this chapter examines the broad development of Martí's thought during the almost quarter of a century following his first deportation to Spain while at the same time offering an explanation as to why such changes occurred.

The key to understanding the evolution of José Martí's sociopolitical thought definitely lies in the conclusions he derived from his observations of the "New World," where he spent twenty of his last twenty-five years. Undoubtedly the time spent by Martí in Europe (from January 1871 to January 1875) was of importance in the overall development of his character and, as was mentioned in the first chapter, Martí read widely. Nevertheless, based on the remarkable paucity of writing, whether of a political or literary nature, by Martí from the time he arrived in Spain until his arrival in Mexico some four years later, his sociopolitical thought experienced little change. On the other hand, a more dramatic set of incidents resulting in a noticeable progression of his ideas was to occur immediately after Martí returned to Latin America.

Cintio Vitier correctly emphasizes the quasi-religious effect on Martí's political consciousness that resulted from his "peregrinación por América Latina" ("pilgrimage through Latin America");[5] Martí truly underwent a mystical experience as he traveled through Spanish America. His flight from the arid and rather uninspiring background of Spanish scholasticism (and also from an essentially reactionary political tradition) was suddenly and dramatically replaced by a return to "his" continent, as Martí joyfully discovered his Latin American roots. In particular, as Andrés Iduarte has demonstrated, this reawakening of Martí's passionate interest in Latin

America was especially encouraged by his experiences in Mexico, where he spent the first two years after leaving Spain.

> The importance of Mexico in the sentimental, intellectual, and political life of the Cuban is indeed great. He lived happily as a man, earned his way, loved and was loved, and felt like a citizen without losing one iota of his pride in being Cuban (indeed he engaged in continuous controversies over the independence of Cuba). He learned from the organizers of the Juárez reforms, saw the frozen Indian race and dreamed of melting this petrification. He lived with illustrious and sage Indians like Ignacio Ramírez and Ignacio Manuel Altamirano and spoke of the potential of their people. He came into contact with the stately remains of the Aztec and Maya-Quiché cultures and found in all these aspects a magnificent past, a combative present, an Indian refinement, and a political revolution. This was to prove the essential base to develop his faith in "Our America."[6]

The years that Martí spent in Mexico, together with the eighteen months he lived in Guatemala, and to a lesser extent his five-month stay in Venezuela in 1880, were truly of inestimable importance for Martí both as a Latin American and as a budding revolutionary. He gained inspiration from the example of these former Spanish colonies, now sovereign nations, and also became convinced of his ability to complete the Latin American epic initiated by Simon Bolívar, because, as he noted defiantly in 1881, "it is well known that a stanza is missing in the 1810 poem of independence" (VII, 284). His was at all times a balanced stock-taking of Latin American reality—its needs and wants, its numerous problems, and its many inherent qualities. Moreover, before any other writer of this modern era Martí saw the necessity of establishing close commercial, political, and cultural ties between all members of the Latin American community, and he also discouraged in no uncertain terms the tradition of many nations of "Nuestra América" to regard themselves primarily as Argentinians, Mexicans, or another nationality, before Latin Americans. For him there was only one spiritual affinity between all the countries of Latin America. He proudly proclaimed: "Our country is really just one; it begins at the Río Grande and extends to the miry hills of Patagonia [at the tip of South America]" (XI, 48).

In short, during this time Martí learned that he too was a Latin

American. It cannot however be termed a case of rediscovery, since Cuba, because of its status as a colony of Spain, had always been encouraged to identify with the *madre patria* rather than with its rebellious Latin American neighbors. Martí also discovered that his continent, besides possessing an abundance of natural beauty and untapped wealth, could also draw upon an amazingly rich tradition of cultures and peoples. In sum, for the first time in his life Martí felt proud, not only because he could identify with this hitherto-unknown Latin American cultural tradition but also because he most definitely admired the apparently limitless potential of the continent, his continent. With some justification, it can be stated that Martí experienced in a deeply personal way what another Cuban, Alejo Carpentier, would later come to define as *lo real maravilloso,* the magic reality of Latin America.

José Martí's dramatic personal identification with "Nuestra América" also assisted greatly the development of his own political consciousness, which during his time in Spain appears to have been dormant. Suddenly in 1875 he found himself in an emotionally charged atmosphere, the twilight of Lerdo de Tejada's presidency. And after observing the maneuvers of Porfirio Díaz to wrest control from President Lerdo, Martí suddenly felt himself politically involved for the first time since his deportation more than four years earlier, and he condemned the high-handed selfish actions of Díaz. Just as he had rebelled in Cuba against what he saw as a cruel and essentially immoral domination of the island by Spain, Martí now reacted with righteous indignation to General Díaz's unjustifiable strong-arm tactics. The subsequent demise of Lerdo de Tejada and the triumphant entry into Mexico City by Porfirio Díaz in November of 1876 convinced Martí that he could not with good conscience remain in such an oppressive environment. Writing in 1878 to his friend Manuel Mercado, Martí explained the reason for his departure. In Mexico he had been extremely contented, Martí explained; but for the usurpation of power by Díaz, he would have been delighted to stay there. However, because he loathed the methods employed by Díaz in Mexico, Martí felt the need to leave, defending his actions by claiming: "For anyone with a beam of light on their brow, it is not possible to live where tyrants rule" (XX, 47). Accordingly he left the country (he would later also leave Guatemala and Venezuela after seeing the unfortunate results of *caudillismo* [tyrannical dictatorship]), but not without a revitalized interest in political reform; the revolutionary spirit, flagging in Spain, had been reconfirmed in Martí after his stay in Mexico, and the process of radicalization had thus been renewed.

The five years that Martí lived in Latin America allowed him time to probe beneath the surface reality of his continent, to discover for himself the reasons behind the traditional instability in both social and political life, and finally to provide suggestions in many cases that would help solve such grave debilities. It was during this time that he became aware of the many continent-wide problems that would have to be solved before Latin America could realize its vast untapped potential. More important, when this consciousness was added to his determination to fight for political independence in Cuba, they together represented the basis for his sociopolitical aspirations for the future Cuban Republic as Martí gradually began to piece together a rudimentary program of reform for both Cuba and "Nuestra América." Consequently, whereas before he had experienced an essentially passionate urge to fight against the Spanish forces and to free his country from the clutches of the *madre patria,* after his *peregrinación* (pilgrimage) Martí had reached a further stage in his apprenticeship. Now he was aware of many specific problems that would have to be solved not only in Cuba but also throughout Latin America.

Among many of the specific lessons that Martí had learned during these five crucial years spent in Latin America was the necessity of avoiding at all costs the dangers of *caudillismo,* which in fact he had witnessed firsthand in all of the countries where he had resided, as well as the accompanying necessity of preventing all forms of military governments in Latin America. His observations on General Díaz in Mexico had convinced him that such regimes were to be vigorously discouraged, and his personal separation in 1884 from his powerful allies, Generals Gómez and Maceo, after he had detected in their behavior an intent to impose a military government on the Cuban people after the island's liberation, testifies to the firmness of his conviction. Moreover, as will be shown in chapter 4, it was also during his stay in Mexico that José Martí expressed his unqualified support for the concept of an active and effective democracy. So it was in Mexico that Martí became a convinced democrat and, as his strict adherence almost twenty years later to the democratic principles of the Partido Revolucionario Cubano shows, it is probable that he hoped to cultivate this form of government in the liberated Republic.

Martí also made substantial observations on a variety of economic, social, and political reforms that he deemed necessary for the full development of Latin America. For an idea of the wide range of reforms planned by Martí during his stay in Latin America, it is only necessary to glance briefly at the far-reaching social changes envisaged by him, which will be examined in following chapters. In essence among the most important of these reform programs were: the need for all citizens, regardless of wealth or social standing, to obtain a decent and necessarily practical education; the need for all Latin American countries to follow primarily an agricultural economy; the pressing need for social harmony and for a fair and equitable distribution of wealth, since this would guarantee true social justice in "Nuestra América"; the need for workers' organizations, the right to strike, and workers' solidarity in order to achieve a just reward for their labors; the need for the Church (Roman Catholic) to be stripped of all power and influence within the sociopolitical community and also to be prevented from offering religious education in the school system.

The reform programs would be dealt with in far greater detail by Martí during his residence in North America, when he would develop and refine his original ideas. It is important to note, however, that it was in "Nuestra América," based on the reality of Latin American society, that Martí first conceived and planned these necessary reform programs. Equally important is the fact that at this time Martí saw their relevance *primarily* to Latin America as a continent, and to a lesser extent to his own country. In every sense of the word, José Martí appeared intoxicated by the vital dramatic reality of "his" America and appears to have temporarily concentrated his attention on offering much-needed solutions to urgent problems faced by the already independent nations of the subcontinent. Nevertheless, the lessons he learned in connection with Latin America as a whole, when combined with his determination to win political independence for Cuba, represented an important foundation for his renewed liberation campaign, which began soon after he arrived in New York in January of 1880. The basis for Martí's sociopolitical aspirations for an independent Cuba was thus established long before his arrival in the United States. For the next fifteen years, supported largely by his observations on the changing nature of North American society, Martí would continue to develop the rudiments of his national programs convinced that after political independence had been won from Spain a totally new direction would have to be followed if Cuba were to be truly liberated.

Despite his pronouncements on the urgent need for social justice, on the right of all those who worked the land to own it, on the need for workers' solidarity, and a host of other progressive proposals, it is important to realize that José Martí was at this time (1880) a generous, idealistic and somewhat naïve liberal. In fact his political programs (if they can be termed such at this particular stage of generalizations) resembled quite closely many of the ideas of the French so-called utopian socialists in the early nineteenth century. Also at this time Martí was still not concerned with applying the relevance of these programs to the particular situation of Cuba; in actual fact, initially and perhaps understandably, he appears to have had few specific interests for his own country other than winning political independence.

Over the course of the next fifteen years, which Martí spent in the United States following a variety of pursuits—teacher, reporter, diplomat, and revolutionary—his political thought clearly matured, as did his plans for the type of social and political innovations that he aspired to introduce into an independent Cuba. Indeed, apart from the impression made on him by his stay in San Lázaro, this period spent in the United States probably represented the most intense series of experiences in his entire life and, without doubt, constituted the most significant influence on the formation of his sociopolitical thought. Consequently a new and crucially important period began for Martí in the 1880s; based upon his untiring scrutiny of North American life and society, he intensified his analysis of the needs and problems of both "Nuestra América" and Cuba, while at the same time his determination to lead Cuba to independence was rekindled. Martí, the Latin American poet and statesman, was soon to become Martí, the international revolutionary.

José Martí's political consciousness developed dramatically during his stay in the United States. By May of 1880, just five months after arriving in North America, he had been appointed acting head of the New York Revolutionary Committee and was steadily increasing his influence among all sectors of Cuban exiles living in the United States. As well as a renewed revolutionary zeal, visible in all Martí's work written in the United States, there were also several noticeable stages in the degree of radicalization of his plans for a liberated Cuba as Martí became affected by a variety of stimuli in North America. This did not necessarily alter his basic plans for the *patria,* since by 1880 Martí had already decided on the predominant characteristics he wanted for the society of a liberated Cuba. Instead, there was a general intensification of these same plans as Martí, basing his arguments on events and general feelings about North American society, became increasingly convinced of the validity of his earlier observations and at the same time increasingly determined that they would be implemented in an independent Cuba. There are two fundamental explanations behind these developments: Martí's disillusionment with the United States, which can be deduced from his extensive correspondence and numerous reports on the subject; and Martí's gradual realization of the unfortunate implications that this conduct of the United States held for Latin America as a whole. A close study of Martí's life and work in North America shows a process of steady disillusionment with the United States as a country from which originally he had expected so much, a disillusionment soon to be paralleled by an increasing fear that the many basic changes (unfortunately for the worse) in the national character of the United States could not help but have adverse effects on his own continent. More than any other single factor it would be this obviously selfish interest of the United States in "Nuestra América" that would prove responsible for the radicalization of his thought.

To appreciate the extent of José Martí's disillusionment it is only necessary to study his initial impressions of the United States which he published in a series of articles, "Impressions of America (by a very fresh Spaniard)" for a New York newspaper, *The Hour.* In the first of these articles, published on July 10, 1880, Martí expressed (in English) his pleasure at being—finally—in a free country. "I am, at last, in a country where every one looks like his own master. One can breathe freely, freedom being here the foundation, the shield, the essence of life" (XIX, 103). Closely linked with this admiration for the many basic freedoms available to all Americans was Martí's astonishment at the industrious and energetic character of the New York inhabitants.

> Activity, devoted to trade, is truly immense. I was never surprised in any country of the world I have visited. Here I was surprised . . . I remarked that no one stood quietly in the corners, no door was shut an instant, no man was quiet. I stopped myself, I looked respectfully on this people, and I said goodbye forever to that lazy life and poetical inutility of our European countries. (XIX, 103)

Obviously, when Martí arrived in the United States in 1880, his was an entirely positive attitude; he had come to a land that he admired and respected deeply and from which he expected so much. The tradition of American freedom that had sprung from the struggle to win independence from the British overlords had left a lasting impression on Martí, who saw an obvious parallel between the U.S. defeat of the British colonialist system and the liberation campaign that he firmly aspired to lead against the Spanish *madre patria* in order to restore dignity and freedom to his own country. Unfortunately this parallel was not to be recognized by a United States that, as Martí was soon to conclude, had departed dramatically from its original tradition of freedom.

One of the principal reasons for this drastic change in the American character, as Martí clearly noted, was the huge influx of European immigrants to the United States during the 1880s, people whom Martí described as bringing with them "their odiums, their wounds, their moral ulcers" (XIX, 106). Unlike the "true Americans" (descendants of the original settlers), this "thirsty foreign population, that must not be confounded with the true American people, shows that anxious desire for money" (XIX, 105), which he regarded as being unhealthy. From this surge of European immigrants a "new American" had already begun to arise, totally disinterested in the noble origins upon which the republic had been founded (and which Martí at *all* times admired), instead concerned primarily with the acquisition of material goods. In a later report in this series Martí revealed his apprehensions in regard to these obvious materialistic concerns. "What will this little girl, so fond of jewelry at seven years, do for it at sixteen? Slavery would be better than this kind of liberty; ignorance would be better than this dangerous science" (XIX, 122).

In many respects these "Impressions of America" can be taken as a scaled-down parallel of Martí's disillusionment with the United States and, by extension, as an illustration of the radicalization of his sociopolitical thought. Some months after claiming that freedom was "the essence of life," in another report Martí told of the "many pitiful sights" he had observed during his evening walk: "a poor woman knelt on the sidewalk, as if looking for her grave" (XIX, 123). While walking around Madison Square he claims to have seen a hundred men, all without work, and possessing neither adequate clothing nor food. These people, "evidently suffering from the pangs of misery" (XIX, 123), mark the beginning of a new phase in Martí's interpretation of the United States. From abundant praise he passed now to a thorough and uncompromising study of the major social problems faced by North America, and this examination in turn afforded him a further understanding of the many fraudulent political practices in the United States. By the end of 1890, disillusionment had firmly set in, and the U.S.A. no longer appeared to Martí as the beacon of hope and the inspiration for a liberated Cuba that he had earlier conceived it to be.

If Martí's disillusionment began in the latter half of 1880, it can be claimed with some justification that a year later Martí had arrived at what would eventually be his definitive stance on North American political life, an interpretation that in fact could be subtitled "What to avoid in a liberated Cuba." Writing in October of 1881, Martí informed his Latin American readers of the existence of powerful business interests that controlled the official policies of both the Republican and Democratic parties and blatantly manipulated these parties in order to further their own ends.

> These controlling corporations have traditionally used a scandalous form of trafficking in order to assure themselves, through electoral victories, of certain positions. They therefore prevented austere, honest individuals (whose integrity would not have allowed this commonplace intrigue or whose competence they feared) from participating in the running of these political parties. (IX, 64)

With a few exceptions, the most notable being the early years (1885 and 1886) of Grover Cleveland's first presidency, when Martí wholeheartedly supported the President's attempts to escape from the clutches of the powerful ruling bloc, this would prove to be the general reaction of Martí to politics as practiced in the United States. His grasp of the major social issues and fundamental problems of U.S. society would also become firm during this time; the Haymarket riots in Chicago and the resulting trial in 1886 and 1887 ultimately illustrated for Martí the pitfalls of North American democracy.

The profound disappointment of José Martí at the apparent disregard for the noble traditions of the United States by the nation as a whole, the many major social problems, and the flagrant abuse of political power (in May of 1884, referring to the Democrats as "considered more honest, simply because they didn't form the government at that time"–X, 31), all combined to increase both his disillusionment with the United States for squandering its potential and his determination that such mistakes must at all costs be avoided in the liberated *patria*.[7] He had arrived in 1880 with the expectation that the United States would prove a valuable inspiration for his own master plan of the liberated Cuban Republic, but by 1885 at the very latest Martí was totally convinced that he had been gravely mistaken. He still advocated studying the reality of North America, but now Martí advised his fellow Latin Americans to use the United States as a model of what to avoid in the future Cuban Republic instead of a source of inspiration.

> In the sins it commits, its errors, where it falls short—it is necessary to study this people, in order that we will not make the same mistakes. . . . It is a great nation, the only one where a man can really achieve greatness. However, both through a constant pride in its prosperity and the fact that in order to maintain its vast appetite it is always overextended, this people falls into a moral vacuum, its better senses poisoned, adoring—wrongly—success above all else. (X, 299)

Based on his observations of the problems faced by North American society, Martí steadily became aware that his hopes had been ill-founded and that the United States, which he had earlier viewed as an invaluable social experiment with great relevance for the future of mankind, had carelessly abused its vast potential. Racial problems were rampant, and Chinese, Indian, and black Americans were widely discriminated against; political life was both cynically regarded and widely abused; industrial magnates and powerful labor groups faced each other menacingly, all leading Martí to predict in March of 1882 that in the United States "a tremendous social battle will be unleashed" (IX, 278). The grand social experiment had failed, Martí concluded: "This North America is like an Egyptian mummy that has been galvanized totally by example and by persistence—it is a country where everything drives us away" (III, 111). According to Martí, the United States had flagrantly ignored its great tradition of freedom and dignity, deliberately replacing it with a cult of self-seeking materialism; a new America had thus arisen, one that was far removed from its noble origins.

As Martí came to realize that the United States did not represent the shining example of hope for humanity that he had earlier conceived it to be, he began to analyze the basic characteristics of the new American nation, concluding in 1886 that the common trait of this society was "widespread spiritual coarseness which afflicts so greatly all affable, delicate minds. Everybody fighting for themselves. Achieving a fortune is the only objective desired" (X, 375). Martí became even more concerned as he probed beneath the surface of this aggressive national character and of this seemingly amoral political conscience, and he began to understand the reasons for such conduct. Moreover, on the horizon there loomed an even more frightening prospect for Martí, one that could only have an adverse effect on "Nuestra América." Added to Martí's displeasure at the internal U.S. structure was his eventual conviction that the United States was also becoming increasingly interested in extending its dominion over Latin America, and his reports accordingly adopted a more concerned tone and in fact became warnings. As early as January of 1882, José Martí informed his fellow Latin Americans about this covetous interest felt by many sectors of U.S. society in "Nuestra América."

> The descendants of the pilgrim fathers had their celebrations. What a difference, though! Now they are no longer humble, nor tread the snow of Cape Cod with workers' boots. Instead they now lace up their military boots aggressively and they see on one side Canada and on the other Mexico. . . . Senator Hawley spelled it out like this: "And when we've taken Canada and Mexico and reign without any rivals, throughout the continent, what kind of civilization will we have then?" A terrible one, in truth—like that of Carthage!
>
> (IX, 205–6)

Mindful of this increasingly dubious interest of the United States in Latin America, an entirely new perspective was added to Martí's outlook as he redoubled his efforts not only to inform readers about North American life in general, but also now to warn them of possible incursions into his continent. Thus Martí's task became one of "defining, advising, warning, of revealing the secrets of the apparently marvellous successes (in actual fact all appearance and no essence) of this country" (VIII, 268). Previously he had been personally disturbed by the internal politics of the United States and by the materialistically oriented direction in which it appeared determined to move; but, after seeing a firm intention on the part of many U.S. interest groups to exploit the countries of "Nuestra América," Martí found himself forced to adopt, quite noticeably, a more radical stance. There were two major conditioning elements in the obvious radicalization of Martí's sociopolitical thought. On the one hand was his deeply felt frustration at what he clearly interpreted as the United States' flagrant spurning of its noble heritage and immense potential, preferring instead to subscribe to a "survival of the fittest" philosophy. On the other hand Martí could definitely see how this widely accepted policy would eventually have dire consequences for all of Latin America. U.S. industry would ultimately need both a cheap source of raw materials and a market for the resulting surplus of its manufactured goods—and Latin America was the obvious choice to satisfy both needs. From 1881 until 1889 these two obsessive preoccupations combined to encourage in Martí a steadily increasing process of radicalization.

A new and highly significant phase in this process was initiated in March of 1889, one that would in fact last until Martí's death in 1895. Concerned less with preparing his famous "Escenas norteamericanas" ("North American Scenes") for his Latin American readers (by early 1892 Martí had ceased to write for the multitude of Latin American periodicals to which he had earlier contributed), Martí now busied himself with preparations for the campaign that he hoped would liberate Cuba. This campaign was threatened seriously, however, in 1889 when talk resurfaced in the United States as to whether that country should purchase Cuba from the Spanish government and convert the island into a U.S. protectorate. Then on March 16, 1889, the *Philadelphia Manufacturer* published a highly critical article entitled "Do We Want Cuba?" (later reprinted in the New York *Evening Post*), to which Martí wrote a blistering reply.

Martí considered these articles to be of extreme importance, demonstrating to his fellow Cubans the little regard in which they were held by many influential Americans. Accordingly he translated all of the pertinent documents into Spanish, publishing them soon afterwards in a pamphlet called *Cuba y los Estados Unidos (Cuba and the United States).*

Of particular concern to Martí was the conclusion of the original article, which given his heartfelt distrust of U.S. interest in Cuba and by extension in "Nuestra América" was totally unacceptable for him. "The only hope we could possibly have to equip Cuba for the dignity of being one of our United States is to Americanize it totally, covering it with people of our own race" (I, 234). For Martí, any attempt to sell his *patria,* his nation, as if it were some negotiable article and of course without taking into account the wishes of the people, was completely unacceptable, particularly when the prospective purchaser was the United States. Martí felt he knew this society well enough to recognize that such a change of overlords could only result to the detriment of Cuba, and consequently he redoubled his efforts for the liberation of the *patria.*

The six-page reply of Martí, "Vindicación de Cuba" ("Vindication of Cuba"), can truly be taken to represent accurately the beginning of this last and most radical stage in his sociopolitical thought. In fact, now that his own *patria* was being bandied around as if it were some piece of merchandise to be bought and sold at will, Martí's frustration with the United States finally exploded. Before, he had been deeply troubled both by the cold-blooded attempts to disregard the best interests of "Nuestra América" and subsequently by the growing U.S. economic penetration into Latin America in general. However, now that the United States was seriously considering the idea of purchasing the island and of "americanizarla por completo" ("Americanizing it completely"), Martí spoke out loudly and bravely against such action, stating the opinion of many Cubans on the United States of America.

> They admire this nation, the greatest of all those founded by freedom. But they distrust those elements that, like worms in our blood, have begun the work of destruction in this extraordinary Republic. They have made the heroes of this country their own heroes . . . but they cannot honestly believe that excessive individualism, this adora-

> tion of wealth, and the continued joy of military victory after the terrible Civil War are preparing the United States to be the typical nation of liberty. In such a state there would be no opinion based on the excessive appetite for power, no acquisitions or triumphs contrary to good and justice. We love the land of Lincoln just as much as we fear that of Cutting. (I, 237)

Cutting, Martí tells us in 1886, was "a shameless, self-seeking journalist" (VII, 46) from Texas. He had broken Mexican libel laws and was arrested "for his own capricious reasons; and because he wanted to spark an invasion of Chihuahua by the state of Texas" (VII, 49), he was viewed as a symbol of the brash, annexationist drive of Texas. Scarcely forty years had passed since the United States had taken approximately one-half of Mexico's surface area, and Martí was afraid that more of the same treatment might be in store.

This tone of consternation at the attempt of the United States to extend its influence into Latin America became increasingly noticeable in Martí's work after this revived interest in purchasing Cuba from Spain. He now realized that in order to win political independence for the *patria* not only did he have to defeat the Spanish forces but also to keep the United States firmly at bay. Writing in April of 1889 (a month after publishing his reply to U.S. interest in Cuba), Martí expressed his profound distress at such a selfish desire to purchase the island, all the more damnable, Martí reminded his readers, because only a century earlier the United States had embarked upon a similar struggle for freedom.

> Who can possibly think about the project—recently made public—of buying Cuba, especially when the blood of our astute neighbors still has not dried in their own country. This was blood shed for the same bill of principles as the United States rose up against *her* owners. How can they even think about this project without extending a handful of helping threads to us, without extending their arms? (XII, 168)

The events of 1889 would completely dispel any remaining doubts that Martí might have entertained concerning U.S. interest in "Nuestra América," and he developed an even more radical position, which can be deduced from his letter to Enrique Estrázulas.

> Now I am beside myself, because what I have been fearing and telling people for years is coming to pass—the conquering policy of the United States. They are now announcing officially, through the mouth of Blaine and of Harrison, their desire to treat all our countries arrogantly as natural dependencies of the United States and to buy Cuba. (XX, 203)

Other major contributing factors to the radicalization of Martí were the first Inter-American Conference, held in Washington from the end of 1889 until 1890 (on which Martí reported in great detail), and the International Monetary Conference in 1891, at which he acted as the official representative for the Uruguayan government. The first of these two conferences gathered together for the first time representatives from almost all the Latin American countries. From the beginning of the Inter-American Conference everything was geared toward convincing the representatives of the value of having closer ties with the most powerful country of the Americas, the United States. There was an elaborate 5,500-mile train journey intended to impress the delegates with an exhibition of American society and industry; the American press continually listed the advantages to be gained by the Latin American countries through closer ties with the United States while at the same time advocating a hardline treatment in dealing with the countries south of the Río Grande;[8] and the delegates appeared flattered by the constant attention they received from the host country. At one point Martí described how "the black valets come and go, ten of them for every guest, brush in hand" (VI, 42).

Faced with this high-powered campaign to win the allegiance of the countries of "Nuestra América," Martí could only urge the Latin American representatives to probe beneath the veneer of progress and material wealth found in the United States. He was by this time totally convinced of the rather dubious motives that lay behind the organization of this conference and explained these personal fears in some detail to his readers. There was no longer any doubt in his mind of U.S. motives when discussing their interest in Latin America, nor did he treat the United States as any great power worthy of imitation.

> For all of Latin America, from independence to the present, there was never any matter that required as much good sense, and vigilance, or

> that demanded a more minute, thorough examination, than this invitation of the United States. This is a powerful country, full of products it cannot sell, and determined to extend its sway over Latin America. The invitation is to the other, less powerful, nations of Latin America, linked by profitable free trade practices with European nations, and its intention is to form a cartel against Europe and the rest of the world. Spanish America was able once to save itself from the tyranny of Spain. Now, after seeing with judicial eyes the antecedents, causes, and purpose of this invitation, it is necessary to say—because it is the truth—that the time has arrived for Spanish America to declare her second independence. (VI, 46)

Although on a much lower key, Martí's direct participation at the International Monetary Conference (held in Washington from January to April of 1891) was of even greater importance to him in warning the Latin American delegates against any overly close ties that they might make with the United States. The conference had been summoned with two purposes in mind: to win the support of the Latin American delegates on the subject of bimetallism, which would allow gold and silver to be circulated on equal terms instead of the traditional system that backed paper currency with only gold; and to encourage the Latin American nations to sever their economic ties with Europe (which was opposed to any such change in currency matters) and subsequently to increase their trade with North America. If the United States' proposal was accepted, the result would be partially beneficial to Mexico and Peru (and of course to the United States, at that time the world's leading silver manufacturer), but almost all of the remaining Latin American countries would receive little if any benefit. More important, if the proposal of the United States was approved, this could very possibly lead to a drastic cutback in trade between Latin America and Europe, with the result that "Nuestra América" would become increasingly dependent on the United States for trade.

An examination of the minutes of the Monetary Conference reveals the active role played by Martí who was a leading member of two important committees, one to study the credentials of the representatives and the other to debate the proposal of the U.S. delegates on bimetallism. It was in the latter role that he delivered one of the most important speeches of the conference. Martí was convinced that few Latin American countries would benefit from the suggested changes and was most definitely concerned about the loss of sovereignty that he thought might result if the proposal dealing with bimetallism was approved. He claimed that this was not the appropriate time to exert pressure on the great European commerical powers to enter into such an agreement. As a result, the committee in which Martí played such an active role recommended:

> While fully recognizing the great convenience and importance to commerce of the creation of an international coin or coins, it is not deemed expedient at present to recommend the same, in view of the attitude of some of the great commercial powers of Europe toward silver as one of the metallic currencies.[9]

This last phase in the radicalization of Martí's thought, initiated by his letter to the *Evening Post,* was characterized by an increasingly militant tone as José Martí devoted his attention both to the task of overthrowing the Spanish control of Cuba and of making his fellow Latin Americans aware of U.S. interest in "Nuestra América." As late as October of 1889, Martí was still prepared to allow the United States the benefit of the doubt. In a letter to Gonzalo de Quesada he stated how the United States "is waiting at our door like an enigma, at the very least" (I, 250). Soon afterward, particularly after the two conferences, he lost all hope of Cuba ever receiving a fair hearing from the North, which he then called "a diverse nation, formidable and aggressive, which does not consider us as its equal and denies us the conditions of equality, . . . a nation which considers itself as Cuba's superior and wants that country as a source for sugar, as well as a strategic bridge" (IV, 424).

The effect of the two Inter-American conferences on Martí should not be underestimated; in many ways they proved to him that his earlier and long-standing mistrust of U.S. interest in Cuba had been totally justified. After the conferences he was infinitely more aware of the definite danger posed to the future of the Cuban Republic by this rather obvious American intent to purchase the island. On a more personal level, he now reacted angrily against the open harassment of the revolutionary groups living in the United States; he realized that without the support of the Cuban exiles his hopes for liberating the *patria* would be greatly curtailed. In particular he was disturbed at the breaking of the tobacco workers strike at La Rosa Española factory in Key West through the illegal importation of Spanish workers from Cuba by the factory owners.

More important, however, was Martí's assessment after 1891 that not only did the United States intend to purchase Cuba and Puerto Rico from Spain, but also that they planned to use the two islands as a base from which to launch an offensive action against the rest of Latin America, thus fulfilling the old dream of continental supremacy. Writing in *Patria* in 1893, Martí claimed that in fact the two islands were "indispensable for the security, independence, and ultimate character of the Spanish American family of the continent. Yet our English-speaking neighbors desire this key to the Antilles, in order to use this base to seal the North and then to press down with all this weight on the countries to the South" (II, 373).

Before 1891, as Alberto Andino has clearly shown, Martí's character was inherently opposed to any manifestation of "colonialism, the exploitation of the humble by the powerful."[10] It was this same highly developed moral conscience that led him to fight first against the Spanish domination of Cuba, and later to condemn in such outspoken form U.S. involvement in "Nuestra América."[11] A further stage in Martí's seemingly inevitable radicalization was now reached; after discerning an increased desire on the part of the American government to annex Cuba and Puerto Rico, Martí now revealed himself as a committed anti-imperialist revolutionary, concerned now not only with winning independence for his own *patria* but also with protecting the equilibrium of the Americas, and indeed of the world.

> The Antilles hold the balance of the Americas. If they were enslaved, they would be a mere bridge in the war of an imperial republic against the jealous, superior world which is making preparations to deny her this power, in other words merely an outpost of this American Rome. If, however, the Antilles remain free (and are worthy of remaining so through an industrious, equitable dedication to freedom), they would be the guarantee of equilibrium on the continent as well as the guarantee of independence for Spanish America (which is still threatened) and of the honor for the great republic of the North.

> It is in developing its own territory (unfortunately in an almost feudal state, divided into mutually hostile sections) that the United States will encounter a more secure form of grandeur than in the base conquest of her smaller neighbors, or in the barbarous struggle which, after taking possession of Spanish America, North America would then unleash against the major powers for the domination of the world. It is not with a light hand but with the knowledge accrued over centuries that the new life of the liberated Antilles has to be built. It is with an august fear that one has to enter that great human responsibility. . . . It is a world that we are seeking to balance—and not just two islands that we are going to liberate. (III, 142)

In this dramatic way did Martí outline his revolutionary hopes. At first glance such a scheme to stop the "república imperial" ("imperial republic") from doing irreparable harm not only to Latin America but also to humanity at large appears truly incredible. Indeed, as Roberto Fernández Retamar has rightly noted, Martí "had proposed for himself nothing less than the task of saving all the continent, and further to contribute to the still-uncertain equilibrium of the world. Probably no one in their right mind, with such meager resources (Cuba at that time had a population of just over one and a half million), has ever set for himself such an enormous feat."[12] However, far from constituting a reckless or foolhardy venture, Martí's plan in actual fact was the natural reaction to what he firmly believed to be an inherently harmful and evil policy, one which could have adverse effects on the entire world. Martí recognized that an independent Cuba, while rewarding Cuban aspirations for a vigorous and essentially moralistic form of government, would also protect the rather shaky foundations of North American integrity: "If the Antilles are free, they will preserve the independence of Our America, as well as the equilibrium of the world" (IV, 111).

Consequently this belligerent denunciation of "los Imperialistas de allá" ("the Imperialists over there"–IV, 168), issued by Martí in 1895, can indeed be interpreted as having originated from the same righteous indignation that had led him to condemn the Spanish colonialist policy in *El presidio político en Cuba* almost a quarter of a century earlier. The basic substance of Martí's thought had changed remarkably little since 1870, for in essence his own rigorous moral conscience would never have allowed him to condone any political act that he considered either unjust or selfish. Seen in this light, his condemnations of, among others, Porfirio Díaz (1876), Máximo Gómez (1884), and Secretary of State Blaine (1889) can all be viewed as further examples of this highly moralistic outlook of Martí, which remained constant throughout his life.

Therefore, while the substance of Martí's thought differed very little indeed during the course of his life, there was instead a fundamental change in the *degree* to which it was taken by Martí. In other words, the many important and at times traumatic experiences in his life did not so much effect the essence of his thought but rather influenced the degree to which he actively supported these fundamental beliefs. The honest, idealistic, and highly sensitive Martí found himself inextricably—and perhaps one can say inexorably—bound to a path of gradual radicalization. José Martí's entire political career can thus be viewed as a continuous enrichment, based upon these formative experiences, of the original high ideals exhibited in *La Patria Libre* in 1869.

Of particular importance in the development of Martí's sociopolitical thought, as has been indicated in this chapter, were the many years he spent both in "Nuestra América" and in the United States. The resulting knowledge from his stay in the Americas, together with his firmly established code of ethics visible from his earliest work, convinced him that his aspirations for the liberated *patria* were truly just. In the famous letter to Manuel Mercado in May of 1895, written just a few days before Martí met his death in battle against the Spanish forces at Dos Ríos, Martí explained the necessity of a long, arduous struggle against both the Spanish and the "unruly and brutal North which despises [us]" (IV, 168).[13] Fortunately, they would ultimately win, claimed Martí, because *honor* was with the Cuban cause. Martí, the revolutionary, anti-imperialist, and internationalist of 1895, was the natural culmination of a process which began when he emerged from San Lázaro prison in 1870; the degree of his radicalization might have changed, but the basic tenets of his thought had remained constant.

III. THE ENVISIONED *PATRIA*

4. Political System

Having outlined the origins of Martí's political career and the principal influences on the development of his thought, the type of society that José Martí aspired to introduce into an independent Cuba can be examined in greater detail. Any attempt to outline the basic political structure desired by Martí for Cuba is facilitated by eliminating at the outset those aspects of government that Martí's views definitely, and most obviously, forbade. Although this may be somewhat self-evident, it must be stated that Martí wanted an essentially republican form of government for his *patria.* Having already experienced first-hand the injustice of an oppressive monarchy in Cuba, he was determined that this form of government should never again be instituted on the island.

His campaign to liberate Cuba was therefore based on a very clear understanding that a monarchial government was unjust as well as archaic and would not be tolerated in Cuba. His thoughts on the subject were exemplified by an article published in the Caracas newspaper *La Opinión Nacional* on September 17, 1881. Léon Gambetta had recently been elected Prime Minister of France, and Martí was clearly overjoyed with the results. "This is the conquest by modern man: to be the hand and not the flour being pounded; to be the horseman and not the steed; to be one's own king and priest; to govern oneself" (XIV, 58).[1] France was indeed fortunate, Martí emphasized, "because this people does not have a king, it is indeed a kingly people" (XIV, 58). In short, as he wrote in 1877, "the prime duty of people at this time, is to be people of their time" (VII, 97).

However, Martí did not blindly accept the republican system per se, nor did he apparently intend to base the Cuban Republic on any particular model then in existence. Martí had observed the frequent abuse of republican principles in other parts of the world—in Spain, in various countries of Latin America, and most noticeably in the United States, where he spent so many years. His report on the behind-the-scenes activities of Práxedes Sagasta in Spain summarized what Martí saw as the many potential abuses facing any nascent republic.

> Sagasta, a shrewd individual . . . is undoubtedly battling in the shade of the monarchy, in order to prepare the republic's advent. But it is not an energetic, practical, active republic that he seeks . . . but rather a nominal, repressive republic—heterogeneous and fleeting. (XIV, 37)

Martí was therefore well aware that the republican system did not constitute an automatic answer to all national problems. It was quite simply that he considered such a form of government to offer the best foundation on which to build his desired society, in order to make it, like Gambetta's France, "un pueblo-rey" ("a kingly people").

As well as being a firm republican, Martí was also convinced that the government he hoped to institute in Cuba would be a civil one, entirely free of any vestige of military control. This danger had to be avoided at all costs; Martí realized it could ultimately lead to a form of oppression not unlike that which he had witnessed under Spanish rule in Cuba. In a letter to his friend Manuel A. Mercado written on November 10, 1877, Martí vividly described the necessarily antimilitaristic nature of any viable government in Cuba. "The power enjoyed by republics should only be in the hands of civilians. All sabers tend to injure. But the tails of dress coats can scarcely be used as whips. This is the way it shall be" (XX, 37).

Seven years later Martí was to see this very danger loom ominously before him as he made preparations for the liberation of the island. His principal associates in the venture were Máximo Gómez and Antonio Maceo, both of whom were popular military heroes because of their active participation in the 1868–78 struggle against

Spain. By 1884, Martí was the accepted leader of the Cuban immigrants in New York; therefore, his assistance was greatly needed by Gómez and Maceo. Martí originally appears to have respected their geniune patriotic intent although he gradually came to suspect that both men were in fact motivated by the idea of their own personal gains after independence had been won. As a result of his disillusionment, Martí reluctantly—for in effect it meant at this point the collapse of his goals for an independent Cuba—withdrew his support from the campaign. His letter to Máximo Gómez in October of 1884 showed his displeasure with what he interpreted as their selfish desire to exploit the revolutionary struggle of the Cuban people for their own personal benefit.

> It is my determination not to contribute one whit, through blind love to an idea on which I am staking my life, to bring a regime of personal despotism to my country—something that would be more shameful and disastrous than the political despotism it is presently burdened with. . . . You do not found a nation, General, the way you command an army camp. (I, 177)

The bravery of Martí's stand on this issue should not be underestimated. Not only was he forced to postpone his planned campaign for the liberation of Cuba in 1884, but Martí also incurred the wrath of the majority of the Cuban revolutionaries living in the United States. Martí was subsequently accused of being a megalomaniac, prepared to halt indefinitely the entire revolutionary struggle simply because he was jealous of the way in which Gómez and Maceo were taking charge of the expedition. In actual fact, a careful examination of Martí's pronouncements concerning all military governments, both before and after the incident, shows that his attitude was constant throughout his revolutionary career. At all times Martí regarded military control as being essentially incompatible with a true form of republican government.

Martí was well aware that the responsibilities and duties inherent in fairly governing a country constituted an exceptionally difficult task, one that could only be undertaken by an experienced and honest political leader. For, as he noted on another occasion, "there is no task more complicated, more subtle, than that of governing; absolutely nothing that requires more skill, submissiveness, and learning" (XIII, 106). Consequently, career military men, because of their very background, were far removed from a proper understanding of the intricacies and compromises needed to convince, rather than order, the members of the society to comply with official policies. Referring to the presidency of General Ulysses Grant, an excellent military tactician but a poor political leader, Martí described how the general typified the dangers of the career soldier turned politician.

> He would chew up frontiers at the same time he silently bit on his tobacco. The presidential chair seemed to him to be a horse to mount; the Nation, a regiment; all citizens, recruits . . . he would imagine the grandeur of the Ceasars, and intimately loved his country, the way a Roman victor loved his golden chariot. (XIII, 82)

Though Martí accepted wholeheartedly that the military had an extremely important role to play in the winning of independence for Cuba, at the same time he clearly stipulated that after the triumph of the liberation movement all military power was to be transferred to the civil authorities.

Having determined that José Martí envisaged both a republican and civil form of government for an independent Cuba, the type of political life that he hoped to implement in the Republic must be considered, in particular the relationship between the government and the people, as well as the roles and obligations expected of them both. It must also be ascertained exactly how Martí interpreted the emotion-laden term "democracy" and whether he expressly supported a system whereby all citizens would vote in regular elections or whether he planned a selective democracy in which only some Cubans fulfilling certain conditions (wealth, revolutionary background, education, etc.) would be allowed a voice in government. Based on such an examination it will be possible to determine if Martí's thoughts on the desired democratic society were vague and loosely worded or actually constituted a consistent and well-planned reform program.

Surprisingly enough, and despite his early revolutionary determination to liberate Cuba from Spanish oppression, few if any references to the idea of democracy appear in Martí's work written during his younger years. Spanish domination of the island was so ruthless, the Cuban people as a whole had such little confidence in their own abilities to govern the homeland, and there were so many immediate injustices to condemn that Martí understandably concentrated his attention on the immediate goal of defeating the Spanish forces. However desirable a democratic government may have appeared to him, he realized that any opposition group had to concentrate on a convincing military defeat of the Spanish Administration as its first objective. Martí therefore devoted himself religiously to this necessary first step in the liberation process.

The first major references to the theory and practice of democracy to be found in Martí's *Obras completas* date from his arrival in Mexico in 1875. It was then that he discovered the government of President Lerdo de Tejada, which he viewed as a fair approximation to the democratic ideal. At the same time Martí was aware that the shady maneuvers of General Porfirio Díaz, whom he considered both ruthlessly ambitious and fully intent upon wresting the government from Lerdo by whatever means he deemed necessary, could very well rob Mexico of all social progress made in that country since the presidency of Benito Juárez.

Consequently, in an article significantly entitled "Catecismo democrático" ("Democratic Catechism"), published by the Mexican newspaper *El Federalista* in December of 1876, Martí left no doubts as to his wholehearted support of the democratic process. He vehemently denounced all military takeovers of the kind advanced by Porfirio Díaz as a means of furthering his own ambitions, while also warning that if a *caudillo* of this type were appointed, the country would suffer greatly. Martí therefore urged all Mexicans not to support their candidates with weapons, since this would only plunge Mexico into a state of senseless anarchy from which, he correctly predicted, a selfish and militaristic regime would emerge. Instead he advised them to follow the alternative solution afforded by the next election, when they could vote for the leader of their choice. This was of fundamental importance for Martí who claimed: "The will of all citizens, peacefully expressed—this is the source that leads to true republics" (VIII, 54). Thus in a country that possessed the necessary electoral machinery for effecting a meaningful political change by truly representative means, as Martí conceived Mexico in the mid-1870s to be, this type of military takeover was, for him, totally unwarranted and unacceptable.

Martí's interest in the practice of democracy, awakened by his stay in Mexico, was further strengthened after his arrival in the United States in 1880. However, from that time on, though he was still in favor of the *theory* of democracy, his appreciation of the practical *application* of that theory—at least in the North American context—was highly critical. He contrasted the victories resulting from a democratic election in Mexico with those won by force of arms, writing for *La Nación* of Buenos Aires in 1885. "There, using an army of folded ballot papers, a victory was achieved, one that was more swift and more complete than has ever been won by force of arms" (X, 123).

When describing the practice of democracy in North America, at times he accepted with reservations but more often he roundly condemned the fraudulent practices surrounding the polling booth. Writing for *La Opinión Nacional* in 1881, for example, he criticized severely the phenomenon of "bossism," the controlling of politics by influential party leaders.

> The despicable "boss" was described earlier; the ringleader of the party; the one who prepares the elections, twisting them, taking advantage of them, handing them on a plate to his friends but denying them to his foes—and selling them to his opponents; the person who holds sway over the electoral commissions; the same one who demands financial contributions of employees, enabling him to bring about the elections, which will keep them in their jobs. (IX, 97)

What is perhaps a fair summary of Martí's ambivalent approach is his report written for *La Nación* in 1885, cited above. While admitting the many obvious injustices that resulted from the irregularities at the poll, Martí still considered this unfortunate system infinitely more acceptable than the *total* lack of democracy to be found at that time in Cuba. His conclusion was that such corrupt practices were regrettable, but the franchise at least constituted a step in the right direction: "Oh indeed, many votes *are* sold; but there are more that are not!" (X, 123).

From his severe criticisms of political life in the United States, several important deductions can be made concerning the type of political practices that Martí advocated implementing in an independent Cuba. What had to be avoided at all costs in the *patria* was the selfish approach to politics, which Martí interpreted as typifying the attitude of the U.S. electorate at large and in particular that of both major political parties. He remarked that in North America the idea of working selflessly for the well-being of the nation clearly had been completely subordinated to the protection of personal interests. Honesty and true merit had become totally irrelevant in the North American context, Martí noted; deceit and corruption—at least in the political arena—had become the order of the day. Martí saw that political life in the future Republic had to be channelled away from this model represented by the infamous *políticos de oficio* (professional politicians) and instead had to spring from a new, highly moral, and honest source.

Several *martianos* have suggested that following the Haymarket riots and subsequent trial in Chicago in 1887, Martí's attitude shifted suddenly and dramatically away from the bourgeois liberal approach he had followed until that date. However, from an examination of his writing on both the theory and practice of democracy, it is evident that his attitude was little if at all changed by the Haymarket incident. Writing in 1889 for the Mexican newspaper *El Partido Liberal* on a contemporary study entitled *La democracia práctica (Practical Democracy),* Martí reiterated his total support for the democratic process, despite the difficulties inherent in implanting it in a Latin environment. "There is nothing as autocratic as the Latin race, *nor anything that is as just as a democracy that has been put into practice.* As a result it is not so easy to convince us Latin Americans of the worth of the democratic elective system" (VII, 347) [my italics].

Some three years later, in an article for *Patria,* the official journal for the Partido Revolucionario Cubano, Martí again underlined his intent to fight "con alma democrática" ("with a democratic soul"–II, 147) for the liberation of Cuba. However, there were few specific recommendations made by Martí as to the actual form of democracy; for him the need to awaken and subsequently to mobilize the support of the Cuban exiles for the independence struggle was of far greater importance at that time. Democracy at this stage represented basically an abstraction that was eminently desirable and that would in one form or another be implemented in revolutionary Cuba.

Moreover, after observing the many abuses in the United

States' democratic system, Martí was convinced that a necessary first step before democracy could be introduced in any form into Cuba would be to raise the level of political consciousness of all Cuban voters, "mejorar la masa votante" ("to improve the voting mass"–X, 43) as he put it, so that the population at large would be more adequately prepared to understand the platforms of the political aspirants in an independent Cuba and the theory of democracy itself. Martí demanded that all Cubans should question every political candidate and every official policy, their cooperation in this matter being truly crucial. By this method he hoped to end the Spanish habit of "favoring among the workers a fundamental dislike of politics, so that they will not get involved in Cuban politics" (II, 201), and to transform this apathetic attitude toward political life into an active participation in national affairs. For as Martí wrote: "A rebellious person is worth far more than a meek one. A river, too, is worth more than a stagnant lake" (XXI, 142).

Again using the U.S. political system to illustrate his aspirations for the liberated *patria,* Martí in his *Fragmentos (Fragments)* clearly emphasized the need for his compatriots to take an active, and necessarily selfless, interest both in national politics and in political theory, hoping that in this way they would avoid being manipulated as were their American counterparts.

> I do not want the people of my country to be like these Americans—an ignorant, emotional mass that goes wherever the bosses want it to go, making noises that the people do not understand as they play on the people's passions the way a pianist plays on the keyboard. Anyone who gratifies popular passions is a blackguard. Conversely, the people that renounces its use of reason and allows its country to be exploited is acting unjustly. (XXII, 73)

There are not, however, any sinister implications of thought control in respect to this desire of Martí to raise the political consciousness of his fellow Cubans. Quite simply, Martí hoped that as a result of their own patriotic and selfless reasoning, all Cubans would be able to decide the best form and system of government as well as the most suitable policies for the island. Thus he expected (perhaps somewhat overoptimistically) that following an honest study of the national situation the Cuban voters would be able to choose between the patriotic statesmen (among whom he definitely numbered himself) and those people interested in personal gain, the *políticos de oficio* (professional politicians). Martí's hopes for this direction were extremely straightforward, as expressed in a letter to José Dolores Poyo in December of 1891.

> It is my dream for every Cuban to engage in politics in an entirely free manner, as I understand the Cuban does, and in all deeds to act out of prudent feelings of solidarity, making his own decisions, without being influenced by any harmful or deceitful interests. (I, 276)

In a liberated Cuba, Martí was determined that all forms of manipulation, largely attributable to the political ignorance of the masses, had to be avoided at all costs, so that a dedicated, selfless, and honest government could emerge, supported and totally understood by the Cuban people as a whole.

José Martí considered political consciousness—or at the very least an objective appreciation of politics—as an absolute necessity for his Republic. Equally important for him, though, were the concepts of an effective and legal opposition to the government and of freedom of expression, whether it be of press or speech. All Cubans had to be conscious of every political alternative before electing their representatives, and as a result Martí was adamant at all times that freedom of expression should be guaranteed. "In free countries, the opposition has three major channels: freedom of expression, legislative assembly, and the press" (VI, 242). This early view (expressed in June of 1875) was consistently defended by Martí, always aware of the necessities of such basic liberties.

Indeed, some fourteen years later in a report to *La Nación*, Martí stated clearly that "the fundamental freedom, the basis for all others, is the freedom of mind" (XII, 348). He saw the potential danger of teachers who might exploit their position to indoctrinate students less politically aware than themselves and warned that this would not be tolerated in the future Republic. The teacher, he stated, was not to act as a mold that shaped the students' minds but rather was to be "an honorable guide, who will show in good faith what needs to be shown" (XII, 348). Illustrative of Martí's determination that all Cubans participate in political discussion was his desire that every citizen of the Republic should have the right to criticize any aspect of national government, since this was both a privilege and a duty. There was, however, one proviso—the criticism leveled at the administration was to be an honest attempt to offer constructive suggestions on methods of improving the government. He wrote in 1891: "Peoples have to live criticizing themselves, because critical reflection is healthy; but criticism has to be carried out with only one heart and one mind" (VI, 21). It is therefore possible to conclude, without reservations, that freedom of expression was essential for Martí, who in his *Fragmentos* (mostly written between 1885 and 1895) firmly defended this policy, declaring that "every time they strip a person of his right to think, it is like killing a child" (XXII, 114).

For Martí the direct result of these two basic necessities—a high level of political consciousness and a fundamental freedom of expression—was the definite obligation for all citizens to vote in every election in the *patria*. In the same report to *La Nación* in which he spoke of the need to "mejorar la masa votante" ("improve the voting mass"), Martí also outlined his theories on the common, moral obligation of the entire country to cast their ballot. "As in the case of every right we possess, voting is also a duty; whoever does not fulfill this obligation should be punished with a sentence not less than someone who gives up his weapon to the enemy!" (X, 43).[2] Martí's stance on this issue was quite clearly that a citizen who ignored this civil and moral obligation by failing to vote in an election, whatever his political affiliation, was abdicating from one of his most sacred responsibilities and should be imprisoned because, quite simply, "es un ladrón" ("he is a thief"–XI, 125).

At all times Martí warned his fellow Cubans that their active cooperation was not only desirable but also obligatory. It was their duty to take an active interest in all levels of government, to question every official policy, and to vote in all elections. Futhermore, they were expected to vote not necessarily for what was in their personal best interest but rather for what would most benefit the *patria*. Understandably, this essentially selfless and highly responsible attitude that Martí expected of his fellow Cubans was even more firmly demanded of those prospective leaders who would guide them. Martí's profound disillusionment with the manner in which the noble democratic inspiration of North American politics had been prostituted by an ever increasing number of greedy and self-seeking politicians had ultimately convinced him that a totally new direction had to be followed in Cuba, one that would be dedicated to the well-being of all Cubans.[3]

Writing in 1883 Martí clearly summarized the two very different approaches that could be followed in Cuba after independence had been won. On the one side was what Martí considered the example of the North American political system, at that time controlled by large corporations and rich industrialists, and seemingly unconcerned about the problems facing the less fortunate members of their society. Essentially this appeared to him as a cold, unfeeling system whose maxim, based on Martí's reports, could well have been "might is right."

On the other side was the approach to politics that Martí favored, one that can be described as a humanistic attitude. He was determined that political life in Cuba should not revolve solely around the economic development of the nation and that instead of regarding politics as a profession, an *oficio* (occupation), the Cuban people should always consider it a sacred vocation, a *sacerdocio* (religious vocation).

> Politics is like a religious vocation when one participates because of danger to one's country, because of an expansive soul. There are some people who emerge from themselves, overflowing with love, and need to give themselves to the common good, bringing to earth an invisible sword, always held high, which lights up the battlefields with its radiance. . . . But when politics falls to the level of being merely another occupation, it usually leads to villainy. Such sad spectacle is now being offered by the United States. (IX, 355)

In Martí's liberated *patria* everything would have to be subordinated to the well-being of the nation as a whole; a new form of politics—a selfless and patriotic one—would be introduced.

Another integral feature of the political structure that Martí hoped to institute in Cuba was its essentially Latin American nature. Despite any charge of being an idealistic dreamer that could possibly be levelled at Martí, he was well aware that any form of government implanted on the island had to make a definitive break with all of its artificial (and primarily Spanish) traditions and customs, reverting instead to a system based directly on the reality of

Cuba. For as Martí urged, the government instituted after independence had been won from Spain had to be "la copia legítima" ("the legitimate copy") of the nation that had elected it, in both its objectives and traditions, "and if it is not, an effort has to be made so that it will be" (XIV, 364). Writing in 1891, Martí was even more adamant about this need for a form of government based on the reality of the *patria:*

> The good ruler in Latin America is not the person who knows the systems of government in Germany or France, but rather is familiar with the elements that make up his own country and how he can direct them in their entirety to arrive—using methods and institutions born from their country—at that desirable state in which everyone realizes their potential. . . . The government has to be born from the country. The form of government has to be reconciled with the basic components of the country. Government is really nothing other than the balancing of the natural elements of the country. (VI, 17)

In summary, prior to the organization of the Partido Revolucionario Cubano, of which he was the *Delegado* (leader), Martí's plans for the type of government he aspired to introduce in an independent Cuba revolved around two basic programs, on each of which he placed equal emphasis. The first program, his desire for an essentially just and actively democratic society was sincere but somewhat simplistic because of a lack of concrete planning. The second broad plank in Martí's reform program was the need for "Cuban content" in all spheres of life in the *patria*—economic, social, cultural, and political—and in fact his attitude can be well summarized by his famous dictum: "Let us make wine out of bananas; if it turns out bitter, at least it is *our* wine" (VI, 20). These programs, Martí claimed, would together ensure that the political structure emerging after the liberation of the island would constitute an essentially new and truly Cuban administration. "We are adults and do not want artificial governments cut with scissors and based on a foreign fashion dummy. Instead we want a work that develops from our intelligence and is taken from the mold of our country" (IV, 275).

Prior to 1891, Martí's actual revolutionary efforts were of a somewhat fragmented nature. Thereafter, he was demanding nothing less than the liberation of the *patria* and the introduction (for the first time in Cuba's history) of a democratic and Cuban form of government, yet he had remarkably little experience in an undertaking of this magnitude. The year 1891 saw a redoubling of Martí's attempts to gain the support of the Cuban exiles, and more important, to organize them into a cohesive revolutionary party.[4] The subsequent founding of the Partido Revolucionario Cubano in January of 1892 and his election as its leader would thus afford him the opportunity to unite the Cuban exiles living in the United States and by doing so to develop valuable organizational experience.

The inauguration of the Partido Revolucionario Cubano (henceforward referred to as the PRC) and the role of Martí within the party structure provide a new and vitally significant source of evidence with which to analyze the type of political structure envisaged by Martí for the liberated *patria.* Indeed, because Martí did not live to see an independent Cuba, his role in the PRC is really the sole *practical* evidence of his views on the workings of democracy and on the desired nature of postindependence Cuban society. The validity of such an examination is indicated by Martí himself, who claimed that the party truly represented a microcosm of the type of democratic society that he hoped to found in Cuba.

> The grandeur of the Partido Revolucionario Cubano is precisely that in order to found a republic, it has started with a republican base. Its strength is that, in this work in which all share, all too have the same essential rights. (II, 278)

The success of Martí in consolidating the diverse interests of the exiles into a powerful political party was a very considerable achievement. At that time some thirty-four clubs of Cuban exiles were in existence, according to one source.[5] While the vast majority of these were in Florida, particularly in the towns of Key West (usually referred to as *Cayo Hueso* by the Cubans) and Tampa, there were also sizeable clubs in New York, Philadelphia, and New Orleans. Martí thus had the task not only of winning the goodwill and cooperation of the clubs, obviously at great distances from each other, but also of channeling their support into effective and concerned political action in an attempt to overthrow the might of Spain. Moreover, since many of the clubs had been formed principally as cultural and social centers rather than as hives of conspiracy, Martí also had to impress upon each of them the urgent need for complete revolutionary solidarity among all Cuban exiles. Another serious problem faced by Martí in the task of uniting these diverse associations into a common united front was the wide range of social levels, of religious and political persuasions, and of racial origins comprising the membership of the many Cuban clubs.[6] And, as if these obstacles were not of themselves insurmountable, Martí was also faced with the constant problem of keeping in communication with all of the revolutionary associations, for he was well aware that any successful revolutionary effort would have to depend on the active support of as many of his fellow Cuban exiles as he could muster. Martí's ability to win the support of so many clubs and individual Cubans and to direct this support into an effective and extremely well-planned liberation campaign reveals a great deal not only about his personal charisma and patriotic conviction but also about his organizational ability, an aspect rarely mentioned by *martianos*. Consequently, Martí truly appears to have been an organizer and a propagandist of the first order, far removed from the romantic and idealistic poet that pre-1959 interpretations generally depicted him as.

The type of self-denial and dedication to the revolutionary cause that José Martí expected from his fellow Cubans can in many ways be gauged from his own willing devotion to the cause of independence, in particular after 1891. His home life had long before collapsed; his wife Carmen Zayas Bazán, failing to understand his patriotic zeal much less his apparent determination to wrest control of the island from the Spanish, had already returned to Cuba several years prior, taking with her their young son, José (the object of so many of Martí's poems in *Ismaelillo*). In 1891, Martí renounced all of his official posts, as well as the income that he received from his teaching and from his literary work. Consequently, without family ties or official commitments in New York, Martí was then able to direct his full attention to the task of uniting the Cuban population of the United States and forming them into a revolutionary force capable of liberating their homeland.

Because morale among revolutionary groups in Cuba itself was so low and the Spanish control of the colony was as repressive as ever, Martí realized that the necessary first step in the liberation process had to be taken among the Cubans living abroad. However, the type of expedition that José Martí hoped to form in North America was entirely different from any earlier campaign planned by Cuban revolutionaries. Instead of the traditional filibustering type of scheme, such as that planned in 1884 with Máximo Gómez which in essence was intended to offer arms and military leaders to provide the necessary revolutionary spark in Cuba, Martí's plans were far more ambitious. In fact what Martí hoped to accomplish was the unification of all Cuban exiles in the United States into a cohesive political party with the intention of exporting to Cuba not only the necessary spark for the revolution but also the firmly established outline (within the PRC itself) of revolutionary social and political structures that he subsequently hoped to found in Cuba after independence had been won. In other words Martí did not plan simply to overthrow the Spanish forces, but rather—and far more important—to offer to the *patria* the broad outline for the future society and political administration of the island.

In many ways the charismatic form of democracy favored by Martí for the liberated *patria* can be ascertained from the manner in which he organized the Cuban exiles. Invited by the Cuban population of Tampa to speak in the Ignacio Agramonte Club, Martí traveled from New York and addressed his fellow Cubans on November 26 and 27. Martí's presence whipped up such a frenzy of militant patriotism among the Cuban exiles that the next day he helped to draft a series of recommendations, the "Resoluciones tomadas por la Emigración Cubana de Tampa" ("Resolutions Taken by the Cuban Emigrants of Tampa"), which summarized the widely felt longing among these Cubans for the liberation of their country. Martí had thus acted as a stimulus to their patriotic yearnings, and within two months the Partido Revolucionario Cubano had been formed, the revolutionary constitution of this party (the "Bases del Partido Revolucionario Cubano") clearly modeled from the earlier "Resoluciones."

Both of these brief documents, the "Resoluciones" and the "Bases" were extremely important; for the Cuban revolutionaries they represented something similar to the Declaration of Independence for Thomas Jefferson and his compatriots. The "Resoluciones" were particularly noteworthy because until this time revolutionary fervor among the exiled Cubans had been of a fragmentary nature, with most of the clubs of Cuban exiles rather isolated from each other and lacking a common identity or sense of purpose. The presence of Martí among these same Cuban exiles dramatically remedied this situation as his sincere patriotism, his personal fame as an exceptional poet and newspaper reporter, and his abundant encouragement and energy combined to create a stimulating atmosphere, the end result of which was a single revolutionary party, determined to unite, as the first resolution stated, "in a common, republican, and free action, all the honorable revolutionary elements" (I, 272). Martí personally composed this revolutionary charter and, because of his obvious sincerity and great personal charisma, immediately established himself as a symbol around whom to rally. He was accepted enthusiastically by his compatriots as their undisputed leader.

Moreover, the "Resoluciones" are particularly important because they represented a significant first step towards formalizing, in a single document, Martí's fundamental reform program for the political structure of a liberated Cuba. Martí's own broad aspirations for the future Republic had now been accepted as the official policy of the majority of Cuban exiles and two months later, with the foundation of the Partido Revolucionario Cubano, these objectives were to be unanimously accepted as the official goal of the entire party. Martí had thus gained the wholehearted support of the Cuban exiles and at the same time had convinced them that his ideas on the necessary liberation struggle should form the basis for the future society of the *patria*. The PRC, a united party of Cuban exiles, all of whom had agreed to the revolutionary constitution of the "Bases," finally represented an effective revolutionary force.

The "Resoluciones" are composed of four very brief recommendations, all of which were developed in the "Bases" after the founding of the PRC. The most important of these was the third resolution, which repeated several familiar themes of Martí including the need to accommodate all political activity of the Cuban exiles to the nature of Cuban reality and, more significant, the need to ensure that the revolution was to be fought for the benefit of the entire country.

> The revolutionary organization has to be fully aware of the practical necessities of our country, based on its composition and history, and

> has to ensure against working—either now or at some future time—to the advantage of any particular class. Instead it has to work by uniting all the concerned forces of the country through democratic means and strengthening ties of common action and fraternity among Cubans residing abroad. It also has to seek the respect and support of other republics and has to work toward the creation of a just, open Republic, united in its territory, law, work, and cordiality, in short a Republic created with the help of all and for the good of all. (I, 272)

Because these brief "Resoluciones" represent the core of the subsequent "Bases del Partido Revolucionario Cubano" (and, by extension, of the type of republic that Martí aspired to found in an independent Cuba), it is possible to make some general, but pertinent, observations on several key items of his political hopes for Cuba. Above all it is clear that Martí wanted an inherently egalitarian society, "levantada con todos y para bien de todos" ("created with the help of all and for the good for all"), in which no particular class or group would receive preferential treatment. The inclusion of *all* Cubans, and not just the white exiles, deserves special attention. In the 1868–78 revolutionary struggle initiated by Céspedes, the rebels, fearing a possible uprising against them of the freed Negro slaves and desperately needing the support of the rich plantation owners, had initially decided to refrain from condemning slavery. Now, however, Martí's projected plans for the liberation of the *patria* clearly stated that all Cubans were to be equal before the law, a concept never before accepted in Cuba.

The fulfillment of Martí's desire to "join together in a common, republican, and free action all the honorable revolutionary elements" (I, 272) was taken a step further less than two months later with the foundation of the PRC, once again in Florida. On January 2, 1892, Martí was presented to the population of Key West, after which there followed a meeting of Martí with the leaders of the Cuban separatist groups. Within three days Martí had drawn up the "Bases del Partido Revolucionario Cubano" (as well as a supplement detailing matters of procedure, the "Estatutos secretos del Partido"), which were approved unanimously by the presidents of the various associations, and the PRC was inaugurated.

The "Bases" truly represented an interesting summary of Martí's earlier political statements, now united in a single revolutionary manifesto and regarded as the fundamental reform program for the liberation of Cuba. In all there were only nine "Bases," although each of them clearly showed a determination to change radically the entire spirit of life on the island, rapidly replacing "the authoritarian spirit and bureaucratic composition of the colony" (I, 279) with a far more equitable type of society from which all Cubans would benefit. After what Martí termed "una guerra generosa y breve" ("a generous, brief war"–I, 279), there would be instituted in the Republic an honest and democratic political system. One phrase that sums up admirably the broad sweep of these intended reforms is taken from Article 5 of the "Bases." After the war of liberation "that has to be undertaken for the good and decency of all Cubans," the plans of the PRC were essentially to "hand over to the entire nation this liberated country" (I, 280).[7]

The objectives of the PRC, as presented in the "Bases," were straightforward: to obtain the total and uncompromising independence of Cuba (and to assist Puerto Rico in her struggle for independence), and subsequently to institute a totally new life style in a fully liberated country.

> To found, by means of the honest, cordial exercise of man's legitimate capacity, a totally "new" nation, based on a sincere democracy, capable of overcoming (through substantial work and balance of social forces) the dangers inherent in liberty being gained suddenly by a society that has been designed for a system of slavery. (I, 279)

In this way the "Bases" represented an amplification of the original goals of the "Resoluciones"; the later document also constituted a "statement of intent," almost an approximation of a revolutionary national constitution as well as a general outline of the type of society to be founded in a liberated Cuba.

One of the most interesting aspects of the political structure of the PRC, as Leonardo Griñán Peralta has indicated, is the position of Martí as the *Delegado* of the party.[8] The choice of this word by Martí himself instead of the more common term of *Presidente* reveals a great deal about the way in which Martí viewed his role in the revolutionary struggle, and indeed by implication the role of any future leader in the liberated *patria*. Martí at all times stressed the need for a highly selfless and essentially moralistic form of government—from all citizens of the Republic, and in particular from the *Delegado*.

> Neither in this duty, nor in any other, does this delegation understand that its position is merely to build a revolutionary personage opposed to others. . . . A sincere patriot should sacrifice everything for Cuba, even the glory of falling while defending her against the enemy. (II, 43)

Indicative of the individualistic and selfless form of democracy advocated by Martí was his conviction that he had not only been elected by his corevolutionaries but also had been "delegated" with the task of freeing his homeland from Spanish domination. He did not regard this task as an imposition, nor did he consider this an opportunity to win personal glory or renown. Quite simply, as he wrote to Federico Henríquez y Carvajal in March of 1895, he interpreted his role of *Delegado* as being based on two fundamental premises—great personal sacrifice and unbounded patriotism: "For me the *patria* will never be a personal triumph, but instead agony and duty" (IV, 111). Ideally any ruler of the *patria*, whatever his title, had of necessity to subordinate all personal triumph to the collective well-being of the Republic.

Although one can detect a desire on the part of José Martí to continue serving his country as a director of the nation's destiny after independence had been won, nevertheless it is very obvious that he had not the least intention of imposing himself upon the Cuban people. Above all else, Martí considered himself an instrument of the people, the one delegated by them to liberate the *patria*. Writing in 1893, Martí expressed very clearly that he was totally dependent on the will of his fellow revolutionaries. "What we have to take to Cuba is an idea—not a person. It is not simply Martí who is to land—instead it is the magnificent union of the Cuban emigrants" (II, 278).

A close examination of both the "Bases" and the accompanying "Estatutos secretos" reveal that Martí favored a highly personal form of government, essentially radical in nature, and in which supreme authority lay with one person, the *Delegado*. Equally interesting is the fact that the leader of the PRC was elected annually by all members of every associated organization; and should all of his counseling bodies (the *cuerpos de consejo,* consisting of the leaders of the various revolutionary clubs) so decide, he could be asked to resign before his term of office expired. (Martí was reelected twice after his initial appointment.) Obviously the "Estatutos secretos" of the PRC, with their extremely precise regulations, reveal a rigid adherence to democratic practices, providing detailed information on the duties of the *Delegado,* the treasurer, and the various *cuerpos de consejo,* as well as on terms of office and election procedures.

These details provide a valuable insight into the workings and internal structure of the PRC, particularly useful, as has been stated, because of Martí's determination to base the social and political structure of the Republic on that of the party itself. Although the PRC cannot strictly be classified as following a parliamentary democratic system, nevertheless it strongly favored a form of democratic centralism with the final decision in any matter being taken by the *Delegado.* In an independent Cuba, had Martí survived, undoubtedly he would have striven to ensure the establishment of a similar political model in the Republic, one in which all Cubans would have been actively encouraged to participate in the decision-making process and in which the chosen leader (whether Martí himself or another) would have been accountable at all times to the people at large, who in turn would have been at liberty to vote on the leader's performance at regularly stipulated intervals.

That there are few concrete proposals for the actual means of providing the "sincera democracia" promised by Martí in Article 4 of the "Bases" is a result of the many difficulties inherent in any attempt to "unite in a continuous or common effort, the activities of all Cubans living abroad" (I, 280). Because the Cuban exiles came from such a wide variety of backgrounds and beliefs, quite understandably Martí had to maintain a low profile, hinting at many reforms, not always directly stating them, lest he alienate the support of any one of the diverse groups that belonged to the PRC. Yet despite the apparent lack of explicit and minutely planned schemes for the control of the island after independence had been won, there were many definite intentions of the party, and a general overall plan is evident.

What is contained in both these important documents (the "Resoluciones" and the "Bases") are the barest essentials, the lowest common denominator as it were, of the revolutionary politics that Martí envisaged for a liberated Cuba. There were obviously more immediate concerns to Martí than the drawing up of a detailed political constitution. His first and most crucial task was to unite the Cuban exiles, convincing them that his scheme for the defeat of the Spanish forces by their comparatively limited resources was in fact feasible. José Martí also had to reshape the sense of national confidence, obviously at a low ebb after more than three and a half centuries of Spanish colonialism, promoting a sense of *cubanidad* (a pride of being Cuban), in short, nation-building.[9]

Of fundamental importance in Martí's program for political reform was his deeply patriotic and at the same time highly moralistic approach to government.[10] The whole spirit of political life had to be changed, he consistently argued, so that all Cubans (and not just a limited nucleus of upper-class creoles, representatives of the Spanish controlling forces) would benefit from the wealth of their country. Moreover, if Martí had been allowed his way in the liberated *patria,* an entirely new approach to politics would obviously have resulted, in which all citizens of the Republic would have been expected to take an active interest in politics at all levels. The result that Martí expected from such an approach was the construction of a new society—honest and just—for the first time in Cuba's history. Martí's dream, completely supported by all of his political pronouncements and neatly summarized in the "Resoluciones," was for "the creation of a just, open Republic, united in its territory, law, work, and cordiality, in short a Republic created with the help of all and for the good of all" (I, 272). His concept of the *patria* was really nothing more than this—but neither was it anything less.

5. Moral Foundation

Essential to José Martí's new approach to political life in a liberated Cuba were the innovations that he hoped to introduce in what can be termed the human dimension of the Republic. Martí was well aware of the pressing need for sweeping political reforms in the *patria,* but also realized that in order for them to be successfully instituted it would be necessary from the outset to inculcate into every Cuban citizen certain moral qualities which together would result, he hoped, in a heightened moral consciousness and would eventually lead to the formation of a "new man."

Martí wanted to reshape completely the Cuban national character, injecting into his compatriots first a measure of confidence in both their own potential as well as that of the nation as a whole and then building upon this self-assurance by encouraging them to adopt a deeply patriotic and, more important, a humanitarian interest in their fellow man. Martí maintained that a new humanitarian consciousness was absolutely essential in order to complement and ultimately to guarantee the application of his revolutionary sociopolitical program. Consequently this moral foundation, so rigorously defended by Martí, offers an interesting insight into his plans for a liberated Cuba because it underlies all aspects of his political thought.

Martí was well aware, however, that the necessary first step before attempting to introduce these rather dramatic changes into Cuban society was to convince his fellow Cubans of their common ability—united as the Cuban nation—to fully realize their potential. This role of nation-building, for indeed it was nothing less, as well as Martí's achievements in promoting a united front among his corevolutionaries should never be underestimated; Cuba had been ruthlessly exploited by Spain for more than three hundred years, during which time the creole population had been forced to bear the brunt of official Spanish discrimination. In effect they had always been regarded as second-class citizens, receiving few privileges from their Spanish overlords, while their country was virtually held in contempt by the Spanish forces on the island. Moreover, although these many injustices had always been deeply resented, the Cuban people as a whole had never accepted a common goal in relation to the form of political liberation they desired, nor had a common method for achieving their independence ever been derived. Martí thus saw his initial task as the awakening of a national consciousness, promoting a sense of nationality, of common identity, and subsequently making his compatriots proud of their distinct *cubanidad.*

Because of their status as a colony of the *madre patria,* most native-born Cubans had never considered their homeland as anything other than an appendage of Spain: from the cradle they had been reared in a Spanish environment, had been educated in Spanish traditions, and had been encouraged to identify with the Spanish system of government, with all attempts to stray from this norm harshly suppressed. Martí's intention was to foster a spirit of dignity and self-confidence, in short (as he wrote about another "pueblo abrumado" ["oppressed people"], the North American Indians) to "return to a crushed, exhausted people respect and an awareness of their worth" (VI, 34). Three centuries of Spanish domination had resulted in what can rightly be termed a national inferiority complex. Writing in 1894, Martí noted the pressing need to overcome this complex and to promote a deserved pride in Cuba's vast potential.

> Does Cuba have to be a tavern, an idle beer parlor of San Jerónimo? Or will it be an independent, industrious, Latin American nation? This and nothing less is Cuba's task. (III, 359)

Indeed, if José Martí had been successful solely in this goal, his achievements would have been remarkable.

Martí's earliest writings reveal his clear understanding of the needs of the *patria* to develop its own national identity, judged from his patriotic composition, "¡10 de octubre!" ("October 10!"), written shortly before his sixteenth birthday to honor the Céspedes rebellion. Apparently his earliest plea to his compatriots to liberate themselves from their Spanish shackles and, at last, to appreciate their distinct national identity, this poem portrayed Cuba as "the nation which, for three centuries, has suffered the full weight of oppression" (XVII, 20). Fortunately, Martí gained hope from the activities of the Céspedes expedition and encouraged his fellow Cubans to grasp the true importance of their *cubanidad* and to liberate the *patria* from Spanish domination.

> Finally, and with integrity,
> Cuba breaks the hangman's noose which oppressed her
> And haughtily shakes her free head! (XVII, 20)

Writing more than twenty years later, after the failure of several military expeditions that had attempted to bring about this much needed independence, Martí indicated how life for the vast majority of Cubans in the colony was still as oppressive and as demeaning as it had been some three centuries earlier. He examined the basic lack of human and national dignity in colonial Cuba, concluding: "That is Cuba now, a faded rose, dusty and withered, a rose watered with tears and blood!" (IV, 392).[1] Quite obviously, Martí's task in establishing any sort of national pride was fraught with many serious problems.

José Martí's ambitious plans to arrest both this lack of national self-assurance and the trend toward self-denigration, while at the same time promoting a sense of *patria* to all Cubans, had two definite and self-complementing objectives. First, by overcoming this national inferiority complex he hoped to make his compatriots proud of their *cubanidad* and subsequently to act (preferably against the Spanish control of the island) in order to defend the much maligned national identity. Second, he was convinced that once Cubans became conscious of their cultural heritage, they would be more inclined to treat their compatriots, and ultimately their fellow man, with the dignity that he felt they richly deserved. There would thus be a dramatic change of temperament in his fellow

Cubans, Martí reasoned; once they were liberated from the oppressive colonialist system, they would be more prepared to treat their compatriots, and of course themselves, with both respect and esteem. Consequently, the conditions would be ripe to foster an appreciation of the inherent dignity of one's fellow man, the necessary initial step in the long, complicated procedure of creating a new man.

The importance that the concepts of *dignidad* (dignity) and self-respect held for Martí can be gauged from his much cited statement made in a speech in 1891 to the Cuban exiles living in Tampa: "I want the first law of our Republic to be the worship of the full dignity of man by all Cubans" (IV, 270). In his famous letter to the editor of the New York *Herald,* dated May 2, 1895, José Martí further revealed his high regard for this concept of *dignidad,* while explaining that one of the fundamental intentions of the liberation campaign was to establish and to protect by law the doctrine of human dignity. In the letter Martí related the moral depression into which his country had been plunged.

> Cuba's children . . . suffer in indescribable bitterness as they see their fertile nation enchained and also their human dignity stifled, as every day they have to pay with their free Latin American hands a tax that is almost all they produce, and even worse with their honor—all for the necessities and vices of the monarchy. (IV, 152)

It must be stressed that Martí's attempt to erase the national inferiority complex and to cultivate "la dignidad plena del hombre" ("the full dignity of man") was not the result of any blind nationalism. Martí's aspirations for a moral regeneration of Cuba were unquestionably related to his hopes of reawakening the patriotic zeal of his compatriots; both would obviously facilitate his far-reaching plans for the revolutionary struggle. Martí was also fervently intent upon encouraging, virtually for the first time in the realm of Latin American *belles lettres,* a close spiritual union with the other countries of the continent. With regard to his master plan for the liberation of Cuba, he was convinced that there was much that the island could learn from her already independent sister republics in Latin America.

Therefore in order to protect this concept of *dignidad,* Martí believed that a certain spirituality, which he had discovered on his travels through various Latin American countries, would have to be introduced into Cuba. This fervent desire for a spiritual union with "the countries of Latin America, my sister and mother" (VI, 362) became far more noticeable after he began to reside in the United States in 1880. Less than two years later Martí was totally convinced that, because of their very different origins, Latin America should avoid being unduly influenced by North America.

> There are avaricious races like that of the North whose formidable hunger requires virgin peoples. And there are faithful races like that of the South whose offspring want no other sun to warm them than that of their *patria* and who desire no other riches than the golden orange and the white lily grown in their grandparents' garden.
> (IX, 224)

Based on his observations of the United States, Martí became increasingly disturbed by the obvious preoccupation of a large sector of the North American population with accumulating vast hoards of wealth. Writing for *La Nación* in May of 1884, he informed his readers: "This vice is in the marrow of these North Americans—for them life has no other objective apart from piling up a fortune" (X, 39). The result of this widespread lust for money was aptly termed the "metalificación del hombre" ("metalification of man"–XXI, 16) by Martí, a process that obviously had to be avoided in the future Republic. In another article in *La Nación* two years later, and again using the United States as a model of the pitfalls to be avoided in the *patria,* Martí explained the very definite need for the Cuban nation to develop spiritually as well as economically.

> Here you can see this general crudity of spirit that afflicts even the expansive, delicate minds. Everyone fighting for themselves. A financial fortune as the only objective of their lives. . . . There is not sufficient soul or spirit in this gigantic nation, and without that marvelous coupling, everything is bound to collapse (in any nation) tragically. . . . It is necessary to shake these souls from their status as spiritual dwarfs. In all men the merchant should be cultivated—but so too should the priest. (X, 375–376)

In many ways José Martí's pride in the achievements and rich spiritual nature of "Nuestra América" acted as a foil to his desire for the development of a sense of identity, of national dignity, in Cuba itself, which explains his continuous references to the achievements of "his" America. Comparing "Nuestra América" to the United States in 1887, Martí noted: "Our Latin American nations have done far more in rising to their present position than the United States have in supporting themselves (and perhaps declining in essential matters), given the amazing base from which they started" (VII, 330). Four years later in his famous report entitled "Nuestra América," Martí heaped abundant praise on the independent republics of Latin America, and claimed: "In less time than we so far have had and given the chaotic factors of our reality, there have never been such advanced, compact nations formed" (VI, 16).[2] Accordingly, the Cuban people as a whole should take heart, Martí insisted, for they sought the same goals already fought for and decisively won by the other republics of Latin America.

Martí's respect for both the achievements and essential spirituality of "Nuestra América" was intended by him to serve as an example of what Cuba also could hope to accomplish if she were prepared to take the initial step toward independence. Without a firm commitment made by all his fellow citizens, a commitment to promote this awareness of national dignity while attempting to develop the desired Latin "spirituality," Martí's subsequent plans calling for selflessness and for great personal sacrifice in order that the *patria* at large might benefit would be ill-founded.

The initial step in Martí's master plan, and indeed an absolute prerequisite for a new liberated society, was to increase the level of national consciousness among his compatriots. Only by respecting the *patria*'s great potential would it be possible to overcome the deeply rooted colonialist mentality. Having achieved this awareness of their *cubanidad,* Martí was certain that his fellow countrymen would at last respect their own capabilities and, apprised of these hitherto unseen talents, would unite to overthrow the Spanish overlords. Martí regarded *cubanidad* as the essential base for all future revolutionary activity; for without pride in their nationality and the belief that they were capable of defeating the Spanish forces, the revolution would be short-lived and his ambitious plans for the "new society" would be of no avail. Conversely, informed of their distinctive Latin American spirituality and feeling themselves closely related to their sister republics, Martí was certain that the Cuban people as a whole would be prepared to embark on the program of reforms he saw as essential for the necessary liberation of the island.

José Martí, though, was well aware of the many problems that his nascent Republic would face after political independence had been won. Accordingly he devised a program of rather severe contingency measures which, if successfully applied, he was certain would guarantee both the immediate stability and the subsequent development of the *patria*. His desire to promote a feeling of *dignidad* among his fellow Cubans having proved successful, he then hoped to build upon this newfound national confidence, impressing on his corevolutionaries the urgent need for great personal sacrifice in order to firmly establish the Republic.

It was obvious to Martí that unless an entirely new approach to all major problems facing the Republic was adopted—an approach in which all members would be expected to participate actively—the freedom won after independence would vanish quickly. Therefore he advocated continually that all Cuban citizens should work together conscientiously and selflessly in order to undertake the many responsibilities that would result after independence had been won. This exhortation for all Cubans to cooperate, at all times placing the best interests of the state before their own, he termed *sociabilidad*. As early as 1875, Martí underlined its fundamental importance for the complete restructuring of Cuban society: "Sociability is a law, from which another important one, that of harmony and agreement, springs" (VI, 307).

There does not appear to be any suitable equivalent in English for Martí's concept of *sociabilidad;* certainly the definition of "sociability" given by the *Shorter Oxford English Dictionary* as "the character or quality of being sociable; friendly disposition or intercourse" is inadequate. The *International Encyclopedia of the Social Sciences* disregards the term, although the third usage of the word "socialization" is reasonably close to Martí's interpretation.

> Narrowly conceived, political socialization is the deliberate inculcation of political information, values, and practices by instructional agents who have been formally charged with this responsibility. A broader conception [which is necessary in the case of Martí] would encompass all political learning, formal and informal, deliberate and unplanned, at every stage of the life cycle, including not only explic-

> itly political learning but also nominally nonpolitical learning that affects political behavior, such as the learning of politically relevant social attitudes and the acquisition of politically relevant personality characteristics.[3]

Yet even this explanation does not fully express Martí's understanding of the concept of *sociabilidad*. For him it was quite simply a case of exemplary social solidarity, of persuading all Cubans to lead their lives in an exemplary, selfless fashion, at all times subordinating their own interests to the pressing needs of society at large. Martí himself explained the essence of the term in characteristically direct language. "Our life on this earth is essentially only an obligation to undertake good works. If we are bitten, we stroke our aggressor—afterward our conscience will pay the price of our actions. Let everybody do their work" (VII, 118).

Sociabilidad meant for Martí the process of shared adversity and of mutual assistance, by all Cubans, which he hoped would constitute the basis for a new revolutionary society. He was certain it would unite his compatriots in a common plan of personal sacrifice, while offering them a bright and just future after the island had been stabilized. Martí further hoped to develop the individual consciousness of his fellow Cubans in order to ensure the continued success of such a policy, for just as he expected them to make a determined effort to raise the level of their political awareness, so also did he hope that after studying the strengths and needs of their society they would decide of their own volition to contribute to the *sociabilidad* program.[4] This obviously depended on many variables: dispassionate reasoning on the part of the Cuban people, the necessity of an honest personal conscience in all citizens, and, finally, the ability of Martí to persuade the Cuban nation as a whole to subject themselves to this rigorous soul-searching and subsequently to commit themselves to placing the community's best interests before their own.

Yet Martí appeared undaunted by these rather imposing obstacles, apparently steadfastly believing, based on their appreciation of the need for human *dignidad* in a liberated Cuba and perhaps after reflecting on Martí's own exemplary conduct, that an honest and dispassionate appreciation of the needs of their society would be reached by all Cuban citizens and that eventually all would agree to participate in this new cooperative doctrine. Basically Martí wanted a firm, collective consciousness to appear, which after taking into account the necessities of the Republic would afterward lead to its citizens becoming what Martí termed *hombres radicales* (radical people). For as he explained in 1893:

> A true man goes to the very root. Really that is a radical: someone who gets to the roots. Let no one who does not examine all facets be termed a radical. Moreover, let no one be called a man if they do not contribute to the security and happiness of their fellow humans.
> (II, 377)

Furthermore, this desire to convince his fellow Cubans of the validity of *sociabilidad* was not restricted merely to Cuban or Latin American circles for, as he claimed in 1894, there was only one "superior" race. "It is made up of all those who consult, before anything else, the best interests of humanity" (IV, 325). Therefore, he did not hesitate to include in his preferred group George Washington, "el anciano de (the old man of) Mount Vernon" (VI, 198), beside Bolívar and Hidalgo because all three had obeyed similar duties toward their fellow man. Indeed, his report on the death of the American industrialist-philanthropist Peter Cooper testified that it was possible even in the heady world of high finance to follow this strict doctrine of *sociabilidad.* The obituary written by Martí in many ways embodied the essential qualities of this aspiration.

> He thought that human life is a form of priesthood, and conversely that selfish well-being a type of apostasy. . . . Only one key opens the doors of happiness: Love . . . and he saw that whoever locks in his human potential lives among lions; and whoever rises above this and gives himself to others lives among doves. (XIII, 50)

Thus the two key elements of Martí's program of *sociabilidad* are concisely a reawakened social conscience supported by totally selfless conduct. In actual fact, as Julio Le Riverend has noted, Martí's revolutionary plans intended to bring not only major social and political innovations to the liberated *patria* but also to change the very nature of the members of contemporary Cuban society.

> Objectively, the revolution needs not only a tremendous effort to destroy the old regime but also—above all else—preparations for a to-

> tally new life. In essence, therefore, what is required is the creation of *conciencia,* a sociopolitical awareness, which will produce substantial changes in the conduct of individuals. . . . Martí attempts, and in his time succeeds, to educate some and to convince others that *the Revolution is not merely a change of name but rather a fundamental change in men.*[5] [my italics]

But lest this aspiration of Martí to bring about a "cambio de hombre" ("a fundamental change in man") be regarded as the rantings of an idealistic but impractical dreamer who hoped that his fellow Cubans would suddenly, and as if by magic, decide to work together for the well-being of the nation, it is only necessary to consider Martí's determination—reflected in his intent to introduce legislation if necessary—to ensure that this "cooperative work ethic" was a most definite success. Because an immense amount of reconstruction would be required after political independence had been won, Martí was determined that his compatriots of necessity would have to share in the task of laying the foundation of the Republic. In this task none would be allowed to shirk their responsibilities and duties; all would be obliged to follow the dictates of this program of *sociabilidad.*

Martí frequently emphasized the fundamental immorality of all forms of selfish behavior, even claiming in 1888 that "es un ladrón el hombre egoísta" ("a selfish man is a thief"–XII, 43). In the context of the rebuilding of the *patria,* Martí stated that anyone found guilty of selfishness should be treated as a thief, for in essence the guilty party was depriving the Republic of a much-needed contribution. Moreover, given the urgent need for all Cubans to cooperate in the liberated *patria,* Martí relentlessly extolled the virtue of work, "llegado a ser considerado por él una nueva santidad" ("considered by him a new form of sainthood").[6] The message that Martí preached was extremely clear; he never departed from the premise that all men have an absolute obligation to dedicate whatever talents they possess to the betterment of the society to which they belong. Their abilities, Martí claimed, only represented "a debt that has to be paid. The Creator issues them, and men are to collect the resulting advantages" (XIV, 273).

Martí maintained at all times that this debt to society had to be paid by each and every compatriot; there were to be no exceptions. Anyone who attempted to avoid paying his contribution to the common good was not only to be severely reprimanded but also to be physically forced to work for the benefit of his society. Laziness, as he stated very clearly, was truly a heinous offense, "un crimen público" ("a public crime"), and all nonproductive members of the society would be forced to contribute to the *patria*.

> Laziness is nothing less than a public crime. Just as people do not have the right to be criminals, so too they do not have the right to be lazy. Not even indirectly should society assist those who do not contribute directly by working. . . . We should detest all lazy individuals and oblige them to take up a clean, useful life. (VIII, 379–80)

Martí never presented a chronological outline of the order in which he wanted his plans for this moral foundation of the Republic to be implemented, although it can be discerned that the initial necessities for his country were first to raise the level of national awareness and second to encourage the formation of a strict moral conscience in his fellow Cuban, which he hoped would ultimately lead to a general nationwide acceptance of his far-reaching *sociabilidad* program. The resulting mixture of selfishness and of patriotism would constitute the basis of what, as early as 1878, Martí saw as the essential "nueva religión" of the Republic. "The new religion: virtue not as a result of punishment and duty, but rather through patriotism, conviction, and toil" (VIII, 120).

In order to stabilize this innovative program, Martí hoped to fuse other fundamentally important features into the daily life of the *patria:* the lofty concepts of justice and freedom. Both of these terms obviously contain a multitude of possible meanings and nuances and can be used to support virtually any individual or group action or belief. There is simply no definitive explanation of what constitutes either of these concepts. In the case of Martí, however, it is quite obvious exactly what he understood these terms to mean: both stem from the same profoundly moralistic and inherently selfless basis of his thought.

Justice for Martí was never simply a high-sounding rhetorical slogan used to arouse the masses and subsequently secure their support. Rather, he always viewed justice in a personal perspective, a quality which he hoped to inculcate into his compatriots so that eventually this search for *lo justo* (whatever is just) would assist them in developing their own highly attuned moral consciousness. Justice was thus a concept which Martí urged his fellow Cubans to develop for their own self-realization and which he firmly advocated using as the yardstick for all major political decisions made in the Republic. Once again, as has been noted in relation to Martí's desire for popular acceptance of *sociabilidad,* Martí's aspirations for a thorough national awareness of *lo justo* required, perhaps overoptimistically, the conscious determination by the Cuban people as a whole to selflessly enact the theories that he had presented to them. By means of dispassionate reasoning and selfless conduct, Martí hoped to establish a foundation for the Republic centered on the perpetual search for justice.

In essence, Martí's policy of justice offered his corevolutionaries no more and no less than a chance to be honest with themselves and fair to each other. Based on his determination to construct the liberated Republic upon a pristine and compassionate foundation, Martí interpreted this program of justice as a necessary means of strengthening his doctrine of *sociabilidad,* because in actuality both were interdependent on the other.

Given Martí's conviction that there was never an absolute, morally right or just cause, obviously he could never conscientiously afford blanket support to any individual or cause; the individual merits of all possibilities had to be considered before any decision could be taken. Justice thus implied for Martí the necessity, yet again, of an honest examination of any problem in order that an unbiased and just solution could be found.

Perhaps an example will serve to illustrate this apparently simplistic yet fundamentally honest interpretation of what in fact constituted *lo justo* for Martí. In his many years of providing his Latin American readers with the famous "Escenas norteamericanas" ("North American Scenes"), one of the themes most commonly found was that of the increasingly bitter struggle between capital and labor and the multitude of related social problems that resulted from this conflict. Martí's support of the humble and exploited sectors of society had always been obvious, as indicated in his lines of poetry made famous by the song "Guantanamera": "With the poor people of this earth / I want to cast my fate" (XVI, 67). It would thus appear natural for Martí to defend the noble actions of the exploited workers in their struggle for a decent working wage and simultaneously to condemn this unfeeling and immoral exploitation by their employers. However, this was not the case. Martí's approach to such conflicts, and to all major social and political issues, depended entirely on a conscientious appraisal of the claims and counterclaims of both the participating factions. His report on a tram drivers' strike in 1883 illustrates his careful weighing of all arguments both for and against the strike. "There are indeed unjust strikes. Simply being unfortunate is not reason enough to be in the right. . . . But the tram-drivers' strike was just" (X, 396); and as a result Martí supported their case. For him there was no shortcut to justice.

The essential ingredients for a proper application of justice were thus selfless conduct and an objective process of reasoning, obviously a policy that was easier in theory than in practice. At first this concept of Martí appears to suffer from an overabundance of impractical details, because it was an absolute necessity according to Martí to consider all possible facets of any individual problem before deciding which, if any, solution to a particular problem was correct or just. This, however, was not as impractical as it may seem; eventually the new man (Martí never estimated how long it would take for his master plan to develop), imbued with a heightened awareness of his many social responsibilities and of his innate dignity as a citizen of the Republic, would learn to appreciate the inherent justice of any particular situation and would thus be able to decide accordingly.

Ideally, Martí hoped that this sense of justice would be implemented by his compatriots in all everyday situations and in all dealings with their fellow citizens. This understanding of justice was an ongoing process about which, Martí warned his fellow Cubans, they could never become complacent. Nor were there to be any special rights or privileges for any particular individual or group; all citizens would be expected to follow closely this preoccupation with justice and of course to base their conduct upon it. Eventually, Martí was firmly convinced, an objective communal application of justice would result, one that would benefit all members of the *patria:* "All workers who have reasoned out their position, and who are dignified, calmly and forcefully energetic, will never be defeated by anyone—*provided their cause is just*" (VIII, 352–53) [my italics].

The second major feature of Martí's "nueva religión" was nothing less than freedom itself, regarded by him as being of paramount importance for the stability and the self-respect of the Republic. Political independence was obviously the first necessary step in the liberation process, but as Jorge Mañach has correctly noted this same political independence actually constituted only one manifestation of the wider concept of freedom, of the many basic liberties that would be available to all Cubans in the Republic.[7] Freedom, justice, and dignity, three intangible but essential concepts, would be for the first time within the reach of all citizens.

The determination to implement freedom in the *patria* represented for José Martí even more of a personal crusade than his preoccupation with the concept of justice. This may well be explained by his experiences in Cuba where no attempt was ever made by the Spanish authorities to claim that their domination of the island—in all political, social, economic, and even cultural matters—was just. On the other hand, the Spanish administration did make an attempt, albeit at irregular intervals, to promote a facade of liberty; the most noteworthy example was the tragically short-lived rule of Governor Dulce. Martí's bitter disappointment at this pretense of liberty, withdrawn almost as soon as it had been introduced, made him more determined than ever that in a liberated Cuba this exceedingly thin veneer would be replaced by a true form of political freedom. Martí openly despised the artificial philanthropic pose of the *madre patria* and frequently condemned the few meager liberties *generously* bestowed on the island as "migajas de libertad" ("crumbs of liberty"–XIV, 183) and "merienda de ratones" ("a snack fit only for mice"–XIV, 462), which he claimed were an affront to the intelligence of the Cuban people.

In their place he proposed a new and effective concept of freedom such as his countrymen had never before experienced. Writing for *La América* in 1883 he explained the nature of the "libertad ilustrada" ("enlightened freedom"–VIII, 381) that he offered them. It was not, he took great pains to explain, that rather simplistic view of the domination of the privileged elite by the working classes. He stated: "We know that is simply a new and terrible tyranny" (VIII, 381). Nor was it to be what he termed "that nominal, widely proclaimed kind of freedom, which in many people seems like . . . what the cross of noble Jesus did on the banners of the

Inquisition" (VIII, 381). Instead it was to be a practical liberty, based on the needs of the *patria* and a general respect for the rights and privileges of one's fellow man, a respect which, Martí insisted, would result from a selfless appreciation of the society.

> That freedom in customs and laws which springs from an adequate balance of rights, provides a general respect as mutual guarantee, and frees itself from the traditional dependence on that supreme, unerring director of human nature: the instinct of self-preservation. (VIII, 381)

The appeal that the idea of freedom held for Martí is probably best judged by his lyrical description, published in *La América* in September of 1883, in which he described freedom as "the essence of life . . . the inescapable basis for all useful works" (IX, 451).[8] Yet despite the emotional pull on him by the idea of introducing the noble doctrine of liberty into his country, Martí was well aware that there were several possible interpretations of that term. As the *Encyclopedia of Philosophy* points out:

> When men speak of their being free or claim freedom for themselves, they are referring not only to the absence of coercion and restraint imposed by others (freedom *from*) but also to that on behalf of which freedom is being claimed (freedom *for*).[9]

As this observation relates to Martí's vision of a liberated Cuba, obviously Martí wanted both freedoms for the *patria*. The first is self-evident: to free his country from the clutches of Spanish domination, from the oppressive colonialist system that exploited the island so ruthlessly, from a general position of servility not far removed from slavery. On the positive side in balance ("freedom *for*") Martí also possessed very explicit ideas in regard to what he desired for his countrymen to attain. Among the benefits that he firmly believed would accrue from an honest application of his concept of freedom was an intellectual and political freedom that would offer his fellow Cubans for the first time in their history the opportunity to discuss both the validity and the defects of official policy, to offer constructive criticism as to how the government could be improved, and thus to participate in the governmental decision-making process. In short, Martí's plans were essentially to convert his fellow citizens into "people who are aware of their society and who are educated, responsible, and capable of assuming the weight of a major task for society's benefit."[10]

The physical benefits of freedom that Martí hoped to provide for his compatriots will be outlined in some detail in the next chapter on Martí's specific plans for the revolutionary society of Cuba. In general, however, freedom was not merely an empty concept for Martí; he made it obvious that the entire struggle for political independence only constituted a means of bringing about a more healthy, educated, and just society.[11] Indeed Martí's interpretation of freedom was essentially a socially-oriented view that was rather vague and naïve at times, while at others was truly thought-provoking because of its quite startling relevance to modern times (as for instance his plans for a concentrated mass literacy campaign, on which an almost identical scheme was modeled by the Castro government in 1961, the "Year of Education"). A study of the basic freedoms that Martí dreamed of implementing in a liberated Cuba further reveals that all had to be subordinated to what Martí considered the most pressing needs of society, thus emphasizing even more the social orientation of his policies.

In other words, after the liberation of the island there would be many hitherto-unknown liberties available to all Cubans, liberties, as Martí qualified, that would respond to fundamental social needs. Thereafter Cubans would be able not only to enjoy the intangible benefits (*dignidad,* pride in their racial and national origins and culture, a sense of identity) but would also be free to enjoy social privileges previously reserved for the Spanish-born *peninsulares:* a thorough education, an honorable and respected position in society, and full-time employment. These were all new freedoms for Cuba, and all were planned to reshape totally the structure and the very fabric of Cuban society. It is important to note that had his compatriots chosen to ignore a program regarded by Martí as essential for the development of the *patria,* he was fully prepared to actually force their acceptance through legislation had he continued to be reelected *Delegado.* He was determined that all Cubans should cooperate in the rebuilding of the Republic and thus in the liberation process. Consequently these newfound freedoms, available to all Cubans regardless of color or social standing, were not without severe social obligations to be imposed on all citizens.

The success of Martí's plans to introduce such ambitious reforms into the Republic obviously hinged closely on the popular acceptance of the rigorous sacrifices inherent in his *sociabilidad* program; yet Martí was confident that his fellow Cubans, after mature reflection, would accept the validity of his theories. Nevertheless, Martí was well aware, from his fifteen-year stay in the United States, of the facility with which seemingly excellent human and social liberties could be abused and realized these many new freedoms that he hoped to implement in Cuba would require much care and attention. As in so many other aspects of life in revolutionary Cuba, the successful application of an important governmental policy depended almost entirely on the cooperation and goodwill of all citizens. All Cubans would therefore be expected to ensure that these new liberties were not subject to manipulation or abuse and would also be expected to exercise them constantly in order that they be better appreciated. For as Martí graphically explained in 1881:

> In the gymnastics of nations, as in the case of individuals, one only starts lifting large weights after having lifted (for an extensive period) lesser weights. One's strength grows through constant, regular exercise, and conversely is lost when it is compelled to sudden explosions of energy. It is not this occasional, galvanic strength, fictitious and external, which nations need to prosper with certainty. Instead, what is required is one's own muscular strength, well-exercised, well-distributed, permanent, internal. Freedom is a reward which history bestows as a prize for this labor. One cannot enter the enjoyment of a reward without first having deserved it as a result of a solid, useful task. (XII, 146)

In order to better appreciate Martí's dedication to achieving this "libertad verdadera" ("true liberty"), it is useful to study his reaction to the campaigns waged by two mild opposition groups in Cuba—the Autonomists and the Annexationists—both of whom he saw as endeavoring to foist upon the Cuban people a partial liberty, one that would leave the vast majority of Cubans under an equally unsympathetic regime. Martí's conviction that freedom was a privilege to be enjoyed by all Cubans, not merely the prize possession of a selfish minority group, led him to condemn vociferously the self-centered attempts of both the Autonomists and the Annexationists to maintain their own advantageous economic, social, and political position without considering the best interests of the country at large.

The Autonomists, a monied Cuban elite with even greater social and financial prospects to anticipate if their plans proved successful, were attempting to convince the Cuban people that rather than risk the well-being and economic stability of the island by plunging into a needless and violent war against Spain they should submit to the well-intentioned dictates of the *madre patria,* because the benevolent motherland had promised that gradually Cuba would be allowed to adopt an autonomous position, similar in status to that bestowed on the Dominion of Canada by Great Britain. Martí fought vigorously against this group, for he could clearly see the danger of what he termed "the disastrous imperial rule by a creole oligarchy" (II, 264), who were determined to preserve their special privileges at all costs as they gradually filled the lucrative posts vacated by the crown's representatives and continued to exploit the vast majority of the citizens of an "autonomous" Cuba. Freedom, Martí countered, should not be a hollow-sounding term tossed around high-handedly by this influential group but instead should offer practical applications to everyday situations and should be enjoyed in all of its forms by every Cuban citizen.

For similar reasons Martí violently condemned those other members of the creole elite, the Annexationists, who also attempted to dissuade their fellow Cubans from forging a path toward full political independence, claiming that Cuba was in no condition to govern itself because it lacked both the economic stability and the national maturity for such an undertaking. Their solution was to encourage the country to change masters, allowing itself to be absorbed by the nearby United States of America and thereby become a protectorate of that country. The Annexationists also enjoyed a favored status on the island; and convinced that annexation of the island by the U.S. could only improve their own standard of living (because in effect they would simply replace all the Spanish administrators and owners), they consistently preached to their compatriots that they should forget the short-term need of political liberty and instead reflect upon the economic advantages to be enjoyed as a dependency of the United States. This condition of exchanging one national dependency for another was completely unacceptable to Martí, who called the Annexationists "the arrogant minority who understands by 'freedom' their free domination of their fellow citizens, whom they judge of lesser lineage" (III, 104). Martí advocated that freedom not only had to be decisively won as a result of the determined effort of all Cubans—Martí frequently referred to the need for "the respect that has been attained by winning one's own independence" (II, 347), it also had to be enjoyed equally by all of his compatriots. As the opening paragraph of the "Resoluciones tomadas por la Emigración Cubana de Tampa" states, Martí quite simply wanted "to found, with the remnants of a colony which had thrown slaves upon slaves, a useful, pacific nation composed of men who were truly free" (I, 271).

Manuel Pedro González, commenting on the vast moralistic and humanitarian essence of José Martí's plans for sociopolitical reform in Cuba, has voiced a common reaction of many people who attempt to unravel the fundamental thread of Martí's work.

> The values emphasized by Martí in his work are of such an unusual and noble nature that the reader—or listener—who is not aware of Martí's thought becomes sceptical and suspicious and may suspect as a supporter's praise or hyperbole what is in fact merely an account of the authentic, sublime essence of Martí in its intellectual, artistic, and ethical application.[12]

Martí the idealist, it is thought by many, was totally removed from the reality of his time, a blatantly unjustifiable optimist, similar to the stereotyped concept of Cervantes' Don Quixote—noble but quite mad. Because of the amazing variety of Martí's talents and ideas, the unusual blend of vivid lyrical description and great poetic ability with a program of radical social reform, and in particular because of his determination to create a selfless, new man—José Martí has been widely misunderstood.

The key to understanding this deeply rooted idealism, which in the modern era seems somewhat incongruous, lies in Martí's fundamental concept of the new man, whom he obviously interpreted as a being with boundless potential. Martí, as Carlos Alberto Montaner has pointed out, firmly held "an anthropocentric vision of the cosmos. For him, man is the center of the cosmic order and the justification of all creation."[13] Characteristic of Martí's firm belief in the essential virtue of man is his reply to a fellow

Cuban exile when he was asked why he pursued such lofty goals: "There is no one who does not have some moral worth . . . you only need to know how to find it."[14] Given the faith in his fellow man that Martí most definitely possessed and his conviction that the best guarantee for the success of his radical reform program was a revitalized moral consciousness, his campaign to build a new man and by doing so to build the liberated *patria* upon a moral foundation appears quite sound. His planned revolution, unlike that of the other Spanish colonies, was not simply a move to gain political independence. "For Martí there simply cannot be a revolution without the creation of an ethical awareness, in which man plays an essential part."[15] Without this necessary moral foundation it is quite probable that the more radical of his plans would have come to naught; conversely with the creation of what Martí envisioned as a "new revolutionary man," the revolution would have had an excellent chance of surviving. The creation of the "nueva conciencia ética" ("new ethical awareness") was the very keystone to the revolution that Martí aspired to lead *after* political independence had been won, and it also constituted an absolute prerequisite for his extensive program of social reform. The liberation of the *patria* had to begin with a raising of national and social consciousness, in short the liberation of the Cuban citizen.

6. Social Structure

Because José Martí was killed before he was able to effect his reform program, an analysis of Martí's social reform must be based on his stated intentions rather than his actions. Had he survived the war against the Spanish forces, undoubtedly he would have fought tirelessly to institute sweeping social changes in the *patria*. Indeed, a study of Martí's exemplary selfless life, when compared with the strength of his convictions, reveals quite dramatically that he did in fact practice what he preached, thus affirming a commonly cited claim that José Martí was "el hombre más puro de la raza" ("the purest man of the race").[1]

Focusing on the type of society and social structure that Martí aspired to establish in a liberated Cuba, there are four basic and clearly defined social innovations that he supported wholeheartedly and would have attempted to introduce in Cuba after independence had been won. (It is noteworthy that these programs present the logical conclusion of Martí's desire for a moral basis of the *patria* because their successful application was dependent largely on a national determination to implement such previously unheard-of reforms.) First, Martí was determined to eliminate all racial inequality in an independent Cuba. Second, he was equally convinced that a meaningful form of social equality should be introduced, thus reducing the glaring inequalities and hence the grave social tensions that he had observed in North America. The third broad plank of Martí's social reform program was to strip the highly influential Catholic Church of all earthly power on the island, and Martí strongly encouraged his compatriots to develop a lay, anticlerical perspective. Finally, as the keystone to these three policies, Martí stipulated that all citizens should be both informed and well educated, so that they would fully appreciate the justification for the necessary programs and cooperate in their implementation.

In regard to Martí's concern with the blatant injustice of racial discrimination, as a young boy he had been deeply affected by the sight of black slaves being maltreated (chapter 2). Martí's attitude toward racial prejudice was thus conditioned by his experiences in Cuba, but, more noticeably, by his residence in the United States, where he condemned the discrimination practiced against Indian, black, and oriental Americans.

In the North America of that period the rate of immigration had soared as millions of oppressed and poverty-stricken people seeking a better life flocked to the continent every year. Understandably this flood of immigrants, the "huddled masses yearning to breathe free,"[2] placed enormous pressures on both the economy and the society of the United States, particularly in the port cities where they first arrived. Incentives were subsequently offered to the recent arrivals to encourage them to leave the cities for the virgin wastes and settle on farmland in the more remote areas; money was often awarded such settlers and a substantial parcel of land was usually given to them.

This solution may well have relieved much of this social pressure within the cities but unfortunately, as Martí lost no opportunity to remark, in the vast majority of cases this land so graciously awarded to the settlers in fact belonged solely to the original settlers of North America, the indigenous Indian tribes, who in one fell swoop saw themselves deprived of both their land and their principal means of livelihood. Thus, Martí pointed out, the Indian tribes were the first "Americans" against whom racial discrimination was widely practiced in the United States. Writing for *La Opinión Nacional* in 1881, Martí criticized the crude and callous attempts by the American government to force the Indian people "to abandon forever their pleasant villages, leafy glades, and happy valleys" (IX, 37). Equally disturbing for Martí were the alternative arrangements instituted by the federal government; the Indians were subsequently herded together on reservations, where the government agents appointed to ensure their well-being in fact paid little attention to their charges, concentrating instead on devising schemes to steal the money provided for the Indians' maintenance (IX, 297).

Martí detested the cruel treatment meted out to the Indian peoples by their supposed protectors and violently condemned the supercilious attitude of these white agents toward a people who, he constantly reminded his readers, were also human beings and who therefore merited at the very least their respect and compassion if not their understanding and support.

> The agents do not see the Indians as they should—a pleasant, rudimentary people, one whose flowering has been cut short by a sudden clash with the gathered civilization of the Europeans now living in America. These agents now regard them as mere beasts. (X, 287)

Martí's grief at this brutal form of racial discrimination and his firm opposition to allow it in the liberated *patria* can be deduced from a report published in *La Nación* in August of 1885, in which he presented a harrowing description of living conditions for the Indians, and concluded: "How can we face up to our future national history with this crime on our shoulders, with this impediment?" (X, 273).

In his chronicles to *La Nación,* and despite an infrequent spark of optimism at the racial harmony that might result from the commonly held belief in the "melting pot" theory,[3] Martí also revealed his strong personal disgust at the obvious abuse of other nonwhite minority groups in the United States and in particular the black and Chinese immigrants. In Martí's view the black population in North America was in a similar situation to their black counterparts in Cuba; both groups were exploited to the limits of their endurance while being maltreated by their white "superiors." Consequently, given Martí's uncompromising opposition to the pitiful conditions that black Cuban workers were forced to live under, it is not surprising to behold his fierce condemnation of the immoral treatment received by black Americans, particularly in the South.

> The hunting of blacks is now increasing with a vengeance in the South. . . . The number of blacks is growing there, whereas the number of whites is not. Moreover, the hordes of white immigrants who

> come here head for the developing northern states. As a result the southern whites, rather than be dominated by the blacks (or intermarry), have decided to exterminate the blacks, to frighten them, to drive them from their area like foxes. (XII, 335–36)

Later in the same month, November 1889, *La Nación* published another report of Martí in which, to give his Latin American readers some idea of the extent of racial discrimination in the United States, Martí related the case concerning Frederick Douglass, who had recently been sent by the U.S. government as Minister to Haiti. Unfortunately his mission had been plagued with ill fortune from the outset; on the trip to Haiti, "the Republican officers of the warship on which Douglass was traveling refused to accompany him since, in their words, 'they could not sit at the same table as a mulatto'" (XII, 351). Clearly the land of opportunity was not without serious racial problems.

The other nonwhite minority group that Martí defended against the abuses of widespread discrimination were the Chinese immigrants, for whom Martí expressed great personal admiration. By dint of hard work and frugal living they generally managed to save sufficient money to buy property wherever they settled, a fact which unfortunately aroused the envy and subsequently the resentment of other less industrious workers. "The Chinese arrives at the mines. He builds houses, an inn, laundry, store, and theater; and with less money than a European working there, he lives a prosperous life—something about which the European becomes irritated and jealous" (X, 306). Even more infuriating for Martí, however, was the decision of the U.S. Congress, in an attempt to alleviate racial tension, to actually prevent all Chinese immigration to San Francisco, the most popular center of settlement for immigrants from the Orient.

> It was a duel to the death between a city and a race. In order to maintain slavery over the blacks, the South had earlier provoked a war. In order to expel all the Chinese the West would have done likewise. . . . This is the anger of a city of artisans, needing their high salaries, against a race of workers who can defeat them because they work for lower salaries. Here we see the anger of the strong man for the mild one. (IX, 282–83)

These reports on racial strife in the United States reveal Martí's fervent disapproval of all attempts by any majority group to impose itself on or to discriminate against any racial minorities. Martí was specifically referring to the United States, but his impassioned plea for racial equality was perfectly clear and was obviously applicable to the Cuban situation as well. In the liberated *patria* of José Martí all Cubans regardless of color would be assured of equal privileges.

Martí himself, because of his situation as a creole (person of Spanish descent born in Latin America), was automatically relegated to the status of second-class citizen within his own country. Because Martí was planning to overthrow completely the Spanish domination of his homeland, it would not be surprising to find anti-Spanish references in his work. Martí, however, took extreme care to ensure that no reprisals would be taken against the Spanish inhabitants of Cuba and continually expressed his hope that, after political independence had been won, all inhabitants of Cuba, regardless of racial or national background, would be able to live in harmony. To a certain degree Martí's attitude can also be attributed to his desire to maximize the basis of his support on the island; in his campaign to liberate Cuba, Martí obviously needed all the help that he could muster. Consequently, his overtures to the Spaniards living in Cuba could, theoretically at least, be interpreted as an adroit political maneuver to acquire additional support.

More probable than this explanation though was Martí's patently clear conviction (repeated on a number of occasions) that all human beings, regardless of race or nationality, were essentially and innately equal and therefore all deserved the same common respect and recognition from their fellow man. When viewed in this light, even "the enemy" were to be accorded the fullest respect, both during and after the struggle for independence, and eventually were to be cordially invited to remain in Cuba should they so desire. Martí's intentions were quite clear: "to fight against them to the death, but afterward to invite them to remain, as free as we are, in our liberated home" (IV, 253). Even though the Cuban creoles had been consistently discriminated against during the three centuries of Spanish domination of Cuba, Martí was adamant that there should be no repercussions against those Spaniards who chose to stay on the island as Cuban citizens; both *criollos* and *peni-*

sulares shared a similar cultural tradition, and all would be guaranteed equal opportunities in an independent Cuba.

> I am Cuban and have suffered greatly because of that. But my father was Spanish—from Valencia, and my mother too—from the Canary Islands. As a result I have a burning affection for my two motherlands—the one where they were born and the other where I was—without any feelings of injustice or hate that would spoil them.
> (XXII, 12)

In short, as Martí stated on at least two separate occasions, "All virtuous Spaniards are also Cuban" (XX, 371; IV, 389).

Martí further defined his position in regard to the issue of racial equality in several articles written in the early 1890s. In essence, his plan called for all Cubans to be judged on their moral qualities and on their contribution to the *patria,* and by extension to their fellow Cubans, rather than on the color of their skin. In a letter to Serafín Bello, he wrote: "Any colored individual has the innate right to be treated on the basis of his qualities as a person without any reference at all to the color of his skin" (I, 255). In an article entitled "Basta" ("Enough"), published in *Patria* in March of 1892, he further criticized all attempts to categorize citizens on the basis of their color by both militant black and white groups. For him this was both irrelevant and obnoxious: "It should cease, that continuous allusion to the color of people's skin should cease" (I, 338).

Martí discounted, in frankly unscientific fashion, the possibility of racial tension in a liberated Cuba, claiming that "there is no racial hate, because there are no different races" (VI, 22), and poked fun at attempts made by anthropologists to classify racial origin and identity. Martí judged such efforts to label the different racial classifications entirely artificial, and he haughtily called them the "razas de librería" ("bookstore races"–VI, 22). Such a high-handed and summary dismissal of the distinct racial types obviously reflected his belief in the *family* of man and his extremely strong personal desire to ensure racial harmony and equality in the Republic. All divisions on the basis of color would be unacceptable in Martí's Republic.

Probably the best synthesis of Martí's thoughts on the question of racial equality, and by extension the basis for his future colorless society, was his article "Mi raza" ("My Race") published in *Patria*. Martí first criticized all attempts to label any other human group or racial identity as inferior because, as he noted somewhat ironically, even "the white, blue-eyed, golden-haired Gauls were sold as slaves, chains around their neck, in the markets of Rome" (II, 298). Martí then explained in no uncertain terms his personal views on the subject of racial identity, disagreeing vehemently with the attempts to classify human beings.

> Man has no special privileges just because he may belong to one race or another: the word "man" implies all these privileges for everybody. The black man is neither superior nor inferior to any other man. All—white and black—are morally redundant when they say "my race." All that divides men, all that categorizes them in groupings, segregates or pens them in a cage, is a sin against humanity.
> (II, 298)

Consequently, somewhat from the pragmatic point of view, Martí definitely required the help of as many of his fellow Cubans as possible; but largely from the moral viewpoint, Martí clearly indicated that not only would racial tolerance be encouraged in Cuba but also that he fervently hoped to see a cessation of all references to Cuban citizens by their national or racial origin. In the liberated *patria* all were to be equal citizens and racial discrimination intolerable. Thus, as Jesús Sabourín has rightly noted, "all of Martí's work is a splendid, unquestionable, and very useful antiracist testimony."[4] Essentially, then, what Martí passionately desired for a liberated Cuba was the emergence of a true *hombre* and a true *cubano:* "A true man is more than simply a 'white,' 'black,' or 'mulatto'" (II, 299).

Therefore, based on both an examination of Martí's chronicles dealing with racial tension in the United States and his direct references to the desired nature of Cuban society, it is evident Martí was determined that revolutionary Cuba should not be divided by the question of national or racial origins of the Republic's citizens. By means of a similar method it is evident that Martí not only demanded a colorless Republic but also a classless society, one in which all Cubans would belong to the same social level and in which no social class (be it rich or poor) would dominate. Martí's awareness of and displeasure with the fundamental injustice of class divisions can be seen in his "Diario de Montecristi a Cabo Haitiano," in which he poked fun at one of the more farcical manifestations of class inequality in Cuba.

> It's to do with Arthur who was recently married. His wife went to stay with her relatives in Santiago to have the baby. The question comes from Arthur: Why is it that, if it's to do with my wife, they say she "got knocked up," and if it's Jiménez's wife, then they say she is "with child?" (XIX, 186)

At first glance this desire for a classless society, the second fundamental reform program of Martí for the *patria,* clashes with the general impression given by Martí's "Escenas norteamericanas," in which he almost invariably defended the position of the workers in their conflicts within the capitalist system. Certainly an analysis of the number of industrial disputes treated by Martí would support this view. It must be remembered, however, that for Martí there was never any particular viewpoint that was morally right. Every individual dispute had to be dispassionately judged on its individual merits before any decision could be made.

This obsession with ensuring that in all conflicts justice be wrought can be gauged from Martí's views on the most valuable of weapons possessed by the worker—the right to strike. There was neither immediate justification nor automatic defense simply because of a strike movement, he explained when commenting on the difficult problem of strikes. He assessed the act of striking as "damnable when it is an instrument for the workers to express unfair demands, necessary and praiseworthy when it is used to reject the capitalists' exaggerated demands" (VI, 229). Martí did not defend either of the two sides without first examining carefully the central issues and then deciding which of them was morally justifiable. Social justice, with the emphasis being placed on justice, would thus be applied to all members of the liberated *patria* and would be based directly on the individual moral conscience as noted in chapter 5.

In the context of North American society of the 1880s, which constituted the fundamental laboratory for most of his social deductions, Martí was greatly disappointed by what he interpreted as the "money cult" of that society. Equally troubling to Martí was the seemingly inevitable struggle in North America between capital and labor in which—albeit with many reservations—he generally supported the latter. Martí recognized an obvious social injustice being perpetrated when he contemplated the exorbitant profits being amassed by enterprising capitalists, almost all of whom were totally unconcerned that their employees were hard-pressed to earn a decent living wage. Commenting on a strike of railway porters in 1882, Martí emphasized the fundamental injustice of this particular situation.

> For the capitalist, an increase of a few cents in the pound on food items is merely a figure in the annual balance sheet. For the worker, however, that few-cents increase could possibly result in his being deprived of several basic essentials. Here the workers are requesting a salary that will allow them to dress and eat adequately—and the capitalist is denying them it. (IX, 322)

Martí undoubtedly experienced immense personal sympathy for the exploited workers and for the oppressed and less fortunate members of American society in general. As he noted in *La América* in September of 1883, "One cannot look at a worker in these large cities without feeling pity, respect, and affection" (VIII, 437). However, despite Martí's identification with the lot of the workers—and not as will be seen shortly with the working class—and despite his despair at the path of blind materialism on which American society as a whole seemed bent, Martí at all times refused to sanction the use of violent means to rectify this situation and bring deserved benefits to the workers. Social justice, however desirable, was to be implemented by pacific means.

Martí's views on the immorality of violence to bring about social justice are given in an undated article, "Un viaje a Venezuela" ("A Voyage to Venezuela"), in which he sharply criticized both the selfishness of the upper class and the means advocated by the lower classes to wrest control from their "superiors," referring to this in fact as "the infantile, contemptible struggle between a scornful, dominating caste which opposes the lower classes' attempt to discover life and those same lower classes who disturb the pure fountain of their rights with an excess of passion" (XIX, 155–56). That Martí was opposed to the use of violence as a means of bringing about social justice is further substantiated by his reports on the infamous Haymarket incident in Chicago in which many innocent bystanders were killed after several bombs were thrown during a workers' rally. Although Martí later changed his opinions quite dramatically about the supposed perpetrators of the crime (after he became convinced that there was clearly insufficient evidence to incriminate the accused), he could never forget the barbarity of the act. His revulsion was further strengthened after material was located replete with detailed instructions in the art of preparing explosives. "Many books in which, for ten cents, techniques for killing and setting fire to buildings are taught. All those who are noble of spirit feel fits of rage on seeing this perversion of human nature!" (X, 450).

At this time, Martí was unable to condone the use of hateful violence as a means of engendering social change, no matter how justified the change might be. Instead he preferred a constructive political approach, for "only those who despair of reaching the peaks of their goals want to cast down those peaks. . . . This hate of all that has been built, when not the insanity caused by suffering, is the fury of beasts" (X, 451), he wrote in 1886. It was for this reason that Martí condemned attempts to change society by violent means and fully endorsed both the goals and the nonviolent conduct of workers' groups such as the Orden de los Caballeros de Trabajo (Order of the Knights of Labor–XI, 18).

In regard to this preoccupation with the use of violence as a means of implementing social justice, his moving epitaph on the death of Karl Marx best exemplies Martí's views. Although Martí praised in glowing terms Marx's boundless humanitarian feelings, his sincere determination to help the oppressed—Martí related how at all times Marx "se puso del lado de los débiles" ("took the side of the less fortunate"–IX, 388), and his acute social conscience, describing Marx as an "hombre comido del ansia de hacer bien" ("a man burning with the desire to do good works"–IX, 388), Martí could not support either Marx's theories concerning the necessity of class struggle or his defense of violence as a means of implementing social justice. Martí thus possessed a truly dialectic interpretation of Marx with whom he did not agree completely, but nevertheless whom he deeply admired.

> Karl Marx studied the means of establishing the world on a new base. He awakened those who were sleeping and showed them the way to cast off the broken-down structure. But he acted precipitously and a little in the shadows and could not see that the only children to be born healthy, the only ones in history born from the nation's bosom or at home from the mother's breast, are those children who have had a natural, full-term gestation period. (IX, 388)

Just as Martí denied the very existence of different races in Cuba, so too did he attempt to convince his followers that there were no natural social classes, at all times preferring to emphasize his determination that in a liberated Cuba, as Manuel Pedro González and Ivan A. Schulman have correctly observed, all Cubans would possess the same rights and privileges, and would thus all belong to the same class.

> What he is fighting for is a horizontal society, one in which no one would have special privileges and there would not be any dominant castes, be they of upper or lower class . . . a classless society, one that was leveled both by education and economic status.[6]

Ultimately Martí was aspiring to introduce "la libertad ilustrada" ("an enlightened liberty"–VIII, 381), which would guarantee equal rights to all Cuban citizens regardless of color or social standing.

Writing in *Patria* in 1894, Martí took great pains to explain that the vast majority of his fellow Cubans, previously blatantly discriminated against because of their creole status, would benefit from this innovative program, while at the same time notifying all of his supporters that there would not be preferential treatment for any sector of the population. "If the revolution were, from the shadows, to band together either with the humble or the arrogant, it would be both criminal and unworthy of our dying for it. . . . Let our motto be 'Liberty without anger'" (III, 141). In the liberated Republic, Martí hoped to prevent both "los soberbios" and "los humildes" ("the arrogant" and "the humble") from exploiting the country to their own advantage, as the Spanish overlords had previously done and as the Autonomists and Annexationists also desired. Both sectors of Cuban society would therefore be awarded equal social privileges and in return would be expected to devote their time and their attention to the well-being of the *patria*.

Between 1892 and 1894, Martí developed this concept of "libertad sin ira" ("liberty without anger"), particularly in the journal *Patria,* official organ of the Partido Revolucionario Cubano, which Martí edited. His platform, although of a low-key nature, nevertheless was perfectly clear in its objectives for a liberated Cuba. In particular, based again on his observations of the capital versus labor struggle at that time being enacted in North America, Martí criticized all endeavors to apply labels denoting class origins or social position, because for him—as with racial labels—such an act was both unnecessary and demeaning. Appearing in the first issue of *Patria,* an important article entitled "Nuestra ideas" ("Our Ideas") clearly showed Martí's displeasure even at the idea of class divisions in an independent Cuba.

> It distresses one to see men reduced by the exclusive term *workers* to a narrow category that is more harmful than it is useful. Indeed this isolation of men belonging to a particular occupation or social circle (apart from the appropriate judicious agreement of that same interest) leads to a banding together and resistance of men from other occupations and other social circles. (I, 320)

It could be argued, as in the race issue, that this desire of Martí to stifle all references to social class was intended primarily as a practical means of directing the attention of his compatriots to the singular task of liberating the island. Certainly the task of protecting the unity of the revolutionary group must have been a prime concern of Martí. Another possible, practical explanation for his low-key references to "los soberbios" ("the arrogant") is that Martí wanted to avoid alienating potential rich contributors to his campaign; however, this is doubtful because the majority of funds collected by Martí for the liberation campaign came from small offerings gathered by low-income Cuban workers residing in the United States, and primarily from the tobacco workers in Florida.

Thus in formulating his plans for the future society of the Republic, it is probable that José Martí denied the inevitability of class structure not only because he wanted to stave off all possibility of a division among the Cuban exiles at a time when unity was an absolute necessity but also—and undoubtedly the underlying reason for his stance—because he firmly desired a liberated *patria* in which all Cubans would participate actively. He wrote in October of 1894: "A nation is composed of the rights and opinions of *all* its children and not merely the rights and opinions of just one class of these children" (III, 303).[7] Moreover, after living in the United States during a period of such astronomic economic growth closely paralleled, as he emphatically conveyed to his Latin American readers, by an ever-increasing spiral of racial and social tensions, Martí most definitely wanted to avoid that same unfortunate situation in Cuba. His description of American society in 1893 showed very clearly the type of tensions that he knew would have to be prevented at all costs in the Republic of Cuba. "Here we see the rich banding together while the poor do likewise. North America is closing in on itself and is full of hate. We have to get out of here" (II, 367).

Martí's observations on the many social problems of the United States explains to a large extent his strong personal aversion to the very idea of allowing separate classes; and in July of 1892, Martí confessed how "our lips burn with these words, so unnecessary, 'workers' and 'class'" (II, 52). He continually emphasized the basic immorality of exploiting fellow human beings; and on at least three occasions promised that in Cuba, if given his mandate, all forms of unduly harsh exploitation would be made illegal (in a letter to Gerardo Castellanos: II, 86; and in articles published in *Patria:* II, 255; III, 303). Probably his most outspoken condemnation of any type of class system was that found in *Patria* of June 1892, which in many ways resembles closely his angry and categoric denunciation of artificially devised racial differences, the "raza de librería" ("bookstore races").

> In *Patria,* the rich who fulfill their patriotic obligations, and there are many rich people who have done so, will be honored. Similarly, the poor, and there were many of them too, will also be honored. Our function is to develop national harmony. *There are only two classes among men: the class composed of good men and that of evil men. It angers*

> *me to hear people talk about classes.* By recognizing that they exist, we contribute to their strength. If we refuse to recognize them, however, we help to destroy them. (I, 52–53) [my italics][8]

The third major feature of Martí's intended reform program was his determined anti-Catholic, and in fact anticlerical, stance. Had he been allowed, undoubtedly Martí would have attempted to make massive inroads into the Church's influence in Cuba. The earliest critical references to the Church are found in Martí's first personal notebook, dating from his initial deportation to Spain following his stay in San Lázaro political prison. Martí very bluntly stated then his desire for a secular state in Cuba: "I want to educate my nation so that they will save anyone who is drowning and will never go to Mass" (XXI, 16). Later in the same notebook Martí was even more explicit in his criticism of the Church but also proffered his hopes for spiritual regeneration in the Republic.

> Catholicism was built to meet a social objective. Consequently, when that society has been crushed and another, new society has been created, the social objective has to be different; Catholicism must perish. . . .
>
> One thing, however, must not perish—the divine moral sense, that sublime blend of love and honor, inspiration for all religions and seed of all beliefs. This is the axle around which the moral world turns. . . . This is our omnipresent, sage godhead. This God-conscience, together with the God-*Patria,* represent for our society the only things to be adored. (XXI, 28–29)

Martí's writings on the Church consistently express a highly bitter, almost vengeful, attitude toward the Church's interference in nonspiritual matters. Typical of these was his comment in 1875: "Christianity has died at the hands of Catholicism. To really love Christ, we have to tear him away from the vile hands of his children" (VI, 313). Of particular ongoing concern to Martí was the doctrine of resignation preached by the Church. Angrily Martí depicted Church leaders as feeling "strong among the masses, due to their faith which questions nothing" (XI, 143). The Church's suppression of the process of reasoning was totally unacceptable to the freethinking Martí, who was convinced even by this early stage that the Church's attitude would have to change dramatically in order for it to participate in a liberated Cuba.

Martí's vitriolic attacks on the Catholic Church continued unabated for the rest of his life and his stance varied little. In essence his criticism was that "they have taught us to believe in a God who is not the true one. The true one believes in imposing work as a means of reaching a state of repose, investigation as a means of reaching the truth, and honor as a means of reaching purity" (XIX, 363). His interest in ecclesiastical abuses waned somewhat after he arrived in the United States in 1880 but resurfaced in dramatic fashion in 1887 when a Catholic priest, Father McGlynn, against the wishes of his archbishop, defended the economic and social program of a progressive political candidate, Henry George, and was subsequently summoned to Rome after the archbishop reported the priest's insubordination and lack of respect. Apparently based solely on his support of Henry George (according to Martí the Catholic hierarchy supported another more conservative candidate), the unfortunate priest was excommunicated.

In two scathing articles, "El cisma de los católicos en Nueva York" ("Discord among the Catholics in New York") and "El conflicto religioso en los Estados Unidos" ("The Religious Conflict in the United States"), Martí denounced the selfish meddling of the Church leaders in political matters over which they should not have had any control. He became even more irate after observing the Church leaders suppress the competition for their "official" candidate and advise their "flocks" to support their choice. Martí was shocked by this trafficking in votes and by the blatant forming of dubious alliances by these clerics with both "the powerful economic elite for this offered them an alliance that protected their worldly possessions and with politicians dependent on winning the Catholic vote" (XI, 143).[9] Father McGlynn obviously owed obedience to his archbishop in all ecclesiastical matters, Martí argued, although the priest's opinion on politics and economic theory were, or should be, his own concern. Writing in a personal notebook some seven years later, Martí's indignation at such unjustified interference in nonliturgical matters had not moderated.

> I think that the concept of priests getting involved in politics, of entering houses with their indisputable, infallible authority in regard to

> the essential, external matters of God and then using that position to exercise their influence over political matters, essentially of a temporal, local nature, is the worst form of stealing. It is akin to an illegal seizure of the faithfuls' souls. (XXI, 409)

For Martí the conduct of the Catholic hierarchy, which he closely identified with the interference of Church officials in the McGlynn case, was unforgivable on two counts: it tended to deprive people of their right to choose their own political affiliations by applying undue pressure on the "faithful"; and the Church was obviously prepared, when faced by an alternative stance, to exploit its religious position in order to suppress dissent and thereby eliminate all competition. Such an usurpation of what Martí regarded as essential freedoms would definitely not be permitted in a liberated Cuba; the Church in order to survive there would have to reform drastically.[10]

In contrast to Martí's virulent attacks on the Catholic Church, his few statements on the Protestant religions were rather favorable, to a large extent because they did not wield the same dominating influence over their congregation and were thereby unable to manipulate the political leanings of their members to the degree that their Catholic counterparts could. Martí praised the Protestant churches for their ability to present Christianity in a truly modern, highly relevant light. Typical of his attitude was the article, published in *La Nación* in 1890, on a Methodist church and congregation in Chatanqua that he considered successful.

> There it joined the ranks of the less fortunate and adapted itself to modern times in which domination by the churches and closed-doors to all who disagree is no longer accepted, and it will not enter—like a blind mole—wars for one set of beliefs or another. Instead they look to nature for the secrets of their life. . . . The church here, to avoid perishing in this modern world, walks in tandem with it. (XII, 438)

This theme of the necessity for religion to adapt to the times is also encountered in Martí's moving report on the activities of a famous American minister, Henry Ward Beecher. Christianity as it had been traditionally presented, claimed Martí, was losing all relevance to the modern era and consequently was gradually dissipating. Because Martí maintained that it was no longer possible for religions to stand isolated simply because of matters of dogma, he advocated the unification of all churches in order to attack the prevailing social problems of the day, hoping eventually to see the emergence of "the new church where, with the sky for its roof, the Catholic Christ will sit next to the Hindu Christ, with Confucius on one side and Wotan on the other, and needing no other clerics than the sentiment of duty" (XII, 418).

Martí's moving interpretation of Christ, basically an attempt to demystify the traditional image and to present the Christ figure in a more modern light, reveals his personal conviction that true Christianity was potentially a constructive force.

> He was an exceptionally poor man, who had several basic objectives: he wanted all men to love each other; those who had wealth to share it with those who did not; all children to respect their parents, provided that the parents took care of them; everyone to work (because no one has the right not to work); all to help their neighbors and to refrain from doing them harm.
>
> Christ was full of love for men. Therefore, because he told the slaves that they should be slaves only of God, and also because nations he visited shared a great respect for him and the masses followed behind him wherever he spoke his messages, the despots who governed in those places became afraid of him and had him killed on a large cross. (XIX, 381–82)

Theoretically at least, Martí appeared confident that if the power of the Christian movement could be harnessed to a practical application, a new, relevant religion would emerge, one that would be welcomed in the liberated *patria*. Unfortunately however, Martí saw the Christian religions, in particular the Catholic Church, openly rejecting this opportunity to channel their resources for the common benefit of society, preferring instead to follow more materialistic pursuits while hiding behind a facade of religious dogma. Writing in *La Nación* in July of 1884, Martí argued for a new (and truly "Christian") church.

> Would not the faithful of these churches do better by raising up these souls, buying clothes for those who go naked, and taking bottles away from the alcoholics' lips—instead of hearing sermons about the

> beasts of the Apolcalypse and taking pleasure in the insults that pastors trade about the rival churches in their district? Do they really want to raise a temple to God? Then let them come down to this hell of the unfortunate, not with alms and charity (which degrade the poor) but with the skill of their example. (X, 60)

José Martí frequently despaired that Christianity would move to this needed, socially oriented, and therefore essentially practical path. In fact, even before his first deportation from Cuba in January of 1871, he had severed ties with Catholicism in order to join a local Freemason group.[11] Although Martí never claimed membership in any particular religious group nor praised excessively any religious faith, he did praise individuals whom he viewed as practicing in their daily lives a truly Christian faith, which reflected his basically humanistic set of beliefs. Thus it was the practical application of one's religious faith (whatever it be) and never the label applied to any particular religious persuasion that Martí lauded and vigorously defended. Commenting on the foundation of Martí's religious beliefs, Ezequiel Martínez Estrada outlines the major aspects.

> The Christianity that we see in Martí is more a form of humanism than any speculative religion. It is the pre-Christian humanitarian spirit that Simone Weil determined and explained in *Intuitions pre-chrétiennes*. Indeed the essential elements of Martí's Christianity are not those on which Christ acts as a catalyst in order to form a religious credo or dogma but rather those aspects that came before Christ and subsist outside the religious, mystical limits. These same aspects surround both Christ's person and his doctrine and blend together with other similar forms of reverential, pious wisdom, such as that found in Buddhism or the work of the Greek moralists. The principles of Martí's "Christianity" were not faith and obedience but rather cleanliness of spirit, nobility of conduct, and a spirit of self-sacrifice, exercised because of his love, to help his neighbor.[12]

At the time of his first deportation to Spain, José Martí already possessed a fairly clear set of religious beliefs, which would remain with him—with remarkably little alteration—for the rest of his life. He was outspokenly anti-Catholic and by extension opposed to what may be termed the traditional approach to religion in general.

He had developed a deeply felt confidence that the only meaningful and true religion was to be found within the boundless potential of man himself. He wrote as early as 1875: "Man does not have to turn his eyes up to God; he has God in himself" (VI, 286). This rather unorthodox affirmation obviously is closely related to Martí's desire for a more practical form of Christianity; both deliberately deny the relevance of religious dogma in the vital process and place enormous emphasis not only on the social obligations of man but also on his ability to meet them.

> There is a God: it is man. There is a divine strength: it is everything we can see. Man is a piece of an infinite body, which creation has sent to earth, bandaged and tied, to search for his father, his own body. (VI, 226)

The type of religious life that Martí would have supported in the liberated Republic clearly would have required that the established religions subordinate their theoretical content and concentrate on pursuing a more practical goal, adapting their faith to help solve major social problems. That there would have been an official state religion in the *patria* is highly doubtful. From Martí's criticism of the immoral liasons between the powerful landowners and the Church in most of the countries he had visited, it is a logical supposition that he would have opposed an official religion, particularly when he strongly recommended the union of all religious groups, Christian and non-Christian (XII, 418).

Despite Martí's obvious abhorrence of the corruption that he saw in most established religions and despite his determination to encourage the churches to assist the Republic in a practical fashion, Martí would never have sought to curtail freedom of worship. Admittedly he was defiantly outspoken when considering the idea of Catholic education—or any form of religious education—being taught in the Republic's schools. "There is no right to allow either Catholicism or any religion that condemns it to be taught in the schools. . . . Let man's spirit be totally free, and let him place his ear directly on the earth" (VII, 416). Nevertheless, as a report published in *Patria* as late as September of 1894 indicated, Martí felt that religious freedom was an absolute necessity for all Cubans, whatever their religion.

> Let all men of religion be venerated, whether they be Catholic or Tarahumara. Everyone, whether thay have lank, straight, or thick, woolly hair, has a right to the full exercise of his conscience. Any Catholic who criticizes a Hindu's beliefs is a tyrant, as is any Methodist who condemns a Catholic. (VIII, 257)

In conclusion, organized religion would need to be totally reshaped in the Republic of Martí. Though guaranteeing freedom of worship to all Cubans, Martí obviously would have guided the various churches toward socially oriented goals; he would have attempted to make the various religious denominations contribute in a practical manner to the common good, in essence a compilation of the Christian and humanist ethics.

Finally, the fourth, basic characteristic of the society that Martí hoped to establish in a liberated Cuba was the informed and generally educated nature of its members. Mention was made in chapter 4 of the way in which Martí urged his fellow Cubans, and indeed people everywhere, to cultivate an active interest in both political theory and practice. He saw in this process an important guarantee of a healthy and balanced political life far removed from the machinations of the infamous "políticos de oficio." This necessary political education, however, only represented one element of his ambitious plans for the formulation of a totally new and far-reaching educational policy, evident from his notes on the theme of "Educación Popular."

> II—Popular education does not refer exclusively to the poor class. Instead it means that all classes in the nation, the entire people, are to be well-educated. And just as there is no reason why the rich should be educated but not the poor, why should the poor be educated and not the rich? All men are equal. . . .
>
> IV—The most contented nation is the one with the best-educated citizens, both in the development of their thoughts and in the direction of their sentiments. . . .
>
> V—When every man comes to this earth, he has the right to be educated. Afterward, as a form of payment, he also has the obligation to contribute to the education of everyone else.
>
> VI—An ignorant nation can always be deceived by superstition and made to serve. However, a nation that has been educated will always be strong and free. (XX, 375)

A full education of all citizens not only was regarded by Martí as an inviolable right of every Cuban, regardless of color or social standing, but also, far more importantly, it was considered by him to be an absolute necessity for the successful founding of the Republic.

The topic of education was a true obsession for Martí, so convinced was he that in essence it represented a guarantee of the successful implementation of his other social programs in the *patria*. This concern of Martí helps to explain why there are references to an amazingly wide variety of topics dealing with education, amongst which the most commonly found are the needs for a practical agricultural education (VII, 164; VIII, 276–78, 380; XIV, 229); for the development of a carefully planned mechanical education (VIII, 278–79; X, 375; XI, 80, 85); for instituting night schools so that workers could receive a decent education (XII, 459); the need to avoid looking automatically abroad for solutions to Cuban problems (VII, 325) and also to avoid educating Latin American students abroad (V, 260–62); the need for special care in the education of children (XVIII, 302, 382); for establishing kindergartens, free to the public and situated particularly in poorer districts (XII, 414); and finally the fundamental need, given the lack of facilities outside the city, to provide a well-balanced education for the rural dwellers, the *guajiros*, by means of a system of traveling teachers, the "maestros ambulantes" (VIII, 16; XVIII, 284; VIII, 289–91). In short, as he wrote in *La América* in August of 1883, the modern era demanded an innovative and practical form of education.

> The new world requires a new form of schooling. It is necessary to substitute the literary spirit of education with a new, scientific spirit. . . . Whoever fertilizes their soil well, works less, has that earth for longer, and also receives more from it. (VIII, 299)

Of particular note is Martí's desire to provide an education for people who otherwise would be unable to receive any formal training, either because they did not possess sufficient funds to study or because they lived in isolated parts of the island. As an educational observer, Martí is astute both in his insight into the needs of Cuba and in the programs he designed to meet these needs. Indicative of this goal of implementing a socially oriented education were his plans for educating the workers. In general, he saw that both in

Cuba and in United States the poor, uneducated workers were easily exploited, and Martí therefore concluded: "Until the workers are educated men, they will never be contented" (VIII, 352). To meet this goal of converting the workers into "hombres cultos" ("educated men"), he drew up plans for a large-scale development of the North American idea of free night-schools for all those who would otherwise be deprived of the chance to learn. Martí himself, with several years teaching experience in an institution organized by La Liga, a society of black Cuban workers living in the United States, had firsthand knowledge of the benefits that resulted from these night-schools.

> [There should be] night-schools where the worker-student who went out to earn his bread, or the one who has not had the time or place during the daytime, can go after their work to learn from the first letters of the alphabet to the most delicate, complicated aspects of human understanding. (XII, 459)

Equally impressive in Martí's program for assuring all citizens of the Republic a decent education were his plans to "open free day-care centers in all the poorer areas" (XII, 414). In order to solidify the gains made by the revolution, Martí saw that it was vital to provide the future generation with the immediate benefits of the liberation struggle so that they would be better able to continue the revolutionary process. The emphasis that Martí placed on the education of the young can be judged by his opinion that, before providing even food to his compatriots, it would be necessary first to guarantee the young members of the Republic the right to an education. "Bread cannot be given to all those who need it, but those nations that want to be saved have to prepare their children against the ways of crime: on every street, a day-care center" (XII, 414). Finally, to ensure that there would be sufficient staff to supervise the much-needed schools, Martí advocated a system of drafting teachers into an instructional corps and obliging them to work in the newly constructed schools.

> Soldiers have to be recruited for the army, as do teachers for the poor. There should be an obligatory service for teachers, as there is for the military. Indeed, those teachers who do not undertake their years of

> service should not be allowed to vote. To prepare the nation so that it can defend itself and live with honor is the best form of military defense. (XII, 414–15)

For Martí it was also a moral as well as civic obligation to ensure that even in the most remote areas of the island his fellow Cubans should have the right to a basic education. He was deeply aware of the many dangers inherent in the existence of an ignorant mass of people and at one point had intended to write a study on "Education in the rural areas, to avoid the development of tyranny" (XVIII, 284). Martí's two articles, published in *La América* in 1884, argued the need for the establishment of "un cuerpo de maestros viajeros" ("a corps of traveling teachers"–VIII, 16), who would teach a mixture of agricultural sciences and basic philosophy to the country-dwellers. "This is what the teachers have to take to the rural areas—not only agricultural techniques and mechanical instruments but also tenderness, something which is so lacking, but which achieves so much, in men" (VIII, 289). Martí's plan of opening scores of schools, "sprinkled throughout the valleys, mountains, and most distant corners" (VIII, 291), was thus intended to place a fundamental education for the first time in Cuban history within the grasp of all citizens of the Republic, who would then have the opportunity to become "hombres cultos."

The general nature of the education that Martí desired for the Republic was practical. As early as 1881 he had decided that "Nuestra América" badly needed to adopt an educational program based on "the lively, productive forces of the country in which the students will live" (XIV, 229), namely a sound agricultural training "to accustom man to realize his own potential, while harnessing the productive forces of nature . . . this is what has to be the objective of the new breed of educators" (XIV, 229).

Martí was distressed to see the many serious blunders being made in Latin America where, despite having an economy based almost entirely on agriculture, the educational system of the former Spanish colonies still pursued a path of classical education, preferring to ignore the needs of their respective countries and deliberately spurning the opportunity to offer a more practical form of education. Martí was particularly concerned that courses were not given in agricultural sciences. As a result, he explained in 1884, "they are putting a giant's head on an ant's body. What is worse, with the purely literary education that they give in our Latin countries, every day they add to the head and take away from the body" (VIII, 369). Martí's many years in the United States also afforded him a valuable insight into the type of education that he advocated for the Republic; it revealed to him other ways in which a modern, more practical form of teaching could be established. In an article entitled "Reforma esencial en el programa de las universidades americanas" ("Essential Reform in the Program of American Universities"), he summarized this new direction.

> Education has an inescapable obligation toward man (not to meet this obligation indeed is a crime): to fashion him according to the period in which he is living but without diverting him from the magnificent, ultimate human tendency. Let man live in accord with the universe and with his era—for which Latin and Greek are useless. (VIII, 430)

Thus the dominant note of Martí's philosophy of education was that it should be of a relevant, practical nature, or as he wrote in September 1883: "Let primary education be primarily scientific; instead of the history of Joshua, let the history of the earth's formation be taught" (VIII, 278).[13] Martí was initially very excited by the many educational reforms being introduced in the United States, although unsure if Latin American students should study there. In particular he was enthusiastic about the use of manual labor in some of the American colleges he visited and gratefully emphasized the words of the director of Michigan Agricultural College when he claimed: "There is no basic agricultural teaching that cannot be enhanced by manual work undertaken in the college" (VIII, 286).

Yet despite this desire for an invigorated and practical system of education, Martí was aware of the many potential pitfalls inherent in such an approach. He was an ardent admirer of the American intent of familiarizing young students with the reality of their country but at the same time recommended against an exclusively pragmatic form of education: "That kind of education called 'industrial' or 'manual' has many advocates, and some fanatical supporters, who cannot see that by itself it too is a form of partial education" (XI, 80). On other occasions he also criticized this over-reaction to the former classical education, reporting that the materialistically oriented society of North America forced its children to count before learning anything else.[14] The results of this overemphasis on the practical approach were, according to Martí, as disturbing as those of the traditional Latin American system. "Man becomes a machine, working in a routine way, exceptionally qualified in the area in which he specializes but completely closed to any other knowledge of, exchange or sympathy with other human matters. That is the direct result of an exclusively practical elementary education" (X, 375).

José Martí's comments on an extraordinary range of education-related topics show clearly his deep concern with ensuring all Cubans the opportunity to receive an adequate, free education. But this was not merely a well-intentioned and magnanimous gesture, for Martí also realized that the successful introduction of his other programs into revolutionary Cuba depended heavily on having a well-informed, aware populace who, after reflecting on the validity and the necessity of the measures proposed by Martí, would not hesitate to support them wholeheartedly. Therefore, together with Martí's doctrine of *sociabilidad,* this wide-ranging educational policy of Martí constituted the essential and necessary foundation for his entire program of social reform—hence his obsession with ensuring that it reach the most far-flung corners of the Republic and his desire to conscript an "army" of instructors.

Martí's four reform programs, namely his intent to change Cuba into a raceless, classless, nonsectarian, and well-educated society, all reveal his firm determination to construct in the *patria* a life-style totally different from anything before in Cuba. Martí was thus attempting to rebuild the entire social structure of Cuba. As he explained to Néstor Ponce de León in October of 1889:

> In the nation beloved by me
> I would like to see born
> The nation that can be
> Without hate, and without color.
> In the generous game
> of limitless thought,
> I would like to see building the house,
> Rich and poor, black and white. (XVI, 357)

Each of the major social reform programs studied in this chapter was of crucial importance to the radical restructuring of Cuban society intended by Martí in postindependence Cuba, because all were designed to develop in a practical form the major elements of the essential moral foundation studied earlier. Therefore, based on the successful inculcation of these programs, Martí was certain that a new man would gradually emerge from the reconstruction process, one who, Martí hoped, would subsequently unite with his peers to eventually create a new, revolutionary society.[15] Martí's fundamental dream, "to fill our lands with original men, educated to be happy in the land in which they live . . . men of their time, and men of Latin America" (XX, 147), would thus be accomplished. The new society, inherently just and totally comprehending the necessary continual reshaping of the *patria,* would then be instituted.

7. Economic Policies

Unlike Martí's far-reaching and extremely clear aspirations for social reform in Cuba, his program for economic reform was both less developed and less central to his overall plan for the liberated *patria*. This does not mean that Martí was uninterested or unversed in prevailing economic theories;[1] the important role he played as Uruguay's representative at the International Monetary Conference in 1891 dispels all doubt that might arise on this account. Rather it appeared that Martí's major preoccupation, quite understandably, after winning political independence from Spain was to solidify his position (if he were chosen to continue as the *Delegado*) with the majority of his fellow Cubans.

Consequently, José Martí's immediate plans were to gain the committed support of the Cuban people as a whole, defeat the Spanish forces, and then seek to retain (and indeed to build upon) that support by implementing as soon as possible a program of sweeping social and political reform. Undoubtedly economic development was necessary for the stability of the new government but was not as immediate a priority as the need for the *Delegado* to have the unswerving loyalty of the nation as a whole.

As a result of these priorities, one finds few innovations detailed by Martí regarding specific economic reform, much less evidence of any particular economic school or ideology followed by him. Nevertheless there are many astute observations on the basic nature of economic development that he deemed advisable for the *patria*. In general, José Martí's economic aspirations for an independent Cuba stemmed from the same personal, highly moralistic and socially oriented awareness that characterized his program for extensive social reform in Cuba. His moral foundation for the Republic, presented in chapter 5, led Martí to conclude that however necessary economic development might be, it was subordinate to the best interests of the nation as a whole. Cuba would embark eagerly on a program of much-needed economic reform but with the overriding proviso that the fruits of this development be awarded to the people at large and never to minority interest groups, whatever their nationality.

The firm desire on the part of Martí to ensure that the Cuban people as a whole, and not any specific social group, benefitted from the economic policies followed in the *patria* is prominent in all of Martí's work, from his earliest writings to his famous last letter to Manuel Mercado in 1895. As in the case of his philosophical views, Martí was also an economic eclectic, reading widely and supporting viewpoints that he found just and morally acceptable, even when the theories appeared to contradict his earlier statements. Yet there was no fundamental contradiction in Martí's comments on economic and philosophical matters; consistently he supported whatever concept appeared the most honest and justifiable, refusing to restrict himself by adopting a label that denoted any definitive political, philosophical, or economic theory. The broad moral basis, both of Martí's own character and of his aspirations for the new society in a liberated Cuba, cannot be unduly emphasized.

The basic principle of channeling economic development so that it best served the interests of the vast majority of the population obviously originated from his righteous indignation at the Spanish social and political (and thus economic) domination of the island, which for Martí was totally unjustifiable. From his earliest writings Martí was most definitely opposed to the idea of any foreign group controlling the sovereignty of another nation. Indeed, from the age of fifteen José Martí showed clear signs of advocating the struggle against both colonialism and imperialism, a conviction that his later work—and in many ways his entire life—would develop to the fullest. His pamphlet *La República Española ante la Revolución Cubana (The Spanish Republic Faced by the Cuban Revolution)* set the dominant tone for all future pronouncements dealing with the struggle between what can be termed majority–social interests and minority–economic considerations. In this work Martí condemned in vigorous fashion what he viewed as the fundamentally immoral situation of a colonial power crushing so brutally any attempt by the Cuban people to protect their sense of national dignity and exploiting ruthlessly the natural resources of the colony. In the case of his own *patria,* the only conceivable goal for all honorable Cubans was to fight tirelessly in order to overthrow such an immoral system of callous exploitation.

> Our goal is independence—a tremendous punishment for all of your secular errors of colonization, your absolutist policies as conquerors in times of liberty, your oppression during which your severity knew no bounds and your cruelty never moderated. (I, 107)

The oppression and exploitation of weaker nations by larger and more powerful nations is a subject that occurs frequently in Martí's *Obras completas,* and in each case Martí condemned vociferously all manifestations of such colonialist and imperialist actions.[2] His report on what he considered to be the completely unjustifiable position of the Spanish forces in Africa, written some twenty years after his early pamphlet, testifies to the continuity of Martí's thought. In both works there is the same conviction that all nations have the inalienable right to self-determination and the same highly moralizing tone of righteous indignation at any such colonialist or imperialist venture. In the later report, Martí expounds:

> Spain has been in Melilla for four centuries now and has there only the castle where opponents are executed and an old church. The truly honorable heart, which was Spanish and supported Pelayo at the Battle of Covadonga, now supports the Moorish Riff against Spain's unjust possession of this area, one which does not help the world in the least. To possess something implies a series of obligations. To bathe a nation in blood or to dishonor it with bad habits is not any kind of justification to take possession of a country, be it the Riff or Cuba.
> (V, 333)

However, Martí was not specifically anti-Spanish but rather condemned harshly the attempts of all governments to exploit the natural resources of other nations, paying little heed to the desires or necessities of the people from the exploited area and concerned only with what they could obtain for themselves from this arrangement. Martí attacked the British, especially for their activities in Ireland and the Middle East; the French in the Orient; and, most extensively and vigorously, the United States for their continuous incursions into Latin America. No colonizing venture was spared Martí's ire. For these powers seeking to impose themselves upon weaker sovereign nations, Martí expressed the same moral condemnation and offered the hope that justice (meaning in effect full political independence) would be attained. Typical of his thoughts on such colonizing attempts, and undoubtedly the most startling in relation to recent historical events, was his article "Un paseo por la tierra de los anamitas" ("A Stroll Through the Country of the Vietnamese"), published in the fourth issue of the children's magazine that Martí edited, *La Edad de Oro (The Golden Age),* in which Martí portrayed the struggle of the Vietnamese people to liberate themselves from their colonial masters.

> We wear our hair in a bun and our clothes are a pointed hat, wide pants, and a colored shirt; we are yellow-skinned, flat-nosed, frail, and ugly. But we are skillful workers of bronze and silk. And when the French came here to take away from us our Hanoi, our Hue, our cities of wooden palaces, our ports full of bamboo houses and reedboats, our warehouses of fish and rice, we with our almond eyes have died, thousands upon thousands, to close the way to them. Today they are our masters but tomorrow—who knows! (XVIII, 461–62)

Probably the greatest threat to Martí's plans for the economic independence of Cuba was that posed by the United States, which had long enjoyed a very favorable balance of trade with the island. As early as the mid-1870s, Martí had observed the growing U.S. interest in and subsequent exploitation of Latin America, particularly Mexico, and had warned his fellow Latin Americans against the noticeably covetous attitude shown by many North American business interests. The numerous interventions of the United States in Mexico, the infamous "caso Cutting," the omnipresent slurs in the American press, and the general desire of the North to "take over the country for North Americans, with the objective of cultivating it according to the norms of modern civilization" (VII, 42), all contributed to Martí's ever-growing disillusionment with the land of Lincoln.

Because of Martí's unbounded pride in "Nuestra América," his resentment at the increasing exploitation of Latin America by U.S. interests was hardened even more by the continuous barrage of propaganda printed in the United States deriding the Latin American character as impoverished, feminine, and inherently mediocre. The resulting combination of a profound distrust of North American interest in the southern continent and a deep personal attachment to "Nuestra América" is encountered with great regularity in Martí's work of the 1880s and 1890s. From his report published in *La Nación* in December of 1887:

> And so, although the majority of the nations of our America are truly admirable for having risen, despite obstacles that would be fatal in their present circumstances, from the most obscure and troubled origins, not a single day goes by without criticism of us by these ignorant, contemptuous North American newspapers. They make us appear as tiny little nations without any importance, comic-opera countries, tiny little republics without learning or significance, "nations with rickety legs"—as Charles Dudley Warner, speaking of Mexico, said yesterday—"the dregs of a degenerate civilization, without any virility, and without any purpose!" (VII, 330)

Undoubtedly one of the most important reasons for Martí's enduring fame in Latin American letters was his ability to foresee the nature of a growing interest in Latin America by the United States at a time when most of his contemporaries, enraptured by the impressive economic and industrial developments taking place in that country, eagerly accepted the North American model as worthy of imitation in their homeland. José Martí, however, saw that the North American economic concerns were less interested in assisting their Latin neighbors to develop their own resource industries than they were in stripping, and subsequently exporting to the United States for processing, such valuable natural resources as they could find in the Latin American republics. For Martí this conduct was as dastardly as the more blatant Spanish oppression of his homeland, and he protested vigorously against such savage exploitation of "Nuestra América."

Yet despite his concern with protecting Latin America from what Martí generally interpreted as greedy exploitation on the part of U.S. interests and the overly patronizing attitude of that nation, "a very different kind of nation, formidable and aggressive, which does not regard us as their equal and which denies us the conditions of equality" (IV, 424) as he wrote in 1892, Martí was not opposed to the idea of productive foreign investment in Latin America, with a reasonable return being taken by the investor. Indeed, writing for *La Opinión Nacional* in 1881, he strongly recommended that Venezuela should consider "the establishment of a business network . . . between the United States, overflowing with wealth and interested in expanding their market, and Venezuela, a natural, grandiose market, in need of foreign investment" (IX, 34). Some five years later, referring to Honduras, Martí reiterated this point, demonstrating how foreign investment could prove to be a boon for the national economy and should therefore not be summarily dismissed. For it did not merely represent, as Martí noted, "riches for the foreign companies—but also riches without which the national wealth would be impossible. This is not a financial wealth but rather a moral one, given the public security that it breeds" (VIII, 31–32).

Obviously, Martí's basic distrust of the foreign interests that were investing in Latin America was not so great as to preclude all foreign investment per se; Martí realized the possibility that such groups could provide an important stimulus for the much-needed economic growth (and thereby political stability) in this developing area. Moreover, despite his obvious distress at the apparently neocolonialist designs of many influential North American politicians,[3] Martí was nevertheless prepared to consider the feasibility of a mutually beneficial arrangement, agreeable to all. This would require an attitude of respect on the part of the developer for both the traditions and aspirations of the country in which he was investing and in turn would assure the investor of a fair profit in order to repay his interest and trust in the host country.

Although in theory Martí accepted the possibility of constructive foreign investment, in practice he became increasingly sceptical at the capacity of foreign investors, and more particularly of foreign governments, to be satisfied with an "honest return" on their investment, and his later reports adopted a more bitter tone. Nevertheless, as he noted in *Patria* as late as December of 1894, any foreign developers would be allowed to invest in the Cuban economy, provided that they were prepared to abide by regulations to respect national sovereignty and traditions and to accept a just return on their investment.

> Every worker is a saint, and every producer is a root; those who bring useful work and a sincere interest here (be they from a cold or warm clime), have to find a broad opening—as if for a new tree—available for them. However, we will not allow thieves and meddlers to come here with the pretext of bringing us work, with a false interest in our America, and then try to squeeze us into the ground, without money in their pocket or friendship in their heart. (VIII, 36)

Martí was certain that an active economy, which would ensure all Cuban citizens employment, was an absolute necessity. He wrote in 1886: "There is no means of assuring liberty in our nation and honor in our citizens other than promoting public wealth" (VIII, 27). In arguing this point Martí was basing his theory on two unrelated beliefs: his obsession (at times overly romantic) with the noble concept of work, noted in chapter 5, and his conviction that in an economy where a large proportion of the population either did not work or else, as in the case of those many Cubans employed in the sugar industry, only worked for part of the year, there was far greater likelihood of discontentment and thus potential civil unrest than one in which all workers were fully employed. Martí argued that the Cuban economy, after the island's liberation, would depend very heavily on the successful employment of all able-bodied citizens. He had previously observed in Venezuela (XIX, 155), in Spain (XIV, 37), and of course numerous cases in the United States, how volatile political situations had been made far worse by mass unemployment and was convinced that this should not be the case in the Republic.

> Ample, enjoyable, and well-paid work, enough to satisfy the exasperated needs of the poorer classes, is the only solution for this major, future risk. The pentup rage is finally exploding and it is necessary to disarm it. Misery is the cause behind the rage—it is necessary to overcome this misery. Work, on the other hand, puts this rage to flight; we must persevere in the creation and ever-continuing support for work . . . by creating interest in this work, one assures peace. (XIV, 37)[4]

Another fundamentally important feature of Martí's economic policy for the Republic was his conviction that a liberated Cuba, in order to survive economically, would need to trade with all friendly nations. He argued that it would be fatal for the *patria* to restrict itself in any way to trading with only one economic partner, for as he wrote in 1888: "Whoever studies international economics . . . knows well that it is a fatal error for a nation to have all of its commerce linked with one single country" (VII, 373). A few years later Martí was even more specific, warning his fellow Latin Americans of the potential dangers resulting from such an unbalanced situation.

> Whoever talks about economic union is of necessity talking about political union. The nation that buys all your products, in fact orders; and the nation that sells, serves. One has to balance national commerce to assure freedom. The nation that wants to die sells its products to one single customer, and the nation that wants to be saved, to more than one. Excessive influence on one country in the commerce of another becomes a political influence. . . . The nation that wants to be independent has to be independent in its business. It has to distribute this business among several countries that are equally strong. If it has to show preference to one, let it be to the nation that it least needs, which will be less contemptuous. Have neither union of the Americas against Europe, nor with Europe against a nation of the Americas. (VI, 160)

Cuba and the United States, because of their geographical situation, obviously constituted natural markets for each other's products. Therefore, despite his total distrust of U.S. interest in Latin America and despite his conviction of the many fundamental differences between the peoples of the two Americas, Martí realized the many advantages to be obtained from trading—on an equitable basis—with the North. As late as 1894, following the trauma of the two Inter-American Conferences in the United States and his realization of the general animosity toward Latin America (particularly toward Mexico and Cuba), Martí still did not discount the United States as a potential trading partner, referring in fact to "that part of the Americas which is not Latin, whose enmity it is neither wise nor feasible to encourage, and with whom—with firm respect and astute independence—it is not impossible (and, indeed, it is useful) to be friends" (VIII, 35).[5]

Although Martí stated that because of their physical situation if nothing else both Cuba and the United States should attempt to maintain cordial trade relations with each other, nevertheless he was certain that the spiritual composition of the North American character was in the process of being drastically changed—for the worse—and the *patria* should not rely too heavily on U.S. goodwill. The economic boom that had resulted from large-scale industrial development in the United States had not been without serious social drawbacks, Martí argued consistently.

In particular, Martí severely criticized the predominant theory of protectionism, according to which foreign goods arriving in North America were assessed high import tariffs in order to place them at a higher cost than locally manufactured goods, thereby prompting Americans to purchase the local product. The United States, he informed his Latin American readers, not only was guilty of stripping their countries of natural resources but also intended to restrict the flow of manufactured goods into North America and to rid itself of the surplus of these that it already had on its Latin American trading "partners." Thus Martí could foresee the direct effects that such a policy would have on the Latin American economy and so warned his audience accordingly. Martí was firmly opposed to the very idea of protectionism and understandably more so when it implied potential economic doom for "Nuestra América," which is evident from an imaginary dialogue he drew up between two businessmen.

> "But really, if the would-be purchaser has less money than before (because everything that he buys costs more), who is going to buy that excess of articles churned out by the new workshops and factories—especially since his money is going to be worth less?"
>
> "Who? Why, Spanish America? Why else is Spanish America there if not to buy all that we want to sell her?" (XII, 463)

To avoid the flooding of the Latin American market by goods manufactured in the United States, Martí felt that reciprocal trade agreements would have to be clearly formulated with particular emphasis being placed on the need for an evenly distributed balance of trade between the participating nations. Martí also advised his fellow Latin Americans that this apparent intent of many North American industrialists to "dump their excesses in production on the weaker nations of South America" (III, 49) should serve as a warning to the whole of "Nuestra América" to make a determined effort immediately to pursue a goal of basic self-sufficiency so that should trade relations with the United States ever be severed it would indeed be possible to survive without foreign economic aid.

One of the few specific features of Martí's economic program concerned the nature of the national economy that he hoped to develop in an independent Cuba, and for this he had definite ideas.[6] Writing for *La Nación* in November of 1883, Martí focused on the eventual need for industrial development.

> How many ingenious inventions, how much useful training, mechanical improvements, artistic merit, and brilliant theories remain unknown and die as if they had never existed in our Latin American nations. The causes? A lack of interest in industrial development, of capital to finance the necessary experiments, of exhibitions to reward the resulting inventions with prizes, of workshops where the inventions can be perfected, and of resolute spirit with which to face up to the risks of exhibiting them. (VIII, 363)

In his plans for the national economy, Martí was clearly prepared to promote the idea of industrial development after the Republic had been firmly established. Before that time, though, it would be necessary to develop a solid base for steady economic development in the *patria.* However, Martí refused to even consider mining as a viable base for the economy, preferring instead the adoption of an agriculture-based structure as the required foundation for the Republic's economic growth. Martí's outspoken opposition to the concept of a mining-oriented economy is extremely interesting for it reveals, as early as 1875, Martí's very strong social concerns and his determination that economic development benefit the country as a whole and never any specific investor. As a purely financial proposition he considered mining a dubious enterprise because, as he noted in the *Revista Universal,* such an industry depended excessively on the exploitation of nonrenewable resources and therefore constituted a rather precarious mainstay for the economic development of a nation struggling to emerge from three centuries of colonial exploitation. Furthermore, he declared:

> Mining riches are of such a nature that they enrich beyond all belief a small number of people. This sudden enrichment of a tiny minority does not favor the common masses and is not well distributed among them. . . . These mining riches are resources which slip away or slowly disappear. On the other hand, the nation consists of lives that remain here and constantly increase in number. (VI, 310)

The alternative, an agriculture-based economy, was at all times defended by Martí for whom it represented the most certain guarantee for stable, if unspectacular, economic progress.

> Agricultural wealth, as a means of producing necessary prime materials, is achieved far more rapidly than industrial wealth, is more stable than mining (besides being easier to produce and to develop), and it assures the nation that adopts it of a true well-being. Mines tend to become exhausted; and industrial products are often left without a market in which to sell. The value of agricultural products fluctuates to a certain degree, but their consumption is assured and their agent—the land—never tires. (VII, 163–64)

Moreover, as Martí commented in 1884, not only would such an economy provide sufficient food and employment for the Cuban population (given Cuba's benign climate and excellent soil resources), but also would help to generate much-needed funds through the development of certain popular cash crops. Martí took hope from the recent dramatic increase of trade with European countries and in particular from the increase of volume in the coffee trade, predicting quite accurately that it would be extremely profitable to develop and market such exotic products of Latin America not available in Europe.

Martí affirmed consistently the unbounded potential of the Republic and indeed of the continent, provided that they were prepared to follow this slow, but steady, plan of development. "Rather than in our mines, we have more gold and silver in our textile factories, in the medicines that can be derived from our plants, and in our trees that can produce aromatic dyes" (VIII, 367). Apart from a few rather naïve observations (the most famous of which his statement: "There are no contradictions in nature. The earth is sufficient to sustain all who are born here"–VIII, 378), Martí was very much aware of the extreme care required to protect such an economy. Writing in January of 1882, he stressed the absolute necessity for conservation. "All those who cut timber should be subject—as they are in every country that exports wood—to the most rigorous laws and close supervision. They have to ensure that their logging operation will be such that the original forest will be preserved and that seedlings will be planted to replace the woods that are torn out" (XXIII, 149). Furthermore, on at least two occasions he underlined the fundamental importance of "improving our agricultural products" (VIII, 366), specifically of producing new and more profitable varieties of products that were already successful, and of undertaking extensive research in order to protect Latin America's favored position in this field.

> All our countries of Latin America have been so richly endowed by nature, and in all parts we have—close to hand—the earth, this untiring agent of production. Therefore all our efforts should be directed toward favoring agricultural progress, all our decrees should support it, all our strength should seek to realize this goal, and all our intelligence to assist it in any way possible. (VII, 164)

Martí's general moralistic theories and his specific plans concerning the economic development of the *patria* facilitate an examination of the more controversial question of the basic economic school of thought to which Martí subscribed. From the outset it should be stated that examples exist indicating the influence of both the liberal and the socialist philosophies of economic development. However, in the mid-1880s, Martí gradually departed from the traditional liberal approach, adopting an increasingly radical position on many social issues, though he never accepted the socialist or the liberal philosophy as the definitive model to be followed in the Republic, nor did he ever separate himself totally from the mainstream of either philosophy.

In regard to Martí's general outlook on the type of economy that he desired for an independent Cuba, to a substantial degree he supported many features of the traditional liberal approach. These are summarized by J. Salwyn Schapiro.

> The fundamental principle of the classical economists was derived from the idea that natural laws infallibly regulated economic transactions. Therefore, they upheld laissez faire, and even more dogmatically than their master, Adam Smith. In a free market, prices of commodities would be determined by the natural, economic law of supply and demand. An unhampered, unregulated economy would increase production by encouraging enterprise. And it would lower prices through competition. Business would then prosper, and on the prosperity of business would depend the prosperity of the nation. Capitalists would reap profits; laborers would find employment; farmers would receive good prices for their products; and landlords, high rents.[7]

To the extent of the laissez faire practice, Martí appears to have been in total agreement with the liberal philosophy, revealed by his conclusions following much public debate in Mexico on the importation of foreign goods.

> Protectionism: In order to protect some twenty producers of *sarapes* (long, narrow shawls), the introduction of German shawls was prevented in Mexico because of excessive import duties. These German shawls sold for two and a half pesos, while the Mexican ones cost five. . . . What was happening with the protectionist system in Mexico? Who was being protected by it? Was it the population at large, which was paying a good five pesos for a sarape that was not always good—instead of paying half that price for another one that because of competition always had to be good? Who was it protecting: the people at large, the twenty or so manufacturers, or the small number of workers employed in the factories who without any difficulty could contribute something far more useful to the nation, and for themselves too? (XXII, 180)

Martí also appears to have agreed with the basic liberal philosophy of rewarding personal initiative and hard work. Mention was made in chapter 5 of Martí's firm support of a work ethic and his determination to make willful idleness a crime in the Republic. He recommended strongly that all Cubans work hard, both for the *patria* and for themselves, saving the money that resulted from their toils.

> The act of saving is useless for anybody who does not know the pleasures produced by capital—an intelligent, honorable saving that ac-

> cumulates. These people, unfamiliar with saving, have nothing because they essentially desire nothing. They do not work for their well-being because they do not want a more loving home, a softer bed, better quality clothes, or better food than the ones they have now. (VI, 283)

Thus in theory at least, Martí was not a dogmatic anticapitalist. He greatly admired and defended vigorously the right of the individual to better his standard of living through hard work. This desire for "el honesto lucro" ("the honest profit") as he termed it (VII, 163), the result of great personal sacrifice and industry, is probably best exemplified by his report—full of admiration—on the death of the owner of the Delmonico Restaurant in New York, a man who had arrived in North America a penniless immigrant and who had assiduously saved his earnings until he became one of the richest, and most generous, men in New York. Martí related how the man worked until the very day of his death, concluding that he typified "the splendid dignity of work, which radiated throughout his entire figure" (IX, 43).

Despite disagreeing fundamentally with the exploitative measures employed to increase their fortune, nevertheless, Martí did present the noble deeds of several of North America's richest, and in many cases greediest, philanthropists. There are in Martí's work references to the benevolent deeds of Ezra Cornell (X, 228), Vanderbilt (X, 147), Peter Cooper (XII, 47–53), Isaac Williamson (XII, 198), Andrew Carnegie (XI, 362), and Judge Courtland Palmer (XI, 363; XIII, 319), among others.

Martí was in many ways a typical nineteenth-century liberal; he supported free enterprise in general, reward for personal initiative, and a laissez faire trade structure. However, his "liberal" statements come entirely from his early writings, this point of view rarely being defended after the mid-1880s. This does not mean that Martí advanced instantaneously from a liberal perspective to a socialist one; it is only necessary to read his report in 1884 on Herbert Spencer's study, *La futura esclavitud (Future Slavery*, XV, 388–91), to see that Martí's knowledge of socialism was not overly profound.[8] What an objective study of Martí's work does reveal, however, is his gradual realization that nineteenth-century liberalism was no longer applicable to the changing world circumstances on the verge of the twentieth century. Martí's economic thought (as with his sociopolitical observations) was clearly becoming increasingly radical, and liberalism did not constitute the definitive economic philosophy that he desired for the *patria*.

As many *martianos* have noted, when studying the thought of José Martí it is impossible to escape from his at times overbearing, but always sincere, moralizing; his writing on the question of wealth and the right to acquire it was no exception. Martí was realistic enough to admit that all men were not born with the same sociopolitical advantages, and he never sought to correct this inequity by legalistic means. Nor did he ever forbid the practice of one generation inheriting the economic advantages earned by the previous generation (VI, 276). And though he was fully prepared to allow his compatriots to work hard and to save their honestly earned money in order to improve their material situation, he counseled strongly against the misuse of such funds.

> Just as it is a glorious experience to accumulate wealth with open, resolute labor, so too is the development of wealth by violent or deceitful means a concrete proof of personal inadequacy and shame and a crime worthy of a written penalty. Such methods dishonor the individual who uses them and corrupt the nation in which they are used. (XI, 426)

During his many years in North America, Martí had many opportunities to observe closely this process of people accumulating wealth, and he became progressively disillusioned with both the methods by which it was obtained and the use to which wealth was put after it had been earned. As a result of these experiences, although he was not essentially opposed to the idea of earning an "honest" wage or profit, Martí became convinced during the 1880s that, at least in the context of the United States of that time, his concept of "honest pay for an honest day's work" was rather outmoded, especially because of the rather dubious political alliances being made by large influential corporations. During the 1880s, Martí realized, and indeed remarked vigorously, even at that time free enterprise was not excessively *free*.

> Those disrespectful accumulations of wealth, which through sterile competition ruin prospective competitors who have less funds, result from the abuse of public land. The same is true of those monstrous

corporations that flood or shrink the national fortune with their avarice and their wheeling and dealing. So too for those wicked consortia of capital that compel the worker to perish without work or to toil for a grain of rice. And those numerous businesses that elect at their cost senators and political representatives—or else buy them after they are elected—to ensure an agreement with the laws that maintain their enjoyment of this abuse of power. New sections of public land are given with the full authority of the nation to these business enterprises that continue building their tremendous strength with the products resulting from this activity. (XI, 19)

Obviously Martí was aware that his ideas concerning the ability to earn an "honesto lucro" were rather unapplicable in the United States of this era, although this clearly did not preclude their relevance in the society of the liberated *patria*. It seems highly likely that in the Republic, Martí, depending heavily on a steady economic growth, would have used two different, but not necessarily contradictory, approaches to encourage the successful application of this work ethic: the idea of the spiritual "dignidad del trabajo" ("the dignity of work") and the concept of an "honesto lucro," of material rewards for hard work.

In many ways his comments on the two distinctive generations of rich North Americans, "los ricos de la primera y segunda generaciones" ("the wealthy of the first and second generations"), are a fitting illustration of the two types of wealth, one which he was prepared to encourage in an independent Cuba, the other totally repulsive to him. The first generation represented the wealth resulting from personal initiative and hard work and was completely acceptable to Martí, whereas the second generation exemplified the dangers of unrestrained greed after having tasted the material advantages that resulted from the former's toil and following an increasingly materialistic path. What was in fact even more disturbing for him was the way in which such "ricos" not only became totally corrupt themselves but also managed to influence others, eventually dragging large sectors of the population down in their wake. This, Martí warned sternly, would never be acceptable in the Republic.

The first-generation wealthy remember fondly that period when they were shop assistants, stable boys, warehouse laborers loading bales of wool, mere errand boys, and cowhands. But the second-generation wealthy, who ride like young gentlemen on the same horses that their parents led by the reins, regard the self-made men in the ranks of the nouveaux riches as being unseemly and lacking in decorum. This is ironic because it is exactly the same thing that their parents saw as being most seemly, and most honorable. . . . There is a very deep abyss between those who have *inherited* power, who are slim, pale, and dressed in an ornate style—since this is the custom of the English landed gentry, and those who have *earned* power through their labors, and who are healthy, chaste, resolute, stocky, and extremely clean—with the old-fashioned North American cleanliness, sober and solid.

A political aristocracy has sprung from this financial aristocracy. It dominates newspapers, wins elections, and usually prevails in meetings over that arrogant caste, which hides badly the impatience with which it awaits the time when it has sufficient supporters. Then its members will treat the sacred book of the nation harshly and arrogantly, reforming the national magna carta of generous liberty for the benefit and privilege of one single class. Ironically, these vulgar power-mongers were able to build their fortunes because of this same guarantee of freedom, one which they want to injure gravely. (IX, 108)

Martí was unable to see any advantages to be gained from earning excessive quantities of money. Although he did not state that there should be a limit to the amount of money a citizen could earn, nevertheless there was implicit in his comments the feeling that because money could corrupt so easily all Cubans would be encouraged to discipline themselves to request no more than what they honestly considered a just and honorable wage for their work. It was also a means of averting the possibility in the Republic of "una aristocracia política" ("a political aristocracy"). Indeed the reader of Martí's work receives the distinct impression that he felt deeply sorry for people with excessive wealth because invaribly it had eroded their personal happiness.[9] Once again Martí's plans for the future development of the *patria* depended extensively on the successful emergence of the new man within a radically new, revolutionary society.

Notably, there were many important issues on which Martí was in direct disagreement with classic liberal theories; an obvious example was his position on labor and trade unions. The liberal viewpoint considered labor, as J. Salwyn Schapiro has noted, "a commodity, bought and sold like any other commodity in the free market. What the laborer received in wages, the 'natural price,' was a 'subsistence wage,' just enough to maintain him and his family."[10] Such a situation was completely unacceptable to Martí who at all times demanded both respect and an equitable living wage for all workers. Writing in *La Nación* in 1886 on a railway strike, Martí explained the reasons for the workers' actions, totally justified in his view given the uncompromising attitude of their employers whose original desires for an "honesto lucro" had obviously been surpassed by an unfortunate materialistic lust.

> They see that their problems result quite obviously from the insolence and scorn of organized capital, from the illegitimate combinations of capital, from the system of an unequal distribution of profits that keeps the worker as an eternal beggar; they find it unjust that the railway workers' salaries provide only enough money for a crust of bread and a poor mattress—all done so that bosses and their cronies in the companies can share gargantuan profits among themselves (and for every thousand pesos of actual investment in the companies they issued twenty thousand shares). . . . As a result of a legal decision here, an act of violence there, the workers have now risen up, having decided that they will only sit down face-to-face with the capital that employs them. (X, 413)

Martí was determined that in a free Cuba a system based upon the necessity of social justice for all would prevail. In the context of North America of the 1880s this desire to see social justice implemented led Martí to support a number of movements designed to show solidarity with striking workers and to advocate strongly the formation of trade unions as a means of protecting the workers' rights. In fact, from as early as 1875 (when he himself had been nominated as a workers' representative at a conference in Chihuahua), Martí had consistently praised the unity shown by workers' organizations as they strived to obtain what he viewed as essential characteristics of any employment—respect and a just salary. He was proud to describe the "splendid phenomenon which can be seen now among the working class. Using their own strength the workers are now rising up from the state of unprepared wretchedness in which they were previously to a redeeming, intelligent work. Before, they were useful instruments; now they are men who know and appreciate each other" (VI, 625).

Martí's generous support of the principle of trade unions and his justification of workers groups uniting to demand a fair reward for their labors represented a direct refutation of classic economic liberalism. When a workers' cause was obviously justified (but again note, only then), Martí most definitely endorsed the decision to strike and generally was delighted with the extent of solidarity shown by fellow workers.

> What a group of honorable tailors started twenty years ago, seated round one of the tables on which they cut their cloth, is today a technical association, organized like an incredibly vast freemason network. If a railway worker is unjustly dismissed in Texas, already the foundry workers of Pittsburgh, the shoemakers of New England, the tobacco workers of New York are preparing to assist the railway worker financially, until his position is returned to him. (X, 403)

Martí's consistent claims that social justice should be the major concern and the deciding factor in all labor-capital disputes also led him to diverge further from the path of liberalism, particularly after he embraced the notion that both workers and capitalists should share equitably the profits that resulted from the work of both groups. In June of 1886, Martí wrote favorably on the idea of a tribunal that would judge all industrial disputes and whose goal would be "to promulgate laws in agreement with a just distribution of the products of labor" (X, 394). Some three years later, as the danger of severe social unrest loomed ominously, Martí again referred to a similar idea, claiming that in order to stave off severe social and political unrest, it would be absolutely essential to "distribute the national wealth better" (XII, 250).

Consequently, although he did not offer any specific scheme for the redistribution of wealth, either in the United States or in Cuba, obviously Martí did regard this sharing of excessive wealth to be both desirable and necessary. Moreover, it was not intended solely for the benefit of the poorer members of society who would receive extra funding but also for those people relieved of their riches and thereby freed from the corrupting power of money.

Such a policy would thus benefit the nation as a whole. Writing in the *Revista Universal* in 1875, Martí announced the central features of this rather simplistic, although undoubtedly sincere, plan for the solution of social unrest.

> They are hungry: let their hunger be relieved. Let not the teachings of the Roman senator be in vain: open up the granaries to the people when they have no grain in their home. Let each state think about the means of solving the suffering in their region; let them create employment for those who would perish without it; and let those who have ample wealth distribute some of their riches to those who have an empty table and merely a bed on the earth. (VI, 284)

A few years later in his pamphlet *Guatemala,* Martí developed the theme of introducing social justice into the nation by sharing the riches of the wealthy. He presented the basic immorality of having a few citizens possess huge estates while the vast majority toiled on the land of the *hacendado* (landowner) for a mere pittance, without any hope of possessing land of their own. The ideal solution to these obvious inequalities was to redistribute the land among those people living in such pitiable conditions—yet another major divergency from standard liberalism. Once again there were absolutely no plans as to *how* it would be accomplished, nor did Martí ever stipulate that the land would indeed be taken away from its wealthy occupants. He simply stated the essential immorality of such a condition and claimed that the healthiest possible situation for any nation of Latin America (and one he was most definitely planning to use for the foundation of the future Republic) was to have an agriculture-based economy in which all citizens participated as small-property owners.

> Exclusive wealth is unjust. Let this wealth belong to many people—not the upstarts, new hands that are dead, but rather those who honorably and painstakingly deserve it. A nation is indeed wealthy if it possesses many small-property owners. A wealthy nation is not one in which there are a few rich men but rather one in which every citizen has a small share of that wealth. Both in political economy and in solid government, by distributing these things we make the people happy. (VII, 134)

With this analysis of Martí's economic thought as a basis it is possible to make some general observations as to the type of economic programs that he would have attempted to introduce into Cuba after independence had been won. Probably the most obvious feature, basically because it is one of the remarkably few concrete measures proposed by Martí, was his firm desire that the *patria* should commit itself wholeheartedly to following a varied, strictly agriculture form of development, at all times avoiding dependency on either a mining- or an industrial-based economy.

For the general aspirations for a future economic policy, Martí obviously relied on his own deeply moralistic convictions concerning the fundamental "spirit" behind the more specific programs. In essence, Martí hoped and in fact was confident that the new man would arise from the revolutionary struggle in the *patria,* prepared to contribute effectively to the Republic. This new man, politically conscious and innately selfless, would then decide after a process of painstaking rationalization that a new moral direction had to be followed in the nation's economic development. Thereafter an entirely new approach would be introduced in the *patria* as riches and land were distributed to the needy; a code of humanist ethics would eventually be practiced by the nation; and all major decisions would depend on Martí's famous "en lo que sea justo" ("whatever is just") evaluation. The revolution would thus be firmly established.

Conclusion

That José Martí has been utilized as a source of inspiration by the many different regimes of independent Cuba demonstrates his fundamental importance as a symbol of *cubanía* (the essence of the Cuban identity), as the exemplary Cuban whom all citizens of the Republic should emulate. However, Martí's employment by politicians of totally opposing political beliefs suggests a certain lack of consistency in his basic political philosophy, and many critics have interpreted Martí's plans for an independent Cuba in terms similar to the view held by Richard Butler Gray:

> Did Martí, however, have an intimate knowledge of the governmental system upon which to base concrete suggestions for bringing about an orderly transition from a colonial bureaucracy to a republic? It must be remembered that his only experience with the colonial government was at age sixteen, and was confined to the walls of a rock quarry. . . . Martí was never confronted with the problems of running a governmental organization. By profession he was a journalist. One searches in vain, therefore, to find any concrete proposals for the establishment of governmental institutions once the Spanish bureaucracy had been destroyed.[1]

In short, because so many different administrations since the War of Independence have used Martí as their source of inspiration, it is generally concluded that his writings must necessarily have been of an essentially bland, general nature. In actual fact, a thorough study of his *Obras completas* reveals Martí to be a coherent thinker with clear and most definite priorities for the complete reshaping of Cuba after independence had been won from Spain. Moreover, although Martí refused to support any particular ideology or set of political beliefs, there is a fairly noticeable development in his thought. Therefore, although cut short by his untimely death in 1895, Martí's political thought was evolving very clearly and was moving in an increasingly radical direction.

As to the stimuli which brought about this progression in Martí's ideology, a study of his writings, which include his correspondence and diaries, affirm that he was primarily influenced by the dramatic events of his own life. The steady radicalization of both his political thought and his plans for a liberated Cuba was thus caused not by abstract intellectual influences but rather by the events of his youth and by the many years spent in "Nuestra América" and the United States.

Martí conceived of an independent Cuba in which extensive social, political, and economic changes would occur. There was to be a complete reshaping of the social structure, of political life, and of economic planning. More important, Martí stipulated that no sector of society would be exempt from the proposed reforms.

Probably Martí's most revolutionary plans revolved around the restructuring of social life in the *patria*. The previous colonialist system, which had blatantly discriminated against the native-born Cubans and had given great advantages to the *penisulares,* would be abolished immediately. In its place Martí planned a classless and "colorless" state in which for the first time in Cuban history all citizens would be allowed equal privileges. A determined attempt would be made to provide full employment for all Cuban workers, and all citizens would be able to receive a basic education. In return for the many concrete social advantages that would be available to the people as a whole, Martí hoped to convince his fellow Cubans of the validity of a reinvigorated work ethic, of the essential dignity of honest toil.

In regard to the sweeping political reform planned by Martí for a liberated Cuba, he summoned a totally new appreciation of political life from his fellow Cubans. Supplanting the discrimination of colonial Cuba which excluded the *criollos* from direct participation in the decision-making process, all Cubans not only would be encouraged but also would be expected to play an active role in politics, discussing official policies and suggesting alternatives in an attempt to make the political system work for the people as a whole. Equally important was the creation of the Partido Revolucionario Cubano. The structure and the activities of the party, of which Martí was the *Delegado,* illustrate well the general aspirations of Martí in this regard; his intent was that the PRC would be a microcosm of the general political structure to be instituted in an independent Cuba.

Martí's economic plans, although less developed than his program of social and political reform, nevertheless reveal his determination to ensure that profits from Cuban sugar crops would no longer be siphoned to Spain and the United States but in fact would remain in Cuba to provide the necessary funds so that his planned changes for the social sector could be undertaken. Martí foresaw a slow but steady process of economic growth based principally upon Cuba's plentiful agricultural resources, although he stipulated that there would be some industrialization after the Republic had been firmly established. Trade would be encouraged with as many countries as possible, and in particular with European nations, in order to break commercial dependence on a limited number of trading partners.

Perhaps the most important innovation planned by Martí for the liberated *patria,* and undoubtedly the key to the successful implementation of his specific reforms, was his determination to change the national character of the Cuban people. After convincing his corevolutionaries of the necessity for pride in their distinct *cubanidad* (a tremendous feat in itself considering the three centuries of Spanish domination on the island), Martí planned to inculcate into his fellow Cubans a deep moralistic sense of selflessness, which together with his invigorated work ethic he hoped would lead eventually to the creation of a new revolutionary man, totally dedicated to the well-being of the nation. Indeed, as Andrés Iduarte has observed, "the political thought of Martí, from beginning to end, is a moral sermon."[2]

Thus Martí's plan for a fundamental transformation of Cuban society in essence depended on moral imperatives rather than on any ideological stance. Indeed, for Martí all ideologies were vague abstractions, devoid of any saving grace unless they contributed directly to the well-being of society as whole. What Martí advocated for a liberated Cuba was thus a radical restructuring of the economic, social, and political spheres, based not on ideology but on a moral transformation of what can be termed the human dimension of the *patria.* As Martí himself noted: "It is to the substance of these matters that we are going, more than to the forms. . . . It is a case of changing a nation's soul, their entire way of thinking and acting, and not just their external clothes" (V, 368–69).

Therefore, though Martí has been used as a source of inspiration and justification by the many differing regimes of independent Cuba, Martí himself was extremely specific in his objectives for the liberated *patria.* Rather than the bland humanitarian that he has been so often depicted as, the writings of Martí provide ample proof that he possessed a comprehensive blueprint for the social, political, and economic development of an independent Republic. Moreover, such plans as he aspired to introduce in Cuba show clearly that Martí sought to provide new and necessarily revolutionary solutions to the many ills of the *patria:* minor amendments were thus unacceptable to him.

This study has attempted to clarify the undisputable fundamentals of José Martí's sociopolitical thought as seen in his aspirations for the liberated *patria* and further to demonstrate the uniqueness of José Martí as a man and as an intellectual. Not only was Martí one of the most brilliant literary figures in the history of Latin American letters, but also—as the relevance of his observations, more than a century later shows—he was one of the most underrated political thinkers of modern times.

Chronology

1853	January 28	José Julián Martí y Pérez is born in Havana.
1857	January	Taken to Spain by his parents.
1859		Returns to Cuba.
1862	October	Travels to Hanábana with his father. There he is shocked by the treatment of black slaves on the plantations.
1865	March 19	Enters the Municipal School for Boys, directed by Rafael María de Mendive.
1869	January 19	Publishes *El Diablo Cojuelo,* his first political work.
	January 22	Disturbance in the Villanueva Theatre, which results in Mendive's arrest.
	January 23	Publishes *La Patria Libre,* which included his drama *Abdala.*
	October 4	The *voluntarios,* after bursting into Fermín Valdés Domínguez's house, discover an incriminating letter, of which Martí is one of the coauthors.
	October 21	Accused of treason, Martí is imprisoned in the Havana prison.
1870	March 4	Sentenced by a military court to six years in a political prison.
	April 4	Begins to serve his term.
1871	January 15	His sentence having been commuted to one of exile, Martí is deported to Spain.
	January	Publishes *El Presidio Político en Cuba,* an account of his experiences in political prison in Cuba, shortly after arriving in Madrid.
	May	Matriculates at the University of Madrid.

1873	February	Publishes *La República Española ante la Revolución Cubana,* a condemnation of Spanish interest in Cuba.
	May	Transfers to the University of Zaragoza.
1874	January	With the fall of the Spanish Republic, Martí speaks at a public meeting organized on behalf of the widows and orphans of the fallen republicans of Zaragoza.
	June 25, 27	Obtains title of *bachiller.*
	June 30	Graduates as *licenciado en derecho civil y canónico.*
	October 24	Graduates as *licenciado en filosofía y letras.*
	December	Leaves Spain for Paris.
1875	January	Travels to Mexico.
	March 7	Publication of his first work for the *Revista Universal.*
1876	January	Represents Chihuahua workers at labor congress.
	November	President Lerdo (whom Martí supports) flees the capital as Porfirio Díaz enters.
	December 29	Leaves for Veracruz, where he boards a ship for Havana.
1877	January 6	Arrives in Havana, using second Christian name and surname: Julián Pérez.
	February 24	Leaves again for Veracruz, and from there he travels to Guatemala.
	May 29	Appointed professor of modern languages and philosophy at Guatemala's Central School.
	December	Returns to Mexico, where he marries Carmen Zayas Bazán.
1878	January	Returns to Guatemala.
	April 6	Resigns his position at the school after President Barrios unjustly dismissed the director, a fellow Cuban named Izaguirre.
	September	Returns to Havana, where he applies for permission to practice law. His petition is denied.
1879	April 21	Dramatic speech at a banquet in honor of the journalist Adolfo Márquez Sterling, at which he states his total opposition to any "autonomist" plans suggested by Spain.
	September 17	Arrested for "conspiring" and (on the 25th) is deported to Spain for the second time.

	December	Leaves Spain for France, and from there he travels to the United States.
1880	January 3	Arrives in New York.
	January 24	Patriotic lecture given by him to the Cuban exiles living in New York.
	May 13	Proclamation of the Revolutionary Committee of New York (of which he is interim president) to celebrate the arrival in Cuba of the liberating forces led by General Calixto García, and the insurrection known as the "Guerra chiquita." Begins his newspaper contributions to *The Hour* of New York.
1881	March	Arrives in Venezuela, where he teaches.
	July	As a result of a laudatory article on the Venezuelan statesman Cecilio Acosta, he angers President Guzmán Blanco, who expected a similar article to be written about his own accomplishments. Martí decides to return to New York.
	August 20	From New York, he begins to contribute articles to the Caracas newspaper, *La Opinión Nacional.*
1882	April	Publishes *Ismaelillo,* a book of verse dedicated to his young son.
	July 15	Sends his first correspondence to the Buenos Aires newspaper *La Nación.* Completes his *Versos libres,* published posthumously in 1919.
1883		Becomes editor of the New York journal, *La América.*
1884	October 20	Writes to Máximo Gómez announcing his withdrawal from the revolutionary plans being formulated by Gómez and Maceo.
1887	April 16	Named Consul of Uruguay in New York.
1889	March 21	The *Evening Post* publishes his letter "Vindication of Cuba."
	April	Submits his first article to *La Opinión Pública* of Uruguay.
	July	Publishes the first edition of *La Edad de Oro,* a children's monthly magazine.
	December 19	Addresses the delegates of the Inter-American Conference in a meeting organized by the

		Sociedad Literaria Hispano-Americana de Nueva York.
1890	January 22	Inauguration of La Liga, an educational center in New York designed to provide black Cuban workers with the opportunity for a rudimentary education. He is one of the teachers in this organization.
	June 16	Appointed Consul of Argentina in New York.
	July 24	Appointed Consul of Paraguay in New York.
	December 24	Appointed representative of Uruguay to the International Monetary Conference in Washington, D.C.
	December	Elected President of the Sociedad Literaria Hispano-Americana de Nueva York.
1891	March 30	Reads his report at the International Monetary Conference in Washington.
	May 20	His last report to *La Nación* is published.
	June	His collection of poetry, *Versos sencillos,* is published.
	October 11	Resigns his consular posts.
	October 30	Resigns as President of the Sociedad Literaria Hispano-Americana de Nueva York.
	November 27	Invited by the Ignacio Agramonte Club of Tampa, he arrives in Florida and addresses the Cuban workers employed in Tampa.
	November 28	Approval of the *Resoluciones adoptadas por la emigración cubana de Tampa,* dictated by him. Returns to New York.
	December 25	Arrives in Key West, after being invited by a local group of Cuban workers.
1892	January 5	In a meeting with the presidents of the various groups of Cuban exiles, he drafts the *Bases y Estatutos Secretos del Partido Revolucionario Cubano,* which are accepted.
	March 14	Publication of the first issue of *Patria,* the organ of revolutionary activities, which he edits.
	April 8	Elected *Delegado* of the Partido Revolucionario Cubano.
	September	Travels to Santo Domingo where on the 11th he meets Máximo Gómez.
	September 24	Arrives in Haiti.
	October 13	Leaves for New York after visiting Jamaica.
	November 7	Leaves for Tampa and Key West. During his

		stay in Tampa, an attempt is made to poison him but he recovers.
1893	Feb./March	Fund-raising trip through Florida.
	June 3	Arrives in Santo Domingo for the second time, where he confers with Máximo Gómez. Continues to Costa Rica.
	September	A further fund-raising trip to Florida.
	December	Travels to Philadelphia, Key West, and Tampa, explaining the need for a well-planned attack to liberate Cuba.
1894	January 2	Helps to solve a conflict among the *tabaqueros* in Key West arising after Spanish workers were brought from Cuba to break a strike by Cuban tobacco workers.
	April 8	Máximo Gómez arrives in New York to confer with him.
	April 10	Reelected as *Delegado.*
1894	May	Travels to various Cuban centers in the United States (Philadelphia, New York, Key West, Jacksonville, Tampa, and other settlements in Florida) accompanied by Máximo Gómez's son.
	June	Travels through Costa Rica, Panama, and Jamaica, returning to New York in July.
	July	Travels to Mexico, and from there he returns to New York in August.
	December	Plans are perfected to invade Cuba with three well-equipped ships.
1895	January 10	Betrayal and failure of invasion program known as Fernandina Plan.
	January 29	Order authorizing revolution in Cuba is signed in New York by leaders of Cuban exile groups.
	January 31	Leaves for Santo Domingo.
	February 24	The beginning of the War of Independence following the uprising at Baire.
	March 25	Together with Máximo Gómez, he composes the Manifiesto de Montecristi.
	April 11	Sets foot once again on Cuban soil.
	April 16	Proclaimed Major-General by Gómez.
	May 5	Interview at La Mejorana with Generals Maceo and Gómez, at which the general strategy for the war is determined.
	May 19	Killed in action at Dos Ríos.

Notes

Preface

1. Hence the claim by Carlos Alberto Montaner: "For us Cubans, everything can be debated, everything can be divided into opposing views, except the figure of Martí. This complete and absolute subordination to Martí is explained by the phenomenon already outlined: to deny the validity of Martí is tantamount to renouncing an ingredient—possibly the most basic one—of the Cuban identity." *El pensamiento de Martí* (Madrid: Plaza Mayor Ediciones, 1971), p. 3.

2. All quotations from Martí's *Obras Completas* are from the edition published in Havana by the Editorial Nacional de Cuba, between 1963 and 1966. The numbers of both the volume and page are indicated in the text by Roman and Arabic numerals respectively.

3. Juan Marinello, "El caso literario de José Martí," *Once ensayos martianos* (La Habana: Comisión Nacional Cubana de la UNESCO, 1964), p. 74.

Chapter 1

1. Montaner, p. 4. This introductory chapter is based on a recent paper, "From Apóstol to Revolutionary: The Changing Image of José Martí," read at the annual conference of the British Society for Latin American Studies in April, 1977. Expanded versions of this paper have since appeared in *Norte/Sur* and the *Latin American Research Review.*

2. Andrés Valdespino, "Imagen de Martí en las letras cubanas," *Revista Cubana* 1 (July–Dec. 1968):307.

3. Salvador García Agüero, "Secuencias martianas," *Revista Bimestre Cubana* 37 (1936):207.

4. Miguel L. de Landaluce, "Vía crucis de Martí," *Archivo José Martí* 3 (Jan.–Dec. 1942):143–58.

5. Federico de Córdova, "Martí, demócrata," *Universidad de La Habana* 43/45 (July–Dec. 1942):178–96.

6. José Manuel Cortina, "Apología de José Martí," *Archivo José Martí* 6 (Jan.–Dec. 1952):94.

7. Rufino Blanco Fombona, "José Martí," *Archivo José Martí* 6 (Jan.–Dec. 1952):130.

8. Félix Matos Bernier, "José Martí," *Archivo José Martí* 6 (Jan.–Dec. 1952):171. Richard Butler Gray also offers an interesting list of religious terms used to describe Martí, among which are the expressions "Captain of Archangels," "Redeemer," "The Second Son of God," "The Evangel of Tenderness," "The American Christ," "Jesus Martí," and "Martí the Saviour." *José Martí: Cuban Patriot* (Gainesville: University of Florida Press, 1962), p. 133.

9. Néstor Carbonell y Rivero, *Martí, carne y espíritu* (La Habana: Seoane, Fernández y Cía., 1951–52); Andrés Iduarte, *Martí, escritor* (México: Cuadernos Americanos, 1945); Raimundo Lazo, "La personalidad y el mensaje de José Martí," *Pensamiento y acción de José Martí,* ed. Departamento de Extensión y Relaciones Culturales (Santiago, Cuba: Universidad de Oriente, 1953), pp. 31–48; Félix Lizaso, *Proyección humana de Martí* (Buenos Aires: Editorial Raigal, 1953), and *Martí, Martyr of Cuban Independence,* trans. Esther Elise Shuler (Albuquerque: University of New Mexico, 1953); Jorge Mañach, *Martí el apóstol* (Madrid: Espasa Calpe, 1933); Manuel Isidro Méndez, *Martí, estudio crítico-biográfico* (La Habana: P. Fernández y Cía., 1941).

10. Ezequiel Martínez Estrada, *Martí revolucionario* (La Habana: Casa de las Américas, 1967), p. 161.

11. Aquiles Nazoa, *Cuba: de Martí a Fidel Castro* (Caracas: Ediciones Populares del Pensamiento Vivo, 1961), p. 9.

12. Antonio Martínez Bello, *Ideas sociales y económicas de José Martí* (La Habana: La Verónica, 1940), p. 128.

13. Emeterio S. Santovenia y Echaide, *Política de Martí* (La Habana: Seoane, Fernández y Cía., 1943), pp. 61–63.

14. Carlos González Palacios, "Valoración de Martí," *Archivo José Martí* 6 (Jan.–Dec. 1952):28.

15. Félix Lizaso, *Martí, Espíritu de la guerra justa* (La Habana: Editorial Ucar, García y Cía., 1944), p. 46. Emeterio S. Santovenia y Echaide also tones down Martí's reactions to U.S. involvement in "Nuestra América," while blatantly suggesting that Martí both praised and defended the United States before the delegates at the First Inter-American Conference: "The United States had become a country of admirable institutions

and of men who were raising the world to new levels of advancement. Before a great assembly of delegates from nearly all parts of America, Martí spoke eloquently of the greatness of the country in which he lived, and which had given him the hope of freeing his own country." *Lincoln in Martí: A Cuban View of Abraham Lincoln* (Chapel Hill: University of North Carolina Press, 1953), p. 73.

16. Federico de Córdova, "Martí idealista," *Universidad de La Habana* 49 (Jan.–June 1945):23.

17. José A. Giralt, "Martí, apóstol del panamericanismo," *Bohemia,* 29 January 1928, p. 29.

18. A. Curtis Wilgus and Karna S. Wilgus, "Las crónicas de José Martí sobre la Primera Conferencia Internacional Americana celebrada en Washington," *Memoria del congreso de escritores martianos (feb. 20 a 27 de 1953)* (La Habana: Publicaciones de la Comisión Nacional Organizadora de los Actos y Ediciones del Centenario y del Monumento a Martí, 1953), p. 319.

19. Manuel Pedro González, "Aspectos inexplorados en la obra de José Martí," *Bohemia,* 18 July 1969, p. 5.

20. Duvon C. Corbitt, "Historical Publications of the Martí Centennial," *Hispanic American Historical Review* 34 (Aug. 1954):402.

21. See *The Havana Post,* 28 January 1953, p. 13.

22. From the title of a recent article by Blas Roca, "José Martí, revolucionario radical de su tiempo," *Casa de las Améicas* 13 (Jan.–Feb. 1973): 10–21.

23. Hernando D'Aquino, *Sinfonía martiana (Vida y pasión)* (Miami: Ediciones Universal, 1971), p. 9.

24. Ibid., p. 19.

25. Montaner, p. 20.

26. Directorio Magisterial Revolucionario (en el exilio), *Martí y los norteamericanos en su propia palabra* (Miami: Its Ediciones, 1965), pp. 8–9.

27. Rafael Esténger, p. 8.

28. Manuel Pedro González, "Prefacio," *Indagaciones martianas* (La Habana: Universidad Central de Las Villas, 1961), p. 16.

29. Juan Marinello, "El pensamiento de Martí y nuestra revolución socialista," *Cuba Socialista* 2 (Jan. 1962):19.

30. Montaner, p. 20.

31. Roberto Fernández Retamar, "Introducción a Martí," *José Martí: Cuba, Nuestra América, los Estados Unidos,* Fernández Retamar, ed. (México: Siglo Veintiuno Editores, 1973), p. xiii.

32. Carlos Rafael Rodríguez, "José Martí, contemporáneo y compañero," *Universidad de La Habana* 196/197 (1972):15. It is interesting to compare this revolutionary approach with an example of the traditional

interpretation of Martí as viewed by the former president of Cuba, Carlos Prío Socarrás. Writing in 1946, Prío described the way in which he had been inspired by the *Apóstol:* "I too, José Martí, have felt your presence, and in the harshest and most bitter days of the struggle which you dreamed of for Cuba and which liberated our generation, I have seen you watching over my dreams and caressing the little good that there was in me. I learned in time that I could not imitate you, because it is not possible to compare oneself with you. But I did aspire to win for myself the approving silence of your august shadow." "Martí, arquetipo de lo cubano," *Archivo José Martí* 6 (Jan.–Dec. 1946):391.

33. Armando Hart Dávalos, "Discurso de inauguración," *Anuario del Centro de Estudios Martianos* 3 (1980):72. Of particular note in this issue are articles by Paul Estrade, José Cantón Navarro, Valentina I. Shískina, and Philip S. Foner.

34. See also Roberto Fernández Retamar, *Introducción a José Martí* (La Habana: Casa de las Américas, 1978) and *Siete enfoques marxistas sobre José Martí,* ed. Centro de Estudios Martianos (La Habana: Centro de Estudios Martianos, 1978).

35. Cited by Paul Estrade in "Martí, Betances, Rizal, Lineamientos y prácticas de la revolución democrática anticolonial," *Anuario del Centro de Estudios Martianos* 3 (1980):177.

36. Fidel Castro, *La Historia me absolverá* (La Habana: Casa de las Américas, 1974), n.p.

37. Gray, p. 35.

38. Manuel Pedro González, "Aspectos inexplorados en la obra de José Martí," p. 5.

39. This apt description of Martí by the Chilean poetess Gabriela Mistral was taken from the autograph album of a young Cuban girl. The actual inscription was: "Don't forget, if you have a brother or a son, that the purest man of our Latin race, José Martí, lived in your country. Try to form your little friend in the image of Martí, at the same time a fighter and as pure as an archangel." Cited by Gaspar Mortillaro is his article, "José Martí, el hombre más puro de la raza," *Archivo José Martí* 1 (July–Aug. 1940):57.

Chapter 2

1. Pedro N. González Veranes, *¿Quién fue el progenitor espiritual de Martí?* (La Habana: Editorial Luz-Hilo, 1942), p. 11.

2. Introjection is defined as "an unconscious mechanism by which the external world and its objects may be incorporated into the individual. Thus the child identifies with loved objects, its parents for instance,

by identifying with them, introjecting their qualities into its own mental life." *Encyclopedia of Psychiatry for General Practitioners,* Denis Leigh, C.M.B. Pare, and John Marks, eds. (Vaudreuil, Québec: Hoffman La Roche, 1972), 22:230. See also the study by Ephraim Rosen and Ian Gregory, *Abnormal Psychology* (Philadelphia: W.B. Saunders, 1966), p. 72.

3. William D. Isaacson, "What Motivated Martí's Life," *The Havana Post,* 28 January 1953, p. 13.

4. For more detailed information on the failure of this *Reformista* movement, see Julio Le Riverend, "Martí en la revolución de 1868," *Casa de las Américas* 9 (Sept.–Oct. 1968):97–99. Hugh Thomas also comments on this duplicity of the Spanish government that alienated many Cubans who would otherwise have supported the official Spanish position: "The commission adjourned in April 1867, having apparently accomplished an immense amount of work. Every demand of the representatives had been discussed. . . . The Cubans were led to believe that action would follow. It did not. Narváez had never intended the commission to be more than a talking-shop. By this time a new and vigorous reactionary captain-general, Lersundi, had established himself in Cuba. . . . The Reform Movement of moderate men and rich planters cracked. They no longer had any solutions to offer. Back in Cuba it appeared, ironically, that at least one of the proposals of the Reformers was going to be fulfilled. On 12 February 1867, Captain-General Lersundi imposed a new tax of 6% on income, giving himself the alternative of a 12% tax 'if necessary.' This appeared to be a final insult, since the Reformers had proposed this instead of, and not as well as, the old customs and other taxes." *Cuba, or The Pursuit of Freedom* (London: Eyre and Spottiswoode, 1971), p. 240.

5. The center for this revolutionary activity was in eastern Cuba, particularly in Oriente province, where the leading protagonists were low-income farmers who deeply resented the increased taxation recently imposed by Spain. The war lasted for some ten years, inflicting heavy casualties on both sides, and eventually ending in a virtual stalemate. For more detailed information see Thomas, pp. 245–70.

6. "A new economic decline made the reforms more necessary. When these were not introduced, a sector of the landowners simply did not possess adequate means to ride out the storm that was developing in the innards of the slave society. . . . The entire island began to be shaken by this development. Havana was no exception. . . . When the cry of independence was issued at La Demajagua (the estate of Cépedes) on October 10, the capital was stirred." Julio Le Reverend, "Martí en la revolución de 1868," pp. 98–99.

7. Pánfilo D. Camacho, "Martí: una vida en perenne angustia," *Archivo José Martí* 4 (Jan.–July 1948):136.

8. Figures quoted by Thomas, pp. 247 and 249 respectively.

9. The letter, dated October 4, 1869, was addressed to Carlos de Castro y Castro: "Compañero, Have you ever dreamed of receiving the glory of traitors? Do you know how, in antiquity, treachery was punished? We hope that a disciple of Sr. Rafael María de Mendive won't leave this letter unanswered. Fermín Valdés Domíninguez and José Martí (I, 39).

10. Ezequiel Martínez Estrada, p. 75.

11. Andrés Iduarte, p. 23.

12. Manuel Pedro González, *Indagaciones martianas*, p. 57.

13. For the sake of clarity liberties have been taken with the footnotes. For specific references in these works, see the recent article, "El aprendizaje de Martí revolucionario: une aproximación psico-histórico, *Cuadernos Americanos*, año XXXVI, vol. CCX, no. 1 (enero–febrero 1977), p. 109n2.

14. Martínez Bello, p. 28.

15. Iduarte, p. 29.

16. Julio Le Riverend, "Teoría martiana del partido político," *Vida y pensamiento de Martí. Homenaje de la ciudad de La Habana en el cincuentenario de la fundación del Partido Revolucionario Cubano. 1892–1942* (La Habana: Colección Histórica Cubana y Americana, 1942), 1:88.

Chapter 3

1. Julio Le Riverend, "Martí: ética y acción revolucionaria," *Casa de las Américas* 10 (Nov.–Dec. 1969):40. Ezequiel Martínez Estrada arrives at similar conclusions: "When Martí goes to Spain, he has nothing to learn—only to assimilate. He already possesses the keys and the policies to follow and nothing can turn him aside from them." p. 19.

2. I therefore do not accept the validity of the famous claim made by Antonio Martínez Bello that the radicalization of Martí was initiated by his observations on the lack of justice received by the defendants in the Haymarket trial (pp. 159–60). In a more recent article, Jaime Díaz Rozzotto claims that it was the coup of Porfirio Díaz that was in fact responsible for this radicalization: "From this point on the Cuban Apostle, stumbling here, hitting on other solutions there, comes to represent the bridge which goes from the moribund liberalism (of the 19th century) to the anti-imperialist revolution of the 20th century." "Nuestra América, la plena libertad y José Martí," *Cuadernos Americanos* 34 (May–June 1975):85.

3. This is despite the view expressed by Pedro Pablo Rodríguez in his article, "La idea de la liberación nacional en José Martí," in which he grossly oversimplifies the development of Martí's thought by attempting to show the three basic stages into which it can be "divided," namely 1871–1884; 1884–1889; and 1890–1895, in *Anuario martiano* 4 (1972):179.

4. Julio Le Riverend, "Martí en la revolución de 1868," pp. 109–10.

5. Cintio Vitier, "Imagen de Martí," *Anuario martiano* 3 (1971):238.

6. Andrés Iduarte, "América," *Revista Hispánica Moderna* 18 (Jan.–Dec. 1952):88.

7. Lest it be deduced that Martí was guilty of harboring any base "anti-yanqui" feelings per se, one has only to study his *many* reports full of admiration for the founding fathers of the United States. In 1885, for instance, he wrote: "I would sculpt in porphyry statues of the marvelous individuals who forged the Constitution of the United States of America . . . and every few years I would establish a week of national pilgrimage" (X, 183). Some five years later, Martí expressed his profound displeasure with the direction being taken by political life in the United States, while declaring his undying faith in the political judgement of Abraham Lincoln: "From being a redeeming party (as it was at the outset), responsible for an admirable revolt, a dissident republican notes, the party has now become a mere government machine. . . . It will govern with the support of the rich or the ignorant. It will study their desires and will flatter them; and wherever people harbor bitterness, it will promise them satisfaction" (XII, 403). Later he concludes, "If Lincoln were alive today, he would not support either his successors or the indecisive, hybrid Democrats, but rather would agree with those who, preparing a better way, hear with alarm and amazement that a political party elected by a popular majority now proclaims this typical, dread statement: 'This country wants results and is not concerned with how these are achieved'" (XII, 405).

8. "*The Tribune* states: 'The time has come to make our influence felt in Latin America; the applause given by the delegates to Blaine's speech was a veritable ovation.' *The Star* claims: 'The Inter-American Congress belongs to Blaine.' And *The Sun* says: 'These South Americans who oppose Blaine have sold out to the English'" (VI, 41). In his next report to *La Nación*, Martí quoted the *Sun* again, showing his total opposition to the hard-line tactics supported by the North American press: "*The Sun* of New York stated it yesterday: 'Whoever does not want to be flattered by the Juggernaut had better jump on board.' Instead, it would be better to block the vehicle's path" (VI, 54).

9. *Minutes of the International Monetary Commission*, Washington, 1891, pp. 49–50.

10. Alberto Andino, *Martí y España* (Madrid: Colección Plaza Mayor, 1973), p. 151.

11. While commenting on the moralistic basis of Martí's thought, Manuel Pedro González raises an interesting point: "If the situation had been reversed and the United States had been the weak nation and Cuba

or Latin America the oppressing power, he would have struggled with equal fervor and heroism in defense of the United States against the abusive country. Justice and freedom were indivisible for him. In spite of his intense patriotism, he would never have endorsed the doctrine of 'my country, right or wrong.' Such a creed would have been repugnant and barbarous to him, proper only to primitive tribes." *José Martí, Epic Chronicler of the United States in the Eighties* (Chapel Hill: University of North Carolina Press, 1953), p. 21.

12. Roberto Fernández Retamar, "Introducción," *Martí* (Montevideo: Biblioteca de Marcha, 1970), p. 32.

13. Given the fundamental importance of this letter to Mercado, it seems advisable to reproduce the oft-quoted, dramatic beginning: "My very dear brother . . . every day now I am in danger of giving my life for my country and my duty (I understand this and I have the courage to fulfill it) to prevent in time—with the independence of Cuba—the United States from spreading throughout the Antilles, and with this added strength falling then on our Latin American countries. All that I have done until today, and all that I will continue to do, is toward this goal. My work has had to be silent, carried out indirectly, because often in order to realize these objectives they have to be hidden. Indeed, proclaiming these goals would bring about difficulties too severe for us to realize our goals.

"The same obligations, both personal and public of our peoples . . . who are most vitally interested in preventing Cuba from becoming (through its annexation by the North American imperialists and the Spanish) a path to Latin America, would have prevented their visible acceptance of and obvious support for this sacrifice, which is done for the common good of our people. Our objective is to close off this route, which we are stemming with our blood, preventing the annexation of the nations of our America by the unruly and brutal North which despises them.

"I lived in the monster and know well its entrails—and my sling is that of David" (IV, 167–68).

Chapter 4

1. Martí was thus convinced that, apart from being essentially immoral, the Spanish domination of Cuba was also totally anachronistic. He therefore wanted the island to "move with the times," in an attempt to fight for the same independence already won by her sister republics more than sixty years earlier. Speaking to a meeting of Cuban exiles in New York on January 31, 1893, he scorned those Cuban Autonomists who

had spoken at the last session of the *Cortes* in Spain and concluded ironically: "Because in this grandiose Latin America, like men wearing diapers, we are still talking about the Spanish Parliament!" (IV, 313).

2. In 1885, Martí again referred to this duty, after criticizing General Grant for his lack of interest or participation in earlier presidential elections: "In a republic, a person who does not vote is like a soldier who deserts from the army" (XIII, 88).

3. As early as 1881 Martí had predicted the growing menace afforded by what he termed the "political aristocracy" in the United States, which he saw as steadily destroying the noble foundation of the land of Lincoln: "A political aristocracy has been born from that financial aristocracy and controls the newspapers, wins in the elections, and usually has its way in congress" (IX, 108). Obviously this was totally unacceptable to Martí, and it is evident that in the liberated republic he would have attempted to curtail the power and influence of such an "aristocracia."

4. Indicative of this redoubling of Martí's efforts to organize the resistance of the Cuban exiles was the amount of traveling undertaken by him in the United States prior to and subsequent to 1891. Martínez Estrada offers a detailed list of all of Martí's travels, in which the period from 1882 to 1890 is characterized by the observation "It is not known if he traveled." Afterward, between Martí's visit to Tampa in November of 1891 and his arrival in Cuba on April 11, 1895, there are more than 50 journeys through the United States and parts of Latin America. Ezequiel Martínez Estrada, pp. 225–28.

5. Leonardo Griñán Peralta, *Martí, líder político* (La Habana: Instituto Cubano del Libro, 1970), p. 89.

6. In regard to the widely ranging political tendencies of the various groups of Cuban exiles that Martí was attempting to unite, it is only necessary to consider the variety of ideological beliefs held by many of the leading figures of the PRC. They range from regular republicans like Varona, through a large gathering of anarchists, to the socialist group comprising Diego Vicente Tejera and Fermín Valdés Domínguez and other radicals, the best known of which was Carlos Baliño, later one of the main founders of the Communist Party of Cuba. With reference to this extremely wide background of ideological persuasions Blas Roca has noted well the importance of Martí as a unifying factor in the PRC: "In the Partido Revolucionario Cubano, Martí brings together—in a veritable front of national unity—clubs of the most diverse ideology and social composition: from the Enrique Roig Club, in which mainly socialists were gathered, to the Mercedes Varona, composed of women. In the Partido Revolucionario Cubano, Martí joins together people who merely desired political independence from Spain with the radical revolutionaries

who saw in independence the necessary stage for further social conquest, the rich and the poor, black and white, the new forces of revolution and the representation of the 1868 war." "José Martí: revolucionario radical de su tiempo," *Casa de las Américas* 13 (Jan.–Feb. 1973):15.

7. With regard to this necessary "decoro," an illustrative example of Martí's determination that this should be implemented in the Republic is his refusal of a large sum of money, contributed to the liberation cause by a Cuban highway robber. Martí, as Jorge Ibarra and many other *martianos* have shown, did not accept the contribution, despite a pressing need for funds, claiming instead that a liberated Cuba would have to spring from clean roots. Indeed, as Ibarra accurately claims: "All this causes us to think necessarily that Martí did not conceive the party only as an instrument to liberate Cuba from Spanish domination but rather as a means of radically transforming Cuba." "José Martí y el Partido Revolucionario Cubano," *Ideología mambisa* (La Habana: Instituto Cubano del Libro, 1972), p. 172.

8. "A delegate (*delegado*), or representative, and not the president, was what Martí wanted to be; because although it might be true that every leader acts according to his own aspirations . . . it is always good for his followers to see him convinced that he is working because of being delegated or given a mandate by them." Griñán Peralta, p. 85.

9. Speaking in 1896, Martí's corevolutionary, Enrique José Varona, explained the achievement of Martí in uniting the Cuban exiles, given the national psyche at that time: "To rebel always appears easy. To rebel, however, at the time and under the conditions that Martí did so was extraordinary. Cuba lay defenseless, bled white, following two major rebellions. If anything seemed to float in the air, it was a desire for peace, to heal the wounds, and recuperate. . . . The slogan at the time was the need for reconstruction." "Martí y su obra política," reprinted in *Casa de las Américas* 13 (Jan.–Feb. 1973):93.

10. Writing about this moralistic form of government, Alfonso Bernal del Riesgo terms Martí an "ethocrat": "Martí departs from his speeches and his work and goes directly, like an arrow, against the colonial vices that remain in the Republic. And this takes place naturally, without there being any need to convert Martí to any modern political doctrine. He was an 'ethocrat'—from *ethos*, character, morality, and from *cratos*, authority, government." "Estampa psíquica de Martí," *Revista Bimestre Cubana* 41 (1968):241.

Chapter 5

1. It is interesting to note Martí's views on what he considered the absolute duty of all honorable men to fight for their self-respect, their

sense of *dignidad,* whenever they saw liberty threatened: "Every just, honorable man will fight for liberty wherever he sees it offended, because that is the same as fighting for one's integrity. He who sees liberty offended and does not struggle in its defense, or who helps those who offend it—he is not a complete man" (IV, 391). In the context of contemporary Cuba, Martí states that this duty clearly revolved around replacing the immoral and uncaring administration of Spain with a new, moral and necessarily Cuban form of government.

2. In a similar vein is an entry made in a personal notebook of Martí in 1894: ". . . When we drove out the conquerors [Spain], was what they left worth more than the Indian culture to be found here before their arrival? In poetry, what colonial verses are worth the same as the only ode that we know to be of Netzahualcoyotl? In architecture, what church wall or famous frontispiece—including even the baroque Sacristy of Mexico City or the Governor's house—is worth the same as a wall of Mitla?" (XXI, 375).

3. *International Encyclopedia of the Social Sciences,* ed. David L. Sills (New York: Cromwell, Collier and Macmillan, 1968), 14:551.

4. In short, what Martí wanted to inculcate into his compatriots was the same highly moralistic consciousness that he already possessed. As he had already discovered, Martí essentially wanted his fellow Cubans to realize: "The human race really has only one cheek; whenever a man receives a blow on his check, all other men receive it too" (X, 288).

5. Julio Le Riverend, "Martí, ética y acción revolucionaria," p. 48.

6. Willy de Blanck, "José Martí, el gran político cubano que se adelantó a su tiempo," *Archivo José Martí* 5 (July–Dec. 1950):228.

7. Jorge Mañach states: "Although political independence was for Martí that indispensable objective, the word 'independence' is seen very rarely in his writings. This was of a lesser importance, really an implied value in the broader concept of freedom." *El pensamiento político y social de Martí* (La Habana: Edición Oficial del Senado, 1941), p. 17.

8. "Without air, the earth dies. Without freedom, as without essential air itself, nothing can live . . . like bone to the human body, the axle to a wheel, the wing to a bird, and air to that wing, so is liberty the essence of life. All that is done without liberty is imperfect, while conversely, the more that one enjoys it, the more one lives surrounded by fruits and flowers. It is the inescapable essence of all useful work" (IX, 451).

9. *Encyclopedia of Philosophy,* ed. Paul Edwards (New York: Cromwell, Collier and MacMillan, 1967), 3:223.

10. Julio Le Riverend, "Martí y Lenin," *Política Internacional* 8 (1970):62.

11. Jaime Suchlicki, studying this intent of Martí to build such a model society, is correct when he affirms: "Martí can only be understood if we think of him as a student of social problems, rather than a purely political

doctrinaire." "The Political Ideology of José Martí," *Caribbean Studies* 6 (Apr. 1966):31.

12. Manuel Pedro González, *Indagaciones martianas,* p. 53.

13. Carlos Alberto Montaner, p. 7.

14. Blanca Z. de Baralt, *El Martí que yo conocí* (New York: Las Américas, 1968), p. 41.

15. Julio Le Riverend, "Martí, ética y acción revolucionaria," p. 48. Le Riverend concludes that in many ways Martí can indeed be regarded as a true humanist: "He is a humanist in the sense that he has faith in his fellow human beings, he believes them capable of overcoming their own limits and finally being guided for their own good, acquiring an even greater moral awareness, which will then be used as a basis to transform reality."

Chapter 6

1. This quotation was taken from an inscription in an Cuban girl's autograph album written by the Chilean poetess Gabriela Mistral. The actual contents of the message were: "Don't forget, if you have a brother or a son, that the purest man of our Latin race, José Martí, lived in your country. Try to form your little friend in the image of Martí, at the same time a fighter and as pure as an archangel." Cited by Gaspar Mortillaro in his article, "José Martí, el hombre más puro de la raza," *Archivo José Martí* 1 (July–Aug. 1940):57.

2. Emma Lazarus, "The New Colossus" (Inscription for the Statue of Liberty, New York Harbor). For a light, but thorough, introduction to the plight of immigrants to the United States at this time, see chapter 9 of Alistair Cook's *America* (New York: Alfred A. Knopf, 1973), pp. 273–301.

3. "In the United States a new humanity is now coming to the boil. What has been blended together during this century is now beginning to ferment: men now speak the languages of Babel . . . the photographer is now eliminating the unequal, vague factions, until finally they merge into the energetic, dominant type—as we now see in this impressive batch—one that will not rise, perhaps because of a lack of the right kind of yeast, namely kindness. Races, creeds, and languages now become blurred together, mysterious blue eyes and threatening black eyes blend, the Scottish plaid and the Italian kerchief, all stir together. The false, tyrannical differences which have kept men apart are now undone, they turn to liquid and then evaporate. In their place one sees built up and refined the essence of justice which they all share" (XI, 172).

4. Jesús Sabourín, "Martí, raza y humanidad," *Casa de las Américas* 13 (Jan.–Feb. 1973):68. In this regard see also Juan Marinello, "Martí, maes-

tro de unidad," *Actualidad de Martí* (La Habana: Editorial Páginas, 1943), p. 9.

5. Given this ambivalent attitude of Martí, it is unfortunate that many critics, of differing ideological beliefs, have seen fit to highlight only those parts of Martí's report that supported their particular viewpoint. Typical of this abuse is Carlos Márquez Sterling's blanket statement that "Martí found, in the prose of the writer of *Capital,* bitterness and resentment" (p. 179). His conclusion, "Marx, the apostle of hate. Martí, the apostle of love" (p. 406), and in particular his comments on the following page, reveal deep personal political frustrations of which he seeks to rid himself by exploiting his knowledge of Martí.

6. Manuel Pedro González and Ivan A. Schulman, *José Martí, esquema ideológico* (México: Publicaciones de la Editorial Cultura, 1961), p. 385. Given Martí's determination to afford the same fundamental privileges to all Cubans, Jorge Mañach's earlier view of "the diffuse aristocratic spirit of an artist" in Martí is completely mistaken. Mañach (who even misquotes Martí by substituting "world" for "earth" in one of Martí's most widely known phrases) claims: "In the conflict of human fortunes, his natural tenderness makes him take the side of 'the poor of the world,' opposing the outstanding social injustices of his day. But there is also in him the diffuse aristocratic spirit of an artist, and above all else a keen observation of the varied nature of the human race—both of which struggle against the egalitarian spirit of a democrat." *El pensamiento político y social de Martí,* p. 21.

7. José Cantón Navarro is thus correct when he states: "We will be told that Martí could see how indispensable was the union of all Cubans, first to obtain the nation's independence from Spain, and then to protect that independence from the activities of the United States. . . . All that is, in our opinion, completely correct. We do not believe, however, that Martí's ideas concerning the collaboration of all social classes to develop the republic were solely a question of tactics. We believe that he truly aspired to promote a basic equilibrium in Cuban society, one that would be brought about by the rich citizens voluntarily renouncing a proportion of their excessive earnings. This would then assure the workers, as he used to say, of both 'more justice in social distribution' (XI, 355), and 'a more equitable share of the products of their labor—products of which the workers are an indispensable factor' (XI, 339)." *Algunas ideas de José Martí en relación con la clase obrera y el socialismo* (La Habana: Instituto Cubano del Libro, 1970), pp. 82–83.

8. In this way Martí's sentiments can be seen as a rebuttal of Andrés Valdespino's views concerning the social structure desired by Martí for the *patria:* "The idea of Martí being the supporter of a classless society is

difficult to imagine, however, if we study the Apostle's writings. That Martí should censure and condemn the vices, injustice, and exploitation of the capitalist system is one thing—which he did frequently—and another that he should propose a 'classless' society as a panacea to those ills" (p. 321).

9. "Martí always sees the Church in an inseparable partnership with luxury and opulence. He never describes the Church united with the poor, struggling to defend them or to support them in the face of the meanness of wealth." Manuel Pedro González, "José Martí, anticlerical irreductible," *Cuadernos Americanos* 73 (Jan.–Feb. 1954):185.

10. Martí in fact claimed: "Freedom is now face-to-face with the Church . . . can one be a man and a Catholic, or, in order to be a Catholic, does one have to possess the soul of a lackey?" (XI, 243). For a more thorough understanding of the "caso McGlynn" see Martí's reports in volume XI, in particular pp. 141–48, 242–51, respectively.

11. In regard to Martí's relations with the Freemason movement. Ezequiel Martínez Estrada refers to the influence of "Mendive, who was a mason, freemason, and humanist," thus showing yet another sphere of Mendive's guidance (p. 107).

12. Ibid., p. 107.

13. Writing for *La América* that same month he developed this theme, showing the need for "a radical revolution in the field of education" and advocating the replacement of the traditional subjects by more relevant material: "Instead of theology, we should teach physics; instead of rhetoric, mechanical engineering; instead of precepts of logic . . . precepts of agriculture" (VIII, 279).

14. "To count—yes: that is something they teach endlessly. The children cannot read a syllable when they have already been taught—that is, children of five years of age—to count by memory to a hundred" (XI, 85).

15. Roberto Fernández Retamar is thus correct when he claims that Martí was essentially a "revolutionary": "This can only scandalize people who, even in this day and age, have a poor understanding (and one which in turn impoverishes) of what a revolutionary is. . . . It is a person who wants to build a new world in which a new person will live. By admitting that Martí was essentially a revolutionary, we are stating that above all he wanted to transform Cuban reality profoundly, in order to make it agree more with what he thought was just." *Lectura de Martí* (México: Editorial Nuestro Tiempo, 1972), p. 15.

Chapter 7

1. Felipe de Pazos y Roque puts Martí's prowess in economic matters in proper perspective: "Any man who showed the prowess and expertise

of Martí has to be considered profoundly knowledgeable of economic technique; his knowledge was sufficient for Uruguay to name him their delegate to deal with such difficult material as monetary policy and to attend a major international conference; he produced such penetrating and frequent articles on protectionism and free trade, on new industrial and agricultural techniques; he understood so precisely the economic problems of our 'feudal, theoretical republics of Spanish America'; he had intuitive vision and explained with such clarity the dangers of economic expansion by the fair-skinned North over the olive-skinned peoples to the South." "Las ideas económicas de Martí," *Vida y pensamiento de Martí. Homenaje de la ciudad de La Habana en el cincuentenario del Partido Revolucionario Cubano. 1892–1942* (La Habana: Colección Histórica Cubana y Americana, 1942), 2:178.

2. Writing for *La Nación* in August of 1889, Martí explained the essence of his anti-imperialist beliefs, which he illustrated through the example: "The pure Americans who do not believe that the arm which has grown alongside the health of liberty can turn, in a matricidal way, against it. Nor will we go as hagglers through the world collecting amounts from universal business, simply because we have the strongest arms. Political liberty is no less sacred for a dwarf than for a giant. . . . The centuries must not pass by in vain . . . our liberty, announced by the eagle as the definitive liberty, must prove to be something more substantial than the aristocratic liberty of Greece or the hypocritical liberty of the English nation, which keeps one heel thrust into Ireland and a knee pressed down over the heart of politicians bought off by foreign commerce" (XII, 239–40). Antonio Martínez Bello also comments on this universal nature of Martí's anti-imperialism: "Let us not simply believe that, upon assuming a militant attitude toward imperialism, Martí had in mind only the United States. The *Maestro* was acting after taking into account the ambitions of imperial powers on all continents" (p. 86).

3. See for example Martí's report to *La Nación* published in January of 1890 in which he quoted the views of spokesmen for the Ministries of the Admiralty and of Finance. "The Secretariat of the Admiralty is very firm on this: it wants, and quickly, twenty-one battleships, twenty coastal patrol vessels, sixty cruisers, sufficient torpedoes, a reserve squadron—not thirteen million dollars' worth (as the last congress agreed), but twenty-five and a half million. . . . The Ministry of Finance wants a higher tariff so that no foreign goods will be imported, and whatever money that is left over, 'let it be used to expand the foreign market, in paying for warships and fortifications along the coast. . . . We are the bosses—so let the world pay us!'" (XII, 360–61).

4. In a similar vein was Martí's undated article, "Un viaje a Venezuela" ("A Trip to Venezuela"), in which he again defended the need for solid

economic growth in order to guarantee political stability: "They hope to soothe their misfortunes and develop the nation by means of a political constitution. Yet they cannot see that they will not be strong enough to have a political constitution that is respected and that will last, until they are industrious and profitable to the extent that the general interest can order and preserve the formula of liberties which will guarantee that same constitution" (XIX, 155).

5. In a recent article, Ramón de Armas has detailed the outstanding dependence of Cuba on trade with North America, thus showing that Cuba badly needed to retain good economic relations with the United States. "In 1881, the North American consul in Cuba had been able to state: 'Commercially, Cuba has become a dependency of the United States, even though politically it may continue depending on Spain.' By 1884, the United States was absorbing 85% of the total production of Cuba, and some 94% of her production of sugar and molasses." "La revolución prospuesta: destino de la revolución martiana de 1895," *Anuario martiano* 4 (1972):253.

6. In the same article Armas summarizes well Martí's plans for economic reform in Cuba: "An agrarian reform that would permit an economic system to be established, one based on small agriculture landholdings and one that would . . . support (as a long-term objective) the eventual industrialization of the country. A widening of the technical base and diversification of agricultural production as the foundation for the immediate economic development and eventual industrialization already mentioned. . . . A preference for the 'artificial' industries that have an equivalent and worthy exchange value (an 'intelligent' and 'sane' commerce). An acceptance of foreign investment, providing that it responds to national interests, favors the nation's development, and does not represent a vehicle for political penetration and submission." Ibid., p. 236.

7. J. Salwyn Schapiro, *Liberalism: Its Meaning and History* (Princeton: D. Van Nostrand, 1958), p. 33.

8. In a recent article, Paul Estrade claims that at this time the influence of Marx in the Americas was extremely slight. Indeed, in the context of Mexico of this period he describes socialism as "reformismo social más bien" ("more a form of social reformism"–p. 47). In regard to Martí he continues: "We will not summon once again that partial 'socialism.' This is due to several causes: the dogmatism of North American socialism in the 1880s, his limited understanding of Marxism (as can be clearly seen in his obituary on the death of Karl Marx and by his repeated denial of the class phenomenon in society). In Mexico his ideas do not dazzle because of their originality or their radicalism. Nevertheless they do exist, co-

herent, sane, and kneaded by a certain social praxis. His ideas, therefore, place him in the most advanced group of his time." "Un 'socialista' mexicano: José Martí," *Casa de las Améicas* 14 (Jan.–Feb. 1974):50.

9. Julio Le Riverend, underlining Martí's fundamental dislike for money, correctly notes: "Martí thought that man should really renounce personal wealth if he possessed the proper political awareness and determination to live out a life in agreement with far-reaching principles and objectives." "Martí: ética y acción revolucionaria," p. 42.

10. Salwyn Schapiro, p. 33. Therefore, as Professor Schapiro continues, "buyer and seller, employer and employed, landlord and tenant were to be free to negotiate the terms of their contracts, and contracts thus negotiated would generally prove beneficial to both parties. Combinations, whether of labor or capital, were deemed conspiracies and, as such, violations of the freedom of contract. For this reason economic liberalism opposed trade unions as stoutly as it did industrial monopolies" (p. 34).

Conclusion

1. Richard Butler Gray, p. 66. Earlier in his work Gray had been similarly patronizing: "By no stretch of the imagination can Martí be considered to have thought out a consistent political theory. He had little time for closet philosophy in the matter of politics. He was, first and last, from his revolutionary tract *Patria Libre* to the Manifiesto de Montecristi, an active revolutionist," p. 59.

2. Andrés Iduarte, p. 307.

Bibliography

Works by Martí

Martí, José. *Obras completas.* 27 vols. La Habana: Editorial Nacional de Cuba, 1963–66. Vol. 28: 1980.

Anthologies of Martí's Works

Martí, José. *The America of José Martí: Selected Writings.* Edited by Juan de Onís. New York: Noonday Press, 1953.

______. "Antología." *Revista Hispánica Moderna* 18 (Jan.–Dec. 1962):189–248.

______. *Antología mínima.* Edited by Pedro Alvarez Tabío. 2 vols. La Habana: Instituto Cubano del Libro, 1972.

______. *Argentina y la primera conferencia panamericana.* Edited by Dardo Cúneo. Buenos Aires: Ediciones Transición, 1955.

______. *Cartas a Manuel A. Mercado.* Edited by Francisco Monterde. México: Ediciones de la Universidad Nacional Autónoma de México, 1946.

______. *Cuba, Nuestra América, los Estados Unidos.* Edited by Roberto Fernández Retamar. México: Siglo Veintiuno Editores, 1973.

______. "Dice José Martí." *Lunes,* 30 January 1961, pp. 19–43.

______. *El pensamiento político de Martí.* Edited by Emilio Roig de Leuchsenring. La Habana: Capitolio Nacional, 1960.

______. *Escritos desconocidos de José Martí.* Edited by Carlos Ripoll. New York: Eliseo Torres and Sons, 1971.

______. *Ideario.* Edited by Isidro Méndez. La Habana: Editorial Cultural, 1930.

______. *Ideario.* Edited by Luis Alberto Sánchez. Santiago, Chile: Ediciones Cultural, 1930.

______. *Inside the Monster: Writings on the United States and American Imperialism by José Martí.* Edited by Philip S. Foner. New York: Monthly Review Press, 1975.

______. "José Martí 1853–1895." In *Conciencia intelectual de América: Antología del ensayo hispanoamericano 1836–1959,* edited by Carlos Ripoll, pp. 215–66. New York: Las Américas Publishing Co., 1970.

______. *José Martí en los Estados Unidos.* Madrid: Alianza Editorial, 1968.

______. *José Martí: sus mejores páginas.* Edited by Raimundo Lazo. México: Editorial Porrúa, 1970.

———. *Martí, ciudadano y apóstol, su ideario.* Edited by Homero Muñóz. Miami: Editorial AIP, 1968.
———. *Martí on the U.S.A.* Edited by Luis A. Baralt. Carbondale: Southern Illinois University Press, 1966.
———. *Martí y la primera revolución cubana.* Edited by Ernesto Goldar. Buenos Aires: Centro Editor de América Latina, 1971.
———. "Otros textos martianos." *Anuario del Centro de Estudios Martianos* 1 (1978): 22–40.
———. "Otros textos martianos." *Anuario del Centro de Estudios Martianos* 3 (1980): 3–69.
———. "Tres cartas de José Martí." *Boletín del Archivo Nacional* 67 (Jan.–Dec. 1974): 165–68.

Bibliographies of Martí's Work

Anderson, Robert Roland. *Spanish-American Modernism, A Selected Bibliography,* pp. 107–28. Tucson: University of Arizona Press, 1970.
Biblioteca Municipal, La Habana. *Guía Bibliográfica sobre José Martí.* La Habana: Publicaciones de la Biblioteca Municipal, 1937.
Blanch y Blanco, Celestino. *Bibliografía martiana 1954–63.* La Habana: Ediciones de la Biblioteca Nacional, 1966.
Blondet, Olga. "José Martí: bibliografía selecta." *Revista Hispánica Moderna* 18 (Jan.–Dec. 1952):151–61.
Carmona Romay, Adriano G. *Fuentes para el estudio del pensamiento de José Martí en materia municipal.* La Habana: Editorial Martí, 1953.
Corbitt, Duvin C. "Historical Publications of the Martí Centennial." *Hispanic American Historical Review* 34 (Aug. 1954):397–405.
Facultad de Humanidades y Ciencias, Universidad de la República. *Aportes para una bibliografía de José Martí.* Montevideo: Universidad de la República, 1954.
García Carranza, Araceli. "Bibliografía Martiana (1976 y 1977)." *Anuario Martiano* 1 (1978):346–402.
———. "Bibliografía Martiana, Enero–Diciembre 1979." *Anuario del Centro de Estudios Martianos* 3 (1980):412–26.
Godoy, Armand. "Una bibliografía y una carta inédita." *Repertorio Americano,* 10 June 1933, p. 339.
González, Manuel Pedro. "La revaloración de Martí. Anotaciones en torno a su bibliografía." *Universidad de La Habana* 4 (1953):5–22.
———. *Fuentes para el estudio de José Martí.* La Habana: Dirección de Cultura, 1950.
Peraza Sarausa, Fermín. "Martí, los libros y sus libros." *Revista Interamericana de Bibliografía* 3 (Sept.–Dec. 1953):242–51.
———. *Bibliografía martiana, 1853–1953.* La Habana: Comisión Nacional Organizadora de los Actos y Ediciones del Centenario y del Monumento de Martí, 1954.
———. "Bibliografía martiana, 1956–1968." *Revista Cubana* (New York) 1 (July–Dec. 1968):487–99.
Roig De Leuchsenring, Emilio. "La benemérita labor de los escritores martistas." *Archivo José Martí* 6 (Jan.–Dec. 1953):178–84.

Journals on José Martí

Anuario Martiano. 4 vols. La Habana, 1969–72.
Archivo José Martí. 6 vols. La Habana, 1940–53.

HOMENAJES: COMMEMORATIVE TRIBUTES TO JOSÉ MARTÍ

Banco Nacional de Cuba. *José Martí en la Comisión Monetaria Internacional Americana. Washington 1891. Minutes of the International American Monetary Commision [sic]. Actas de la Comisión Monetaria Internacional Americana.* La Habana: Banco Nacional de Cuba, 1957.

Bibliothèque de l'Ecole des Hautes Etudes Hispaniques. *En torno a José Martí (coloquio internacional).* Bordeaux: Editions Bière, 1974.

Departamento de Extensión y Relaciones Culturales, Universidad de Oriente. *Pensamiento y acción de José Martí.* Santiago, Cuba: Universidad de Oriente, 1953.

"Edición extraordinaria en homenaje a nuestro apóstol José Martí." *Bohemia,* 1 February 1953, pp. 1–127.

El Archivo Nacional en la conmemoración del centenario del natalicio de José Martí. La Habana: Archivo Nacional, 1953.

Embajada de Venezuela en Cuba. *Venezuela a Martí.* La Habana: Editorial Lex, 1953.

González, Manuel Pedro, ed. *Antología crítica de José Martí.* México: Editorial Cultura, 1960.

Hispanic Institute in the United States (Columbia University) and Departamento de estudios hispánicos, Universidad de Puerto Rico. *José Martí (1853–1895). Vida y obra. Bibliografía.* New York and Río Piedras: Ucar, Carcía y Cía., 1953.

"Homenaje a José Martí." *Carteles* (La Habana), 1 February 1953, pp. 26–150.

"Homenaje a José Martí en el 38 aniversario de su muerte." *Repertorio Americano* (San José, Costa Rica), 20 May 1933, pp. 289–302.

"Homenaje a José Martí en el centenario de su nacimiento." *Anales de la Universidad de Chile* 111 (1953):1–165.

"Homenaje a José Martí en el centenario de su nacimiento." *Boletín de la Academia Cubana de la Lengua* 1 (Oct.–Dec. 1952):481–787.

"Homenaje a José Martí en el centenario de su nacimiento." *Revista Cubana* 29 (July 1951–Dec. 1952):7–517.

Homenaje a Martí en el cincuentenario de la fundación del Partido Revolucionario Cubano. 1892–1942. La Habana: Municipio de La Habana, 1942.

"José Martí." *Revista Bimestre Cubana* 41 (1938):161–303.

"José Martí (1853–1895). Vida y obra. Bibliografía." *Revista Hispánica Moderna* 18 (Jan.–Dec. 1952):1–164, 189–248.

Memoria del congreso de escritores martianos (feb. 20 a 27 de 1953). La Habana: Publicaciones de la Comisión Nacional Organizadora de los Actos y Ediciones del Centenario y del Monumento de Martí, 1953.

"Número extraordinario: homenaje a José Martí." *Revista Cubana* (New York) 1 (July–Dec. 1968).

Secretaría de Instrucción Pública y Bellas Artes. *Homenaje al Apóstol Martí, 28 de enero de 1928.* La Habana: Carasa, 1928.

Seminario José Martí. *Estudios martianos (Memoria del Seminario José Martí, celebrado bajo los auspicios de la Fundación José Martí y el Departamento de estudios hispánicos, Facultad de Humanidades de la Universidad de Puerto Rico).* San Juan: Editorial Universitaria, 1974.

Seminario juvenil de estudios martianos. *Estudios sobre Martí.* Edited by Juan Sarría and Juan José Soto. La Habana: Instituto Cubano del Libro, 1975.

"Sobre Martí, a ochenta años de su muerte." *Casa de las Américas* 15 (May–June 1975):1–68.

"Todo Martí." *Lunes,* 30 January 1961, pp. 1–63.

Vida y pensamiento de Martí. Homenaje de la ciudad de La Habana en el cincuentenario de la fundación del Partido Revolucionario Cubano. 1892–1942. 2 vols. La Habana: Colección Histórica Cubana y Americana, 1942.

Critical Studies on Martí

Acosta, Agustín. "Ya sería un viejo . . ." *Boletín de la Academia Cubana de la Lengua* 4 (Oct.–Dec. 1952):776–78.

Acosta, Leonardo. "La concepción histórica de Martí." *Casa de las Américas* 11 (July–Aug. 1971):13–36.

______. "Martí descolonizador. Apuntes sobre el simbolismo náhuatl en la poesía de Martí." *Casa de las Américas* 13 (July–Aug. 1972):29–43.

______. "Los apologistas de la conquista y la refutación martiana." *Casa de las Américas* 13 (Jan.–Feb. 1973):53–65.

______. *José Martí, la América precolombina y la conquista española*. La Habana: Casa de las Américas, 1974.

Agramonte, Roberto. "Martí y el mundo de lo colectivo." *Archivo José Martí* 3 (Jan.–Dec. 1942):126–42.

______. *Martí y su concepción del mundo*. Río Piedras: Editorial Universal, 1971.

Aguirre, Mirta. "Los principios estéticos e ideológicos de José Martí." *Anuario del Centro de Estudios Martianos* 1 (1978):133–87.

Aguirre, Sergio. "Frustración y reconquista del 24 de febrero." *Cuba Socialista* 2 (Feb. 1962):1–21.

Alpizar Poyo, Raoul. *Ideario filosófico de José Martí*. La Habana: Imp. Ojeda, 1944.

Alvarez Ríos, Baldomero. "La revolución de Martí." *Bohemia*, 24 February 1952, pp. 8–9, 138–39.

Andino, Alberto. *Martí y España*. Madrid: Colección Plaza Mayor Scholar, 1973.

Ardura, Ernesto. "Martí y la libertad." *Archivo José Martí* 5 (Jan.–June 1950):90–95.

Armas, Ramón de. "José Martí y la época história del imperialismo." *Anuario del Centro de Estudios Martianos* 3 (1980):237–57.

______. "La revolución prospuesta: destino de la revolución martiana de 1895." *Anuario Martiano* 4 (1972):315–25.

______. "La república cubana de Martí." *Casa de las Américas* 13 (Jan.–Feb. 1973): 44–50.

Arrom, José J. "Martí y el problema de las generaciones." *Thesaurus. Boletín del Instituto Caro y Cuervo* 28 (Jan.–Apr. 1973):29–45.

Augier, Angel. "Anticipaciones de José Martí a la teoría leninista del imperialismo." *Anuario del Centro de Estudios Martianos* 3 (1980):258–78.

______. "Martí: tesis antimperialista en la cuna del panamericanismo." *Casa de las Américas* 14 (Jan.–Feb. 1974):52–64.

Baeza Flores, Alberto. "Agonía y deber en José Martí." *Atenea* (Concepción, Chile) 69 (July 1942):90–101.

Balseiro, José A. "El sentido de la justicia en José Martí." In *Memoria del congreso de escritores martianos (feb. 20 a 27 de 1953)*, pp. 388–98. La Habana: Publicaciones de la Comisión Nacional Organizadora de los Actos y Ediciones del Centenario y del Monumento de Martí, 1953.

Baralt, Blanche Zacharie de. *El Martí que yo conocí*. New York: Las Américas Publishing Co., 1968.

Batista y Zaldívar, Fulgencio. "Batista Speaks at Palace Reception Closing Year of Centennial of Martí." *The Havana Post*, 29 January 1954, pp. 1, 10.

Benítez, José A. "Martí and the United States: The political and economic abuses of growing Yankee imperialism." *Granma* (Weekly Review), 13 December 1981, p. 8.

______. "Martí and the United States: The portrait of the United States and the execrable image of Yankee imperialism." *Granma* (Weekly Review), 22 November 1981, p. 2.

Bernal del Riesgo, Alfonso. "Estampa psíquica de Martí." *Revista Bimestre Cubana* 41 (1938):233–42.
Bisbé, Manuel. "El sentido del deber en la obra de José Martí." *Revista Bimestre Cubana* 37 (1936):330–41.
Blanck y Menocal, Guillermo. "Política de Martí." *Revista de La Habana* 6 (Aug. 1945):508–21.
______. "José Martí, el gran político cubano que se adelantó a su tiempo." *Archivo José Martí* 5 (July–Dec. 1950):219–28.
Blanco Aguinaga, Carlos. "Sobre el concepto leniniano del término demócrata revolucionario." *Anuario del Centro de Estudios Martianos* 3 (1980):106–17.
Blomberg, Héctor Pedro. *Martí, el último libertador.* Buenos Aires: Editorial La Universidad, 1945.
Boza Masdival, Eduardo. "La patria que soñó Martí." *La Quincena* (La Habana) 7 (Feb.–Mar. 1961):9.
Bueno, Salvador. "Rafael María Mendive, el maestro de Martí." *Bohemia,* 25 January 1963, pp. 34–35, 83–84.
______. "Martí y Petofi." *Casa de las Américas* 13 (Jan.–Feb. 1973):80–87.
Caballero, Armando O. "El primer partido revolucionario-antimperialista de la historia." *Anuario Martiano* 2 (1970):425–31.
Cabral, Alexandre. "La influencia de la primera deportación en el pensamiento revolucionario de José Martí." *Anuario del Centro de Estudios Martianos* 3 (1980): 118–32.
Camacho, Pánfilo Daniel. "Martí, una vida en perenne angustia." *Archivo José Martí* 4 (Jan.–June 1948):133–50.
______. *Martí y el partido revolucionario cubano.* La Habana: Imprenta "El Siglo XX," 1953.
Campoamor, Fernando G. "Martí, hombre total." *Revista Cubana* 9 (1937):205–12.
______. "Martí, líder revolucionario." *Bohemia,* 4 April 1969, pp. 12–19.
Cantón Navarro, José. *Algunas ideas de José Martí en relación con la clase obrera y el socialismo.* La Habana: Instituto Cubano del Libro, 1970.
______. "Martí y el anarquismo." *Bohemia,* 19 February 1971, pp. 20–25.
______. "Rasgos del pensamiento democrático y revolucionario de José Martí." *Anuario del Centro de Estudios Martianos* 3 (1980):91–105.
Carbonell, Miguel A. "Martí: su obra literaria y su obra política." *Boletín de la Academia Cubana de la Lengua* 1 (Oct.–Dec. 1952):763–75.
Carbonell, Néstor. "Martí y la Argentina." *Archivo José Martí* 4 (Jan.–June 1948): 151–66.
______. *Martí, carne y espíritu.* 2 vols. La Habana: Seoane, Fernández y Cía., 1951–52.
______. "Martí, sus últimos días." *Archivo José Martí* 6 (Jan.–Dec. 1952):350–79.
______. "Un capítulo en la autobiografía de Martí." *Archivo José Martí* 6 (Jan.–Dec. 1952):283–302.
Carilla, Emilio. "Perfil moral de José Martí." *Humanitas* (Tucumán, Argentina) 1 (1953):317–35.
Carricarte y de Armas, Arturo R. de. *La cubanidad negativa del apóstol Martí.* La Habana: Manuel I. Mesa Rodríguez, 1934.
Casaus, Víctor. "El *Diario* de José Martí: rescate y vigencia de nuestra literatura de combate." *Anuario del Centro de Estudios Martianos* 1 (1978):189–206.
Caso, Quino. "El sentimiento amoroso en la obra literaria de Martí." *Cultura: Revista del Ministerio de Educación* (San Salvador) 12 (1958):133–39.
Castellanos García, Gerardo. *Martí, conspirador y revolucionario.* La Habana: Ucar García y Cía., 1942.

Catalá, Raquel. "Martí y el espirtualismo." In *Vida y pensamiento de Martí. Homenaje de la ciudad de La Habana en el cincuentenario de la fundación del Partido Revolucionario Cubano, 1892–1942,* 1:297–339. La Habana: Colección Histórica Cubana y Americana, 1942.

Ceniceros, José Angel. "Martí; o, la tragedia como destino glorioso." *Archivo José Martí* 4 (Jan.–Dec. 1947):61–92.

Centro de Estudios Martianos. *Trajectory and Actuality of Martí's Thought.* La Habana: Centro de Estudios Martianos, 1961.

Chacón y Calvo, José María. "Una figura continental." *Archivo José Martí* 1 (July–Aug. 1940):28–31.

Collor, Lindolfo. "José Martí." *Archivo José Martí* 6 (Jan.–Dec. 1952):118–22.

Corbitt, Roberta Day. "José Martí's Views on the United States." *Kentucky Foreign Language Quarterly* 2 (1955):152–59.

———. "This Colossal Theatre: The United States Interpreted by José Martí." Ph.D. dissertation, University of Kentucky, 1956.

Cordero Amador, Raúl. "América y Martí." *Archivo José Martí* 6 (Jan.–Dec. 1952): 426–32.

Córdova y de Quesada, Federico de. "Martí, demócrata." *Universidad de La Habana* 43/45 (1942):178–96.

———. "Martí americanista." *Universidad de La Habana* 46/48 (1943):82–102.

———. "Martí idealista." *Universidad de La Habana* 49 (1945):23–42.

———. *Martí, líder de la independencia cubana.* La Habana: Imprenta "El Siglo XX," 1947.

Cortina, José Manuel. "Apología de José Martí." *Archivo José Martí* 6 (Jan.–Dec. 1952):87–105.

Cox, Carlos Manuel. "Marx, Martí y Marinello." *Claridad* (Buenos Aires) 14 (1935):n.p.

Cúe Cánovas, Agustín. *Martí, el escritor y su época.* México: Ediciones Centenario, 1961.

D'Aquino, Hernando. *Sinfonía martiana (Vida y pasión).* Miami: Ediciones Universal, 1971.

Darío, Rubén. "José Martí." In *Antología crítica de José Martí,* edited by Manuel Pedro González, pp. 3–11. México: Editorial Cultura, 1960. Reprinted from *Los raros.* Barcelona: Mauca, 1905.

Desnoes, Edmundo. "Martí en Fidel Castro." *Lunes,* 30 January 1961, pp. 61–62.

———. "José Martí, intelectual revolucionario y hombre nuevo." *Casa de las Américas* 9 (May–June 1969):115–21.

D'Estefano del Día, Miguel A. "Ho Chi Minh y José Martí, revolucionarios anticolonialistas." *Casa de las Américas* 15 (May–June 1975):59–67.

Díaz, Carlos J. "José Martí y el Partido Revolucionario." *Verde Olivo,* 27 January 1963, pp. 33–34.

Díaz Ortega, Enrique. "Humanismo y amor en José Martí." *Archivo José Martí* 5 (Jan.–July 1951):331–40.

Díaz-Plaja, Guillermo. "Martí." *Archivo José Martí* 6 (Jan.–Dec. 1952):441–42.

Díaz Rozzotto, Jaime. "Nuestra América, la plena libertad y José Martí." *Cuadernos Americanos* 34 (May–June 1975):77–87.

Directorio Magisterial Revolucionario (en el exilio). *José Martí, apóstol de la libertad; un mensaje y una doctrina.* Miami: Its Ediciones, 1965.

———. *Martí y los norteamericanos en su propia palabra; pensamiento, sentimiento, vinculación y devoción por los Estados Unidos.* Miami: Its Ediciones, 1965.

Donghi de Halperin, Renata. "Nuestra América y su vocero: José Martí." *Cursos y Conferencias* (Buenos Aires) 30 (1947):329–46.

Edelman y Pintó, Federico. "Los que conocieron a Martí: visión de Federico Edelman y Pintó." *Archivo José Martí* 2 (Dec. 1941):82–85.

Entralgo Cancio, Alberto. *Martí ante el proceso de Jesús.* La Habana: Editorial La Verdad, 1956.

Espinoza, Enrique. "Martí, ahora." *Boletín de la Academia Cubana de la Lengua* 1 (Oct.–Dec. 1952):561–66.

Esténger, Rafael. *Martí frente al comunismo; glosas de contrapunteo entre el hombre libre y el autómata marxista.* Miami: Editorial AIP, 1966.

Estrade, Paul. "La Pinkerton contra Martí." *Anuario del Centro de Estudios Martianos* 1 (1978):207–21.

______. "Martí, Betances, Rizal. Lineamientos y prácticas de la revolución democrática anticolonial." *Anuario del Centro de Estudios Martianos* 3 (1980):150–77.

______. "Un 'socialista' mexicano: José Martí." *Casa de las Américas* 14 (Jan.–Feb. 1974):40–50.

Fernández, Wilfredo. *Martí y la filosofía.* Miami: Ediciones Universal, 1974.

Fernández Retamar, Roberto. "De 'Introducción a Martí'." *Casa de las Américas* 16 (Nov.–Dec. 1975):33–47.

______. "El mentor directo de nuestra revolución." *Cuba* 8 (Feb. 1969):20–21.

______. *Introducción a José Martí.* La Habana: Centro de Estudios Martianos/Casa de las Américas, 1978.

______. "La conmemoración del Centenario de Martí en Cuba." *Bohemia,* 31 August 1973, pp. 4–9.

______. *Lectura de Martí.* México: Editorial Nuestro Tiempo, 1972.

______. *Martí.* Montevideo: Biblioteca de Marcha, 1970.

______. "Martí y Ho Chi Minh." *Anuario Martiano* 3 (1971):180–89.

______. "Notas sobre Martí, Lenin y la revolución anticolonial." *Casa de las Américas* 10 (Mar.–Apr. 1970):116–30.

______. "Sobre Martí y Ho Chi Minh, dirigentes coloniales." *Casa de las Américas* 10 (Nov.–Dec. 1970):48–53.

Florit, Eugenio. "La poesía de Martí." *Archivo José Martí* 6 (Jan.–Dec. 1952):106–17.

______. "Versos." In *Antología crítica de José Martí,* edited by Manuel Pedro González, pp. 297–342. México: Editorial Cultura, 1960.

Foner, Philip S. "Visión martiana de los dos rostros de los Estados Unidos." *Anuario del Centro de Estudios Martianos* 3 (1980):218–36.

Galich, Manuel. "Martí y el panamericanismo: propósito de un siglo." *Anuario del Centro de Estudios Martianos* 3 (1980):308–21.

García Agüero, Salvador. "Secuencias martianas." *Revista Bimestre Cubana* 37 (1930): 206–17.

García Cantú, Gastón. "México en Martí." *Anuario del Centro de Estudios Martianos* 1 (1978):222–28.

García Galló, Gaspar Jorge. "El humanismo martiano y sus raíces." *Anuario del Centro de Estudios Martianos* 1 (1978):265–80.

______. *Martí, americano y universal.* La Habana: Instituto Cubano del Libro, 1971.

García Marruz, Fina. "José Martí." *Archivo José Martí* 6 (Jan.–Dec. 1952):52–86.

García Riverón, Abilio. "Ideario revolucionario de Martí." *Universidad de La Habana* 76/81 (1948):331–36.

García Serrato, Nelson. "José Martí, héroe de Cuba y de América." In *Memoria del congreso de escritores martianos (feb. 20 a 27 de 1953),* pp. 120–49. La Habana: Publicaciones de la Comisión Nacional Organizadora de los Actos y Ediciones del Centenario y del Monumento de Martí, 1953.

Gay-Calbó, Enrique. "Americanismo en Martí." In *Vida y pensamiento de Martí. Homenaje de la ciudad de La Habana en el cincuentenario de la fundación del Partido*

Revolucionario Cubano. 1892–1942, 1:27–59. La Habana: Colección Histórica Cubana y Americana, 1942.

———. "Martí americano." *Archivo José Martí* 4 (Jan.–June 1948):202–11.

———. "Martí y la conducta humana." *Archivo José Martí* 6 (Jan.–Dec. 1952): 338–49.

Ghiano, Juan Carlos. *José Martí.* Buenos Aires: Centro Editor de América Latina, 1967.

Giacosa Bertoli, Atilio. "El sentido americanista de la actuación consular de José Martí, como representante del Uruguay." In *Memoria del congreso de escritores martianos (feb. 20 a 27 de 1953),* pp. 336–47. La Habana: Publicaciones de la Comisión Nacional Organizadora de los Actos y Ediciones del Centenario y del Monumento de Martí, 1953.

Ginsberg, Judith. "Los juicios de José Martí acerca de la inmigración a los Estados Unidos." *The Bilingual Review/La Revista Bilingüe* (New York) 1 (May–Aug. 1974): 185–92.

Giralt, José A. "Martí, apóstol del panamericanismo." *Bohemia,* 29 January 1928, p. 29.

———. "Martí y *La patria libre.*" *Bohemia,* 26 January 1930, pp. 17, 62.

González, Manuel Pedro. "Aforismos y definiciones, o la capacidad sintética de Martí." *Anuario Martiano* 4 (1972):27–50.

———. "Aspectos inexplorados en la obra de José Martí." *Bohemia,* 18 July 1969, pp. 4–9.

———. *Indagaciones martianas.* Santa Clara, Cuba: Universidad Central de Las Villas, 1961.

———. "José Martí, anticlerical irreductible." *Cuadernos Americanos* 73 (Jan.–Feb. 1954):170–97.

———. *José Martí, Epic Chronicler of the U.S. in the Eighties.* Chapel Hill: University of North Carolina Press, 1953.

———. *Notas críticas.* La Habana: Instituto Cubano del Libro, 1969.

———. "Prontuario de temas martianos que reclaman diludación." *Anuario Martiano* 1 (1969):103–15.

———, and Schulman, Ivan A. *José Martí: esquema ideológico.* México: Editorial Cultura, 1961.

González Casanova, Pablo. "América Latina: marxismo y liberación en los planteamientos pioneros." *Anuario del Centro de Estudios Martianos* 3 (1980):194–217.

González Palacios, Carlos. "Valoración de Martí." *Archivo José Martí* 6 (Jan.–Dec. 1952):16–51.

González Veranes, Pedro N. *¿Quién fue el progenitor espiritual de José Martí?* La Habana: Editorial Luz-Hilo, 1942.

González y Gutiérrez, Diego. *La continuidad revolucionaria de Varela en las ideas de Martí.* La Habana: Edición de la Academia de la Historia de Cuba, 1953.

Gray, Richard Butler. *José Martí: Cuban Patriot.* Gainesville: University of Florida Press, 1962.

Griñán Peralta, Leonardo. *Martí, líder político.* La Habana: Instituto Cubano del Libro, 1970.

Guevara, Ernesto (Che). "Apología de Martí." *Humanismo* (La Habana) 8 (1959/1960):35–40.

———. "José Martí." In *Siete enfoques marxistas sobre José Martí,* pp. 69–76. La Habana: Centro de Estudios Martianos/Editora Política, 1978.

Hart Dávalos, Armando. "Discurso en Dos Ríos." In *Siete enfoques marxistas sobre José Martí,* pp. 115–37. La Habana: Centro de Estudios Martianos/Editora Política, 1978.

Henríquez Ureña, Pedro. "Martí." *Sur* 1 (1931):220–23.
Heredia, Nicolás. "La obra de José Martí." *Archivo José Martí* 5 (July–Dec. 1950): 193–98.
Hernández-Catá, Alfonso. *Mitología de Martí.* Buenos Aires: Club del Libro, 1939.
Hernández Pardo, Héctor. "Raíz martiana de nuestra pedagogía." *Anuario del Centro de Estudios Martianos* 1 (1978):240–48.
Hidalgo, Ariel. "El Canal de Panamá en las proyecciones políticas de José Martí." *Anuario del Centro de Estudios Martianos* 1 (1978):229–39.
______. "Martí y el neocolonialismo imperialista." *Casa de las Américas* 14 (May–June 1974):89–95.
Hill, Roscoe R. "Martí, intérprete de los Estados Unidos de América." In *Memoria del congreso de escritores martianos (feb. 20 a 27 de 1953),* pp. 375–87. La Habana: Publicaciones de la Comisión Nacional Organizadora de los Actos y Ediciones del Centenario y del Monumento de Martí, 1953.
Iduarte, Andrés. "El americanismo de Martí." In *Pensamiento y accion de Martí,* edited by Departamento de Extensión y Relaciones Culturales, pp. 311–58. Santiago, Cuba: Universidad de Oriente, 1953.
______. "Ideas religiosas, morales y filosóficas de Martí." *La Nueva Democracia* (New York) 25 (1944):3–7, 26–32.
______. "José Martí: América." *Revista Hispánica Moderna* 18 (Jan.–Dec. 1952): 83–113.
______. "José Martí: prosa." *Revista Hispánica Moderna* 18 (Jan.–Dec. 1952):71–82.
______. *Martí, escritor.* México: Cuadernos Americanos, 1945.
______. *Sarmiento, Martí y Rodó.* La Habana: Imprenta "El Siglo XX," 1955.
Infiesta Bages, Ramón. *El pensamiento político de Martí.* La Habana: Universidad de La Habana, III curso, 1952.
______. *Martí constitucionalista.* La Habana: Imprenta "El Siglo XX," 1951.
______. "Martí político." In *Pensamiento y acción de Martí,* edited by Departamento de Extensión y Relaciones Culturales, pp. 49–70. Santiago, Cuba: Universidad de Oriente, 1953.
______. *Martí the Statesman.* Coral Gables: University of Miami Press, 1953.
Isaacson, William D. "What Motivated Martí's Life." *The Havana Post,* 28 January 1953, p. 13.
Jimenes-Grullón, Juan I. "Convergencias y divergencias entre Bolívar y Martí." In *Pensamiento y acción de José Martí,* edited by Departamento de Extensión y Relaciones Culturales, pp. 235–56. Santiago, Cuba: Universidad de Oriente, 1953.
Jiménez, Francisco. "Martí y las razas." *Cuadernos Americanos* 188 (May–June 1953): 155–64.
Jiménez, Juan Ramón. "José Martí." In *Antología crítica de José Martí,* edited by Manuel Pedro González, pp. 215–17. México: Editorial Cultura, 1960.
Jorge, Elena. "Visión martiana del movimiento de liberación ruso." *Anuario del Centro de Estudios Martianos* 3 (1980):343–54.
Jornada Martiana. *Martí y la revolución cubana.* Montevideo: Embajada de Cuba, 1961.
Jorrín, Miguel. "Martí y la filosofía." In *Antología crítica de José Martí,* edited by Manuel Pedro González, pp. 459–78. México: Editorial Cultura, 1960.
Karras, Bill J. "José Martí and the Pan American Conferences 1889–1891." *Revista de Historia de América* 77/78 (Jan.–Dec. 1974):77–99.
Kirk, John M. "El aprendizaje de Martí revolucionario: una aproximación psicohistórica." *Cuadernos Americanos* 1 (Jan. 1977):108–22.
______. "From *Apóstol* to Revolutionary: the changing image of José Martí." *Norte/Sur* 7 (1979):88–106.

———. "From 'Inadaptado Sublime' to 'Líder Revolucionario': Some Further Thoughts on the Presentation of José Martí. *Latin American Research Review* 3 (1980):127–47.

———. "José Martí and the United States: A Further Interpretation." *Journal of Latin American Studies* 2 (Nov. 1977):275–90.

———. "José Martí: his reform programmes and social change in revolutionary Cuba." *Bulletin of the Society for Latin American Studies* (Britain) 28 (April, 1978): 3–23.

———. "Reflections on the Educational Philosophy of José Martí and its Application in Revolutionary Cuba." *Proceedings of the Rocky Mountain Council on Latin American Studies Conference* (1978):219–24.

Lamore, Jean. "José Martí frente a los caudillismos de la época liberal (Guatemala y Venezuela)." *Anuario del Centro de Estudios Martianos* 3 (1980):133–49.

Landa y Bacallao, Martín A. *José Martí y Fidel Castro; sus pensamientos afines*. La Habana: Impresora Modelo, 1959.

Landaluce, Miguel L. de. "Vía crucis de José Martí." *Archivo José Martí* 3 (Jan.–Dec. 1942):143–58.

Lazo, Raimundo. "La personalidad y el mensaje de Martí." In *Pensamiento y acción de José Martí*, edited by Departamento de Extensión y Relaciones Culturales, pp. 31–48. Santiago, Cuba: Universidad de Oriente, 1953.

———. "Martí y la política." *Archivo José Martí* 5 (Jan.–June 1950):29–43.

———. *Martí y su obra literaria*. La Habana: Imprenta La Propagandista, 1929.

Le Riverend, Julio. "Martí en la revolución de 1868." *Casa de las Américas* 9 (Sept.–Oct. 1968):95–110.

———. "Martí: ética y acción revolucionaria." *Casa de las Américas* 10 (Nov.–Dec. 1969):38–48.

———. "Martí y Lenin." *Política Internacional* (La Habana) 8 (1970):57–71.

———. "Teoría martiana del partido político." In *Vida y pensamiento de Martí. Homenaje de la ciudad de La Habana en el cincuentenario de la fundación del Partido Revolucionario Cubano. 1892–1942*, 1:83–110. La Habana: Colección Histórica Cubana y Americana, 1942.

Leyva, René Armande. *Trayectoria de Martí*. n.p., n.d. [Miami: AIP, 1960?].

Lizaso, Félix. "Busca y hallazgo del hombre en Martí." *Archivo José Martí* 4 (Jan.–Dec. 1952):225–36.

———. "Hombre para el hombre." *Anales de la Universidad de Chile* 111 (1953): 27–34.

———. "La intimidad literaria de Martí." *Boletín de la Academia Cubana de la Lengua* 1 (Oct.–Dec. 1952):715–33.

———. *Martí, espíritu de la guerra justa*. La Habana: Ucar, García y Cía., 1944.

———. *Martí, Martyr of Cuban Independence* (Translation by Shuler, Esther Elise. *Martí, místico del deber*). Westport, Conn.: Greenwood Press, 1974.

———. *Martí y la Utopía de América*. La Habana: Ucar, García y Cía., 1942.

———. *Proyección humana de Martí*. Buenos Aires: Editorial Raigal, 1953.

———, and Ardura, Ernesto. *Personalidad e ideas de José Martí*. La Habana: Ucar, García y Cía., 1954.

López Gutiérrez, Juan C. "La personalidad de José Martí." *Archivo José Martí* 4 (Jan.–Dec. 1952):212–18.

López Morales, Eduardo. "Apuntes para un estudio de la lucha armada en Ho Chi Minh y José Martí." *Casa de las Américas* 10 (Nov.–Dec. 1970):54–63.

Lubián y Arias, Rafael. *Martí, una demostración de energía moral y volitiva*. Miami: Directorio Magisterial Cubano (Exilio), 1967.

Magdaleno, Mauricio. *José Martí, fulgor de Martí*. México: Editorial Botas, 1941.

Maldonado-Denis, Manuel. "Martí y Fanon." *Casa de las Américas* 13 (July–Aug. 1972):17–27.

______. "Martí y Hostos: paralelismos en la lucha de ambos por la independencia de las Antillas en el siglo XIX." *Anuario del Centro de Estudios Martianos* 3 (1980):178–93.

______. "Martí y su concepto de la revolución." *Casa de las Américas* 11 (July–Aug. 1971):3–11.

Mañach, Jorge. *El pensamiento político y social de Martí.* La Habana: Edición Oficial del Senado, 1941.

______. "Espíritu de Martí." *Revista Cubana* 2 (1968):289–305.

______. "Fundamentación del pensamiento martiano." In *Antología crítica de José Martí,* edited by Manuel Pedro González, pp. 443–57. México: Editorial Cultura, 1960.

______. *Martí, Apostle of Freedom.* Translated by Coley Taylor. New York: Devin-Adan Co., 1950.

______. *Martí el apóstol.* (1933) Reprint ed. Madrid: Espasa Calpe, 1968.

______. "Martí: legado y posteridad." In *Pensamiento y acción de José Martí,* edited by Departamento de Extensión y Relaciones Culturales, pp. 71–101. Santiago, Cuba: Universidad de Oriente, 1953.

______. "Perfil de hombre." *Anales de la Universidad de Chile* 111 (1953):55–71.

______. "Perfil de Martí." *Archivo José Martí* 2 (July 1941):22–34.

Marinello, Juan. "Actualidad americana de José Martí." *Archivo José Martí* 5 (July–Dec. 1945):199–203.

______. *Actualidad de José Martí: Martí, maestro de unidad.* La Habana: Editorial Páginas, 1943.

______. "El caso literario de José Martí." In *Pensamiento y acción de José Marí,* edited by Departamento de Extensión y Relaciones Culturales, pp. 103–24. Santiago, Cuba: Universidad de Oriente, 1953.

______. "El Partido Revolucionario Cubano, creación ejemplar de José Martí." In *Siete enfoques marxistas sobre José Martí,* pp. 139–56. La Habana: Centro de Estudios Martianos/Editora Política, 1978.

______. "El pensamiento de Martí y nuestra revolución socialista." *Cuba Socialista* 2 (Jan. 1962):16–37.

______. "Fuentes y raíces del pensamiento antimperialista de José Martí." *Casa de las Américas* 15 (May–June 1975):5–12.

______. "Gabriela Mistral y José Martí." *Sur* 1 (1931):156–63.

______. *José Martí.* Paris: Editions Seghers, 1970.

______. *José Martí, escritor americano.* México: Editorial Grijalbo, 1958.

______. *Martí desde ahora.* La Habana: Universidad de La Habana, 1962.

______. "Martí en su obra." In José Martí, *Obras completas,* 1:9–20. La Habana: Editorial Nacional de Cuba, 1963.

______. *Once ensayos martianos.* La Habana: Comisión Nacional Cubana de la UNESCO, 1964.

______. *The Philosophy of José Martí and Our Socialist Revolution.* Ottawa: Embassy of Cuba, 1962.

______. "Sobre Martí escritor. La españolidad literaria de José Martí." In *Vida y pensamiento de Martí. Homenaje de la ciudad de La Habana en el cincuentenario de la fundación del Partido Revolucionario Cubano, 1892–1942,* 1:159–86. La Habana: Colección Histórica Cubana y Americana, 1942.

Márquez Sterling, Carlos. *Discursos leídos en la recepción pública del dr. Carlos Márquez Sterling la noche del 20 de octubre de 1938: Martí y la Conferencia Monetaria de 1891.* La Habana: Imprenta "El Siglo XX," 1938.

———. *Martí, cuidadano de América.* New York: Las Américas Publishing Co., 1965.

Martí-Ibáñez, Félix. "El mensaje de José Martí." *Archivo José Martí* 5 (July–Dec. 1945):204–16.

Martínez Arango, Felipe. "Perfil vigente de José Martí." In *Pensamiento y acción de José Martí,* edited by Departamento de Extensión y Relaciones Culturales, pp. 11–17. Santiago, Cuba: Universidad de Oriente, 1953.

Martínez Bello, Antonio. "El 'suicidio' de Martí. Su 'inadaptación'." *Archivo José Martí* 4 (July–Dec. 1948):372–92.

———. *Ideales sociales y económicas de José Martí.* La Habana: La Verónica, 1940.

———. *La adolescencia de Martí (Notas para un ensayo de interpretación psicológica).* La Habana: P. Fernández y Cía., 1944.

Martínez Durán, Carlos. "Martí, maestro de América." In *Pensamiento y acción de José Martí,* edited by Departamento de Extensión y Relaciones Culturales, pp. 421–32. Santiago, Cuba: Universidad de Oriente, 1953.

Martínez Estrada, Ezequiel. "Dos capítulos sobre Martí." *Sur* 295 (July–Aug. 1965):8–19.

———. *Martí, el héroe y su acción revolucionaria.* México: Siglo Veintiuno Editores, 1966.

———. *Martí, revolucionario.* La Habana: Casa de las Américas, 1967.

———. "Martí revolucionario." In *En Cuba y al servicio de la revolución cubana,* pp. 47–57. La Habana: Unión de Escritores y Artistas de Cuba, 1963.

Martínez Sáenz, Joaquín. *Martí, el inadaptado sublime.* La Habana: Editorial Cenit, 1956.

Mas, José L. "En torno a la ideología de José Martí (su identificatión con F. R. Lamennais y el Romanticismo Social.)" *Cuadernos Americanos* 199 (Mar.–Apr. 1975):82–114.

———. "José Martí y el Romanticismo Social (F. R. Lamennais: una posible influencia en el joven José Martí.)" *Cuadernos Americanos* 193 (Mar.–Apr. 1974): 160–81.

———. "Perspectiva ideológica de José Martí en sus crónicas sobre los Estados Unidos." Ph.D. dissertation, University of California at Los Angeles, 1974.

Melis, Antonio. "Lucha antimperialista y lucha de clases en José Martí." *Casa de las Américas* 9 (May–June 1969):126–33.

Mella, Julio Antonio. "Glosando los pensamientos de José Martí." *Casa de las Américas* 13 (Jan.–Feb. 1973):5–9.

———. "Martí y el proletariado." *Verde Olivo,* 13 January 1963, pp. 38–39.

Méndez, Manuel Isidro. "Humanidad de Martí." In *Vida y pensamiento de Martí. Homenaje de la ciudad de La Habana en el cincuentenario de la fundación del Partido Revolucionario Cubano. 1892–1942,* 1:9–25. La Habana: Colección Histórica Cubana y Americana, 1942.

———. "Ideas sociológicas de José Martí." *Archivo José Martí* 1 (Dec. 1940):33–39.

———. *Martí, estudio crítico-biográfico.* La Habana: P. Fernández y Cía., 1941.

Menéndez, Aldo. "José Martí: el ensayo." *Bohemia,* 25 January 1974, pp. 14–21.

Mercado, Alfonso. "Mis recuerdos de José Martí." *Archivo José Martí* 5 (July–Dec. 1945): 217–21.

Mesa Rodríguez, Manuel I. "Letra y espíritu de Martí a través de su epistolario." *Archivo José Martí* 6 (Jan.–Dec. 1952):315–37.

Mikulski, Richard M. "José Martí: His Political Ideas." M.A. thesis, Columbia University, 1948.

———. "Martí en tierra yanqui." *Archivo José Martí* 4 (Jan.–Dec. 1949):428–43.

Miranda Valera, Aurelio. *Martí político (a la luz actual).* La Habana: Instituto del Libro, 1969.

Mistral, Gabriela. "La lengua de Martí." in *Antología crítica de José Martí,* edited by Manuel Pedro González, pp. 23–39. México: Editorial Cultura, 1960.

Monal, Isabel. "José Martí: del liberalismo al democratismo antimperialista." *Casa de las Américas* 13 (Jan.–Feb. 1973):24–41.

Montaner, Carlos Alberto. *El pensamiento de José Martí.* Madrid: Plaza Mayor Ediciones, 1971.

Morales, Salvador. "José Martí y sus ideas económicas." *Anuario Martiano* 2 (1970): 164–75.

______. "La democracia en el Partido Revolucionario Cubano." *Anuario del Centro de Estudios Martianos* 1 (1978):59–78.

Mortillaro, Gaspar. "Martí, el hombre más puro de la raza." *Archivo José Martí* 1 (July–Aug. 1940):57–62.

Navarro Luna, Manuel. "Martí en Fidel Castro." *Bohemia,* 25 January 1963, p. 108.

Nazoa, Aquiles. *Cuba: de Martí a Fidel Castro.* Caracas: Ediciones Populares del Pensamiento Vivo, 1961.

Novás, Benito. "Tributo a Martí." *Anuario Martiano* 4 (1972):143–68.

Onís, Federico de. "José Martí: valoración." In *Antología crítica de José Martí,* edited by Manuel Pedro González, pp. 13–21. México: Editorial Cultura, 1960.

Ortiz, Fernando. "La religión de Martí." *La Nueva Democracia* 38 (1958):52–57.

______. "Martí y las razas." In *Vida y pensamiento de Martí. Homenaje de la ciudad de La Habana en el cincuentenario de la fundación del Partido Revolucionario Cubano. 1892–1942,* 1:335–67. La Habana: Colección Histórica Cubana y Americana, 1942.

______. "Martí y las 'razas de librería'." *Anales de la Universidad de Chile* 111 (1953): 117–30.

Oullion, Juliette. "La discriminación racial en los Estados Unidos vista por José Martí." *Anuario Martiano* 3 (1971):9–94.

Pan American Union. *José Martí.* Washington, D.C.: Pan American Union, 1954.

Pazos y Roque, Felipe. "Las ideas económicas de Martí." In *Vida y pensamiento de Martí. Homenaje de la ciudad de La Habana en el cincuentenario de la fundación del Partido Revolucionario Cubano. 1892–1942.* 2:177–209. La Habana: Colección Histórica Cubana y Americana, 1942.

Pérez Cubillas, José. *Martí, economista y sociólogo.* La Habana: Molina y Cía., 1932.

Pichardo, Hortensia. "Martí y el problema agrario." *Anuario Martiano* 2 (1970): 176–89.

Picón Salas, Mariano. "Arte y virtud en José Martí." In *Memoria del congreso de escritores martianos (feb. 20 a 27 de 1953),* pp. 150–56. La Habana: Publicaciones de la Comisión Nacional Organizadora de los Actos y Ediciones del Centenario y del Monumento de Martí, 1953.

Piedra-Bueno, Andrés de. *Martí.* La Habana: Ministerio de Educación, 1956.

Piñera, Humberto. "Martí, pensador." In *Antología crítica de José Martí,* edited by Manuel Pedro González, pp. 527–37. México: Editorial Cultura, 1960.

Portuondo, Fernando. "Martí, Gómez y el alzamiento del 95 en Camagüey." *Universidad de La Habana* 196/197 (1972):158–69.

Portuondo, José Antonio. "Introducción al estudio de las ideas sociales de Martí." In *Vida y pensamiento de Martí. Homenaje de la ciudad de La Habana en el cincuentenario de la fundación del Partido Revolucionario Cubano. 1892–1942,* 2:227–48. La Habana: Colección Histórica Cubana y Americana, 1942.

______. "José Martí: crítica." *Revista Hispánica Moderna* 18 (Jan.–Dec. 1952): 114–44.

______. "Juárez en Martí." *Casa de las Américas* 13 (Sept.–Oct. 1972):140–44.

______. "Martí y el escritor revolucionario." *Anuario Martiano* 2 (1970):145–63.

———. "Teoría martiana del partido revolucionario." *Casa de las Américas* 15 (May–June 1975):14–23.

Prío Socarrás, Carlos. "Martí, arquetipo de lo cubano." *Archivo José Martí* 6 (Jan.–Dec. 1946):380–91.

Quesada y Miranda, Gonzalo de. "La juventud de Martí." *Archivo José Martí* 6 (Jan.–Dec. 1952):486–99.

———. "Martí en Dos Ríos." *Archivo José Martí* 6 (Jan.–Dec. 1952):272–82.

———. "*Patria* de New York." *Universidad de La Habana* 177 (1966):115–35.

Redondo, Susana. "José Martí: vida." *Revista Hispánica Moderna* 18 (Jan.–Dec. 1952):1–20.

Ríos, Fernando de los. "Reflexiones en torno al sentido de la vida en Martí." In *Antología crítica de José Martí,* edited by Manuel Pedro Gonález, pp. 429–41. México: Editorial Cultura, 1960.

Ripoll, Carlos. *Indice Universal de la Obra de José Martí.* New York: Eliseo Torres and Sons, 1971.

———. *José Martí: letras y huellas desconocidas.* New York: Eliseo Torres and Sons, 1976.

———. *'Patria': el periódico de José Martí, registro general (1892–1895).* New York: Eliseo Torres and Sons, 1971.

Roa, Raúl. "José Martí. El autor intelectual." *Bohemia,* 3 August 1973, pp. 32–37.

———. *Martí y el facismo.* La Habana: Ucar, García y Cía., 1937.

———. "Rescate y proyección de Martí." In *Siete enfoques marxistas sobre José Martí,* pp. 19–36. La Habana: Centro de Estudios Martianos/Editora Política, 1978.

Roca, Blas. "José Martí, revolucionario radical de su tiempo." *Casa de las Américas* 13 (Jan.–Feb. 1973):10–21.

Rodríguez, Carlos Rafael. *José Martí and Cuban Liberation.* New York: International Publishers, 1953.

———. "José Martí, contemporáneo y compañero." *Universidad de La Habana* 196/197 (1972):3–29.

Rodríguez, José Ignacio. "Martí y el Partido Revolucionario Cubano." *Casa de las Américas* 13 (Jan.–Feb. 1973):98–100.

Rodríguez, Pedro Pablo. "Como la plata en las raíces de los Andes. El sentido de la unidad continental en el latinoamericanismo de José Martí." *Anuario del Centro de Estudios Martianos* 3 (1980):322–34.

———. "La idea de la liberación nacional en José Martí." *Anuario Martiano* 4 (1972): 169–213.

Rodríguez Feo, José. "Martí en la Revolución." *Lunes,* 30 January 1961, pp. 10–12.

Rodríguez Hidalgo, Alfonso. "La Biblia en el pensamiento de Martí." *La Nueva Democracia* 41 (Jan. 1961):20–26.

Roig de Leuchsenring, Emilio. "Algunos conceptos martianos de la República." *Archivo José Martí* 3 (Jan.–Dec. 1942):60–79.

———. "El americanismo de Martí." In *Memoria del congreso de escritores martianos (feb. 20 a 27 de 1953),* pp. 285–317. La Habana: Publicaciones de la Comisión Nacional Organizadora de los Actos y Ediciones del Centenario y del Monumento de Martí, 1953.

———. "Formación revolucionaria de Martí." *Carteles,* 24 January 1953, pp. 68–70.

———. "Hostos y Martí, dos ideologías concordantes." *Revista Bimestre Cubana* 43 (1939):5–19.

———. *La república de Martí.* La Habana: Imp. Modelo, 1953.

———. "Libertad y justicia en Martí." *Carteles,* 4 January 1953, pp. 14–16.

———. *Martí, antimperialista* (1953). Reprint ed. La Habana: Imp. Modelo, 1961.

———. "Martí y las religiones." In *Vida y pensamiento de Martí. Homenaje de la ciudad de La Habana en el cincuentenario de la fundación del Partido Revolucionario Cubano. 1892–1942,* 1:111–58. La Habana: Colección Histórica Cubana y Americana, 1942.

Rojas, Manuel. "José Martí y el espíritu revolucionario en los pueblos." *Revista Bimestre Cubana* 41 (Mar.–June 1938):216–23.

Ronda Varona, Adalberto. "La esencia filosófica del pensamiento democrático-revolucionario de José Martí." *Anuario del Centro de Estudios Martianos* 3 (1980):378–91.

Sabourín, Jesús. "José Martí: letra y servicio." *Anuario Martiano* 3 (1971):191–200.

______. "Martí en el Che." *Casa de las Américas* 13 (July–Aug. 1972):5–15.

______. "Martí: raza y humanidad." *Casa de las Américas* 13 (Jan.–Feb. 1973): 68–77.

Salomon, Noël. "En torno al idealismo de José Martí." *Anuario del Centro de Estudios Martianos* 1 (1978):41–58.

______. "José Martí y la toma de conciencia latinoamericana." *Anuario Martiano* 4 (1972):9–25.

Sanguily, Manuel. *José Martí y la revolución cubana.* New York: Tipografía de El Porvenir, 1896.

Santovenia y Echaide, Emeterio Santiago. *Lincoln in Martí: A Cuban View of Abraham Lincoln.* Translated by Donald F. Fogelquist. Chapel Hill: University of North Carolina, 1953.

______. *Política de Martí.* La Habana: Seoane, Fernández y Cía., 1943.

Sardiña y Sánchez, Ricardo Rafael. *Martí político.* Miami: n.p., 1963.

Schulman, Ivan A. "José Martí y el 'Sun' de Nueva York. Nuevos escritos desconocidos." *Anales de la Universidad de Chile* 124 (1966):30–50.

______. "Literature and Society: Martí as Historian of His Age and the Future." *South Eastern Conference on Latin American Studies* 3 (Mar. 1972):131–46.

______. "Modernismo, revolución y pitagorismo en Martí." *Casa de las Américas* 13 (July–Aug. 1972):45–55.

______. *Símbolo y color en la obra de José Martí.* Madrid: Gredos, 1970.

Schultz de Mantovani, Fryda. "Dimensión íntima de Martí." *Archivo José Martí* 6 (Jan.–Dec. 1952):133–44.

______. *Genio y figura de José Martí.* Buenos Aires: Editorial Universitaria de Buenos Aires, 1968.

Shíshkina, Valentina I. "El democratismo revolucionario del ideario de José Martí y su significación internacional." *Anuario del Centro de Estudios Martianos* 3 (1980):84–90.

Shuler, Esther Elise. "José Martí. Su crítica de algunos autores norteamericanos." *Archivo José Martí* 5 (July–Dec. 1950):164–92.

Smith, George. "The Revolutionary Ideas of José Martí." *The Havana Post,* 28 January 1953, p. 13.

Solís, Carlos A. (hijo). "La libertad en el pensamiento de Martí." *Revista de la Universidad* (Tegucigalpa, Honduras) 16 (1953):13–15.

Sosa, Joel. "Concepciones teórico-militares en el democratismo revolucionario de José Martí." *Anuario del Centro de Estudios Martianos* 3 (1980):355–77.

Stolbov, V. "José Martí, demócrata revolucionario." *Anuario del Centro de Estudios Martianos* 3 (1980):77–83.

Suchlicki, Jaime. "The Political Ideology of José Martí." *Caribbean Studies* 6 (1966): 25–36.

Ternovoi, Oleg. "Martí: la república 'con todos y para el bien de todos'." *Anuario del Centro de Estudios Martianos* 3 (1980):335–42.

Toledo Sande, Luis. "Anticlericalismo, idealismo, religiosidad y práctica en José Martí." *Anuario del Centro de Estudios Martianos* 1 (1978):79–132.

———. "Jose Martí hacia la emancipación de la mujer." *Casa de las Américas* 15 (May–June 1975):25–41.

———. "Pensamiento y combate en la concepción martiana de la historia." *Anuario del Centro de Estudios Martianos* 3 (1980):279–307.

Torriente, Loló de la. "El nombre más venerado y más explotado de Cuba." *Carteles*, 5 April 1959, pp. 4–5, 84.

Valdespino, Andrés. "Raíces martianas de nuestra revolución." *Bohemia*, 7 February 1960, pp. 13, 104–05.

———. "Imagen de Martí en las letras cubanas." *Revista Cubana* 1 (July–Dec. 1968):307–31.

Varona, Enrique José. "Martí y su obra política." *Casa de las Américas* 13 (Jan.–Feb. 1973):90–95. Reprint of speech delivered by Varona at the meeting of the "Sociedad Literaria Hispanoamericana de Nueva York" on 13 March 1896.

Vasconcelos, Ramon. "Promesas y entrelíneas del Manifiesto de Montecristi." *Archivo José Martí* 6 (Jan.–Dec. 1952):190–95.

Vázquez Candela, E. "Martí anti-imperialista: hombre de su momento." *Verde Olivo*, 27 January 1963, pp. 35–37.

Vitier, Cintio. "Imagen de José Martí." *Anuario Martiano* 3 (1971):231–48.

———. "Los discursos de Martí." *Anuario Martiano* 1 (1969):293–318.

———. "Los 'Versos Libres' de Martí." In *Antología crítica de José Martí*, edited by Manuel Pedro González, pp. 381–90. México: Editorial Cultura, 1960.

———. "Martí, el integrador." *Anuario Martiano* 2 (1970):190–92.

———. "Martí futuro." *Cuadernos Americanos* 156 (Jan.–Feb. 1968):217–37.

———. "Visión del Maestro." *Cuba Internacional* 4 (May 1972):4–9.

———, and García Marruz, Fina. *Temas martianos*. La Habana: Instituto Cubano del Libro, 1969.

Vitier, Medardo. *Martí: estudio integral*. La Habana: Publicaciones del Centenario y del Monumento de Martí, 1954.

Weber, Fryda. "Martí en 'La Nación' de Buenos Aires 1885–1890." *Archivo José Martí* 6 (Jan.–Dec. 1952):458–82.

Wilgus, A. Curtis and Karna S. "Las crónicas de José Martí sobre la Primera Conferencia Internacional Americana celebrada en Washington." In *Memoria del congreso de escritores martianos (feb. 20 a 27 de 1953)*, pp. 318–35. La Habana: Publicaciones de la Comisión Nacional Organizadora de los Actos y Ediciones del Centenario y del Monumento de Martí, 1953.

Zulueta, Luis de. "Martí, el luchador sin odio." *Revista Bimestre Cubana* 43 (1939): 161–77.

Selected Critical Works and Background Reading

Academia de la Historia de Cuba. *Homenaje en memoria de José Martí y Zayas Bazán, celebrado en sesión pública el día 28 de mayo de 1953*. La Habana: Imprenta "El Siglo XX," 1953.

Aguilar, Alonso. *Pan-Americanism From Monroe to the Present: A View from the Other Side*. Translated by Aza Zatz. New York: Monthly Review Press, 1968.

Aguilar, Luis E. *Cuba 1933: Prologue to Revolution*. Ithaca: Cornell University Press, 1972.

Atkinson, William C. *A History of Spain and Portugal*. Harmondsworth, England: Penguin Books, 1970.

Bueno, Salvador. *Figuras cubanas: Breves biografías de grandes cubanos del siglo XIX*. La Habana: Comisión Nacional Cubana de la UNESCO, 1964.

Castro, Fidel. *La história me absolverá.* La Habana: Instituto Cubano del Libro, 1973.
______. *La história me absolverá.* La Habana: Casa de las Américas, 1974.
Connor, James E., ed. *Lenin on Politics and Revolution: Selected Writings.* New York: Pegasus, 1968.
Cooke, Alistair. *America.* New York: Alfred A. Knopf, 1973.
Crawford, William Rex. "The Cubans and Hostos." In *A Century of Latin American Thought,* pp. 218–46. Cambridge, Mass.: Harvard University Press, 1944.
Erikson, Erik H. *Life History and the Historical Moment.* New York: W. W. Norton and Co., 1975.
______ *Young Man Luther: A Study in Psychoanalysis and History.* New York: W. W. Norton and Co., 1958.
Estévez Romero, Luis. *Desde el Zanjón hasta Baire.* 2 vols. La Habana: Instituto Cubano del Libro, 1974.
Foner, Philip S. *A History of Cuba and Its Relations with the United States.* New York: International Publishers, 1962.
Franco, Jean. *The Modern Culture of Latin America: Society and the Artist.* Harmondsworth, England: Penguin Books, 1970.
Henríquez Ureña, Max. *Breve história del Modernismo.* México: Fondo de Cultura Económica, 1962.
Henríquez Ureña, Pedro. *A Concise History of Latin American Culture.* Translated by Gilbert Chase. New York: Praeger Publishers, 1966.
Ibarra, Jorge. *Ideología mambisa.* La Habana: Instituto Cubano del Libro, 1972.
International Monetary Commission. *Minutes of the International Monetary Commission.* Washington, D.C., 1891.
Leigh, Denis, Pare, C. M. B., and Marks, John. *Encyclopaedia of Psychiatry.* Vaudreuil, Québec: Hoffman-La Roche Ltd., 1972.
Le Riverend, Julio. *Economic History of Cuba.* La Habana: Instituto Cubano del Libro, 1967.
Lieuwin, Edwin. *U.S. Policy in Latin America: A Short History.* New York: Praeger Publishers, 1970.
Livermore, Harold V. *A History of Spain.* New York: Grove Press, 1960.
Matthews, Herbert L. *Fidel Castro.* New York: Simon and Schuster, 1970.
______. *Revolution in Cuba: An Essay in Understanding.* New York: Charles Scribner's Sons, 1975.
Mouat, Kit. *What Humanism Is About.* London: Barrie and Rockliff, 1963.
Nelson, Waldo E. *Textbook of Pediatrics.* Philadelphia: W. B. Saunders, 1964.
Olivera, Otto. *Cuba en su poesía.* México: Ediciones de Andrea, 1965.
Onís, José de. *The United States as seen by Spanish American Writers (1776–1890).* New York: Hispanic Institute in the United States, 1952.
Ortega, Luis. *El sueño y la distancia: apuntes para un ensayo.* México: Ediciones Ganivet, 1968.
Payne, Stanley G. *A History of Spain and Portugal.* 2 vols. Madison: University of Wisconsin Press, 1973.
Pendle, George. *A History of Latin America.* Harmondsworth, England: Penguin Books, 1970.
Pichardo, Hortensia, ed. *Documentos para la história de Cuba.* 3 vols. La Habana: Instituto Cubano del Libro, 1973.
Poumier, María. *Apuntes sobre la vida cotidiana en 1898.* La Habana: Instituto Cubano del Libro, 1975.
Remos, Juan J. *Proceso histórico de las letras cubanas.* Madrid: Ediciones Guadarrama, 1958.
Ribeiro, Darcy. *The Americas and Civilisation.* New York: E. P. Dutton, 1971.
Roberts, J. M. *The Mythology of the Secret Societies.* St. Albans, England: Paladin, 1974.

Rosen, Ephraim, and Gregory, Ian. *Abnormal Psychology.* Philadelphia: W. B. Saunders, 1965.

Rubens, Horatio S. *Liberty, the Story of Cuba.* New York: Bremer, Warren and Putnam, 1932.

Sinclair, Andrew. *Guevara.* London: Fontana/Collins, 1970.

Thomas, Hugh. *Cuba—or The Pursuit of Freedom.* London: Eyre and Spottiswoode, 1971.

Thompson, William R., and De Bold, Richard C. *Psychology: A Systematic Introduction.* New York: McGraw-Hill, 1971.

Vitier, Medardo. *Las ideas en Cuba; proceso del pensamiento político, filosófico y crítico en Cuba, principalmente durante el siglo XIX.* 2 vols. La Habana: Editorial Trópico, 1938.

Zeitlin, Theodore. *Ambition, Love and Politics.* Vol. 1, *France 1848–1945.* Oxford: Oxford University Press, 1973.

Index